# How Party Activism Survives

Political parties with activists are in decline due to various external shocks. Societal changes, like the emergence of technologies of communication, have diminished the role and number of activists, while party elites increasingly can make do without grassroots activists. However, recent scholarship concerning different democracies has shown how activism still matters for representation. This book contributes to this literature by analyzing the unique case of the Uruguayan *Frente Amplio* (FA), the only mass-organic, institutionalized, leftist party in Latin America. Using thick description, systematic process training, and survey research, this case study highlights the value of an organization-centered approach for understanding parties' role in democracy in the twenty-first century. Within the FA, organizational rules grant activists a significant voice, which imbues activists' participation with a strong sense of agency. This explains activists' participation with a strong sense of efficacy. This book is an excellent resource for scholars and students of Latin America and comparative politics who are interested in political parties and the challenges confronting new democracies.

VERÓNICA PÉREZ BENTANCUR holds a PhD from the Universidad Torcuato Di Tella, Argentina and is Assistant Professor of Political Science at Universidad de la República del Uruguay. Her research focuses on Latin American Politics and Gender and Politics. Her work has been published in *Comparative Political Studies*, *Revista de Ciencia Política*, *Revista Uruguaya de Ciencia Política*, and *Revista Debates*.

RAFAEL PIÑEIRO RODRÍGUEZ received his PhD in political science at Pontificia Universidad Católica de Chile and is an associate professor at the Departamento de Ciencias Sociales, Universidad Católica del Uruguay. He has been published in *Comparative Political Studies*, *Party Politics*, *Government Information Quarterly*, *Latin American Politics and Society*, *Latin American Research Review*, *Journal of Democracy*, *Política y Gobierno*, and *Revista de Ciencia Política*, among others.

FERNANDO ROSENBLATT received his PhD in political science at Pontificia Universidad Católica de Chile and is an associate professor at the Escuela de Ciencia Política, Universidad Diego Portales, Chile and a researcher at the Millennium Institute for Foundational Research on Data. His book *Party Vibrancy & Democracy in Latin America* was published by Oxford University Press. He has been published in *Comparative Political Studies*, *Party Politics*, *Latin American Politics and Society*, *Latin American Research Review*, *Democratization*, *Política y Gobierno*, and *Revista de Ciencia Política*.

# How Party Activism Survives

## Uruguay's Frente Amplio

**VERÓNICA PÉREZ BENTANCUR**
Universidad de la República

**RAFAEL PIÑEIRO RODRÍGUEZ**
Universidad Católica del Uruguay

**FERNANDO ROSENBLATT**
Universidad Diego Portales

# CAMBRIDGE
UNIVERSITY PRESS

University Printing House, Cambridge CB2 8BS, United Kingdom

One Liberty Plaza, 20th Floor, New York, NY 10006, USA

477 Williamstown Road, Port Melbourne, VIC 3207, Australia

314-321, 3rd Floor, Plot 3, Splendor Forum, Jasola District Centre, New Delhi - 110025, India

103 Penang Road, #05-06/07, Visioncrest Commercial, Singapore 238467

Cambridge University Press is part of the University of Cambridge.

It furthers the University's mission by disseminating knowledge in the pursuit of education, learning and research at the highest international levels of excellence.

www.cambridge.org
Information on this title: www.cambridge.org/9781108719377
DOI: 10.1017/9781108750851

© Verónica Pérez Bentancur, Rafael Piñeiro Rodríguez, and Fernando Rosenblatt 2020

This publication is in copyright. Subject to statutory exception and to the provisions of relevant collective licensing agreements, no reproduction of any part may take place without the written permission of Cambridge University Press.

First published 2020
First paperback edition 2021

*A catalogue record for this publication is available from the British Library*

*Library of Congress Cataloging in Publication data*
NAMES: Pérez, Verónica (Pérez Bentancur), author. | Piñeiro, Rafael, author. | Rosenblatt, Fernando, author.
TITLE: How party activism survives : Uruguay's Frente Amplio / Verónica Pérez Bentancur, Rafael Piñeiro Rodríguez, Fernando Rosenblatt.
DESCRIPTION: Cambridge, United Kingdom ; New York, NY : Cambridge University Press, 2020. | Includes bibliographical references and index.
IDENTIFIERS: LCCN 2019038143 (print) | LCCN 2019038144 (ebook) | ISBN 9781108485265 (hardback) | ISBN 9781108719377 (paperback) | ISBN 9781108750851 (epub)
SUBJECTS: LCSH: Frente Amplio (Uruguay) | Political participation–Uruguay. | Political activists–Uruguay. | Uruguay–Politics and government–21st century.
CLASSIFICATION: LCC JL3698.F7 P47 2020 (print) | LCC JL3698.F7 (ebook) | DDC 324.2895/07–dc23
LC record available at https://lccn.loc.gov/2019038143
LC ebook record available at https://lccn.loc.gov/2019038144

ISBN 978-1-108-48526-5 Hardback
ISBN 978-1-108-71937-7 Paperback

Cambridge University Press has no responsibility for the persistence or accuracy of URLs for external or third-party internet websites referred to in this publication, and does not guarantee that any content on such websites is, or will remain, accurate or appropriate.

*To Lena and Manu*

# Contents

| | |
|---|---|
| *List of Figures* | *page* ix |
| *List of Tables* | x |
| *List of Boxes* | xii |
| *Acknowledgments* | xiii |
| *List of Abbreviations* | xvii |

| | | |
|---|---|---|
| 1 | Introduction | 1 |
| | Theory | 8 |
| | Methods | 19 |
| | Overview | 27 |
| 2 | Context Matters: The Political and Socioeconomic Setting | 30 |
| | Introduction | 30 |
| | Rise and Decay of the Polyarchy | 31 |
| | The Dual Transition in Uruguay | 35 |
| | The Political Economy of the First Three FA Governments | 40 |
| | Conclusions | 46 |
| 3 | Voluntary Activism in the FA | 47 |
| | Introduction | 47 |
| | The Participation Structure: In-Depth Description of the Deviant Case | 48 |
| | Conclusions | 78 |
| 4 | Origins and Reproduction of the Mass-Organic Structure | 81 |
| | Introduction | 81 |
| | The Origin of the FA as a Mass-Organic Leftist Party | 83 |
| | The Determinants of the Construction of the Participatory Structure | 91 |

|   |   |   |
|---|---|---|
|   | The Reproduction of the Mass-Organic Nature | 99 |
|   | Conclusions | 106 |
| 5 | Party Structure, Efficacy, and Activism | 108 |
|   | Introduction | 108 |
|   | Activists Are Different from Adherents | 110 |
|   | Voice Reduction Affects Activists | 115 |
|   | Organizers Transform Adherents into Activists | 120 |
|   | Conclusions | 122 |
| 6 | The Limits to Strategic Adaptation | 124 |
|   | Introduction | 124 |
|   | Empirical Analysis of Party Decisions | 128 |
|   | The Ideological Transformation of the FA | 131 |
|   | Examples of Limits to Strategic Adaptation | 133 |
|   | Conclusions | 142 |
| 7 | The FA in Comparative Perspective | 145 |
|   | Introduction | 145 |
|   | The Brazilian PT: A Negative Case in Latin America | 147 |
|   | The FA as a Strange Electoral Alliance | 154 |
|   | Conclusions | 159 |
| 8 | Theoretical Conclusions and Political Implications | 160 |
|   | Introduction | 160 |
|   | Review of Empirical Findings | 161 |
|   | The Challenges Ahead | 165 |
|   | A Decadent Organization of the Past or Democracy in the Twenty-First Century? | 169 |

*Appendix – Interviewees* 173
*References* 175
*Index* 189

# Figures

| | | |
|---|---|---|
| 2.1 | The electoral evolution of the left before 1971 | page 34 |
| 2.2 | Electoral evolution in national elections, 1971–2014 | 40 |
| 2.3 | Poverty, extreme poverty, and Gini Index 2002–2017 | 43 |
| 2.4 | Main export items 2005–2018 (Paasche Index Prices in US Dollars 2005 = 100) | 44 |
| 2.5 | Evolution of GDP growth rate, unemployment, fiscal deficit, and inflation in Uruguay (2006–2018) | 45 |
| 3.1 | Self-reported distance from a Base Committee (in blocks) | 51 |
| 3.2 | Sociodemographic characteristics of Base Committee attendees | 53 |
| 3.3 | Active Base Committees in Montevideo in 1971 | 58 |
| 3.4 | Active Base Committees in Montevideo in 2015 | 58 |
| 3.5 | The organizational structure of the FA | 65 |
| 6.1 | National Political Board motions from factions and grassroots members (2000–2016) | 129 |

# Tables

| | | |
|---|---|---|
| 1.1 | FA Brand Across Latin America | page 22 |
| 1.2 | Cited FA Documents | 25 |
| 1.3 | Types of Engagement | 26 |
| 2.1 | Constitutional Plebiscites and Law Referenda since 1980 | 37 |
| 3.1 | Number of FA Members Who Pay Dues (By Year) | 61 |
| 3.2 | New Party Members (By Year, 1986–2017) | 62 |
| 3.3 | Electoral Evolution of FA Factions | 72 |
| 3.4 | Electoral Strength of FA Factions (2014 National Election and 2016 FA Internal Election) | 74 |
| 3.5 | Percentage of Base Committee Attendees by Faction | 76 |
| 3.6 | Faction Representation in Base Committees and Performance in a Recent FA Internal Election (2016) and National Legislative Election (2014) | 77 |
| 4.1 | Descriptive Inference Concerning the Origin of the FA | 92 |
| 4.2 | Causal Inference of the Origin of the FA | 98 |
| 4.3 | Causal Reproduction | 101 |
| 4.4 | Evidence of Descriptive Inference – Reproduction | 104 |
| 5.1 | Socioeconomic, Sociodemographic Characteristics, and Ideology | 112 |
| 5.2 | Willingness to Participate in Different Activities by Type of Adherent | 113 |
| 5.3 | Reported Behavior by Type of Adherent | 114 |
| 5.4 | Linear-Regression Model: Willingness to Participate and Reported Participation | 115 |

5.5 *t*-test Results Comparing Means on Treatment
 (Selective Incentive) and Control 118
5.6 *t*-test Results Comparing Means on Treatment
 (Collective Incentive) and Control 120
6.1 Members Perceptions of Ideological Positions 125

# Boxes

5.1 Survey Experiment                   *page* 117
5.2 Survey Experiment 2                       119

# Acknowledgments

This book was possible thanks to the invaluable help of many people. We want to express our gratitude for the various sources of funding that we received to support this project. Fernando Rosenblatt acknowledges support from CONICYT-Fondecyt #11150151 and CONICYT REDI #170101. Fernando Rosenblatt also acknowledges support from CONICYT-FONDECYT #1190072 and from the Millennium Institute Foundational Research on Data, which were crucial for completing the project. Rafael Piñeiro thanks the Sistema Nacional de Investigadores of the Agencia Nacional de Investigación e Innovación of Uruguay (ANII) for the financial support involved in the Sistema Nacional de Investigadores (SNI_2015_2_1006237). All three of us wish to thank Friedrich-Ebert-Stiftung in Uruguay for its support of our fieldwork.

We took our first steps in the discipline at the Departamento de Ciencia Política of the Universidad de la República. As BA students, we were taught by the generation of political scientists who forged the nascent discipline in Uruguay. It was also a period of scant resources for education. Yet those who formed us as political scientists instilled in us a passion for both politics and the discipline. We were all research assistants at the department, and this first experience of conducting research confirmed and reinforced our interest in pursuing a career in Political Science. Verónica earned her doctorate at the Departamento de Ciencia Política y Relaciones Internacionales of the Universidad Torcuato Di Tella. Rafael and Fernando were among the first cohorts in the doctoral program in Political Science of the Instituto de Ciencia Política at the Pontificia Universidad Católica de Chile. These doctoral programs gave us a unique perspective on the research problems of the discipline, as well as models of how to pursue scholarship in Political Science from the South. While we relish living in Latin America, close to our research subjects, doing Political Science from the South is extremely challenging. We have benefitted, however, from the professionalization and transformation of the social sciences that have taken place in Argentina, Chile and Uruguay, and from their internationalization. These transformations can be seen, for example, in the activities of different global and regional networks (e.g., EGAP and REPAL) and in the organization of local initiatives with regional projection, such as the Escuela de Verano en Métodos Mixtos at the Instituto de Ciencia Política of the Pontificia Universidad Católica de Chile and the Escuela de Invierno en Métodos y Análisis de Datos organized by the Departamento de Ciencias Sociales of the Universidad Católica del Uruguay

We are deeply grateful to many different people in the Frente Amplio (FA). Their guidance and support were crucial to the successful completion of this book. Verónica Piñeiro, Blanca Elgart, Sergio Pratto, Manuel Ferrer, and Andrés Correa helped us access crucial data and were an effective liaison with key interviewees. They had to put up with our repeated requests for data and our anxiety about completing the fieldwork. The book would never have become a reality without their invaluable help. We also want to thank Javier Miranda, President of the FA, and the Grupo de los 41 for their interest in our project and support during our fieldwork. We thank the almost forty interviewees and the FA adherents who answered the survey we administered. This project would never have seen the light of day had they not been so generously giving of their time. We especially thank Gerardo Silvera, Mariana Castelnoble, and Myriam Fernández, grassroots activists of the Mario Benedetti Base Committee, for generously and enthusiastically providing us access to their Base Committee venue, which is featured on the book's cover photo.

The three of us have the privilege to work in institutions that have been very supportive of this project. We are thus thankful to the Departamento de Ciencia Política at the Universidad de la República, the Departamento de Ciencias Sociales at the Universidad Católica del Uruguay, and the Escuela de Ciencia Política at the Universidad Diego Portales in Chile. Rafael Piñeiro wishes to thank Juan Bogliaccini and Rosario Queirolo, chairs of his department during the execution of this project. Fernando Rosenblatt thanks Manuel Vicuña, dean of the Facultad de Ciencias Sociales e Historia, Universidad Diego Portales. Fernando Rosenblatt also wishes to thank his administration colleagues at the Escuela de Ciencia Política, Claudia Pozo, Eva Hamamé, María Cosette Godoy, and Rodrigo

Espinoza for their constant support and patience during the process of developing and completing this book.

We also want to express our deepest gratitude to Sara Doskow, editor at Cambridge University Press, and her colleagues Danielle Menz and Joshua Penney. They were very helpful during the review and in the process of preparing the final draft of this book. Elements of Chapters 1, 3, and 5 of this book were first published in *Comparative Political Studies* Volume 52 #6 (2019). We are thankful to the editors of this journal, David Samuels and Ben Ansell, for permission to reproduce the paper.

Lihuen Nocetto and Santiago Acuña were key assistants throughout the project. Each of them helped us in so many ways that we cannot even recall all their tasks. They not only helped us collect and systematize a vast amount of data, but also assisted us in thinking through our argument, offering insightful comments and showing great attention to detail. They were very committed to the project. Martín Opertti, Victoria Vega, Camilo García, and Tamara Pantoja were all terrific research assistants at different stages of the project. They did an excellent job collecting evidence, transcribing in-depth interviews, processing motions and other FA documents, and conducting a review of newspapers. David Schwartz also played a crucial role in this endeavor. His professional editing services and his willingness to help with all aspects of the book greatly improved our work.

We are very thankful to Emiliano Cotelo and the team of En Perspectiva Producciones for their generosity in sharing their magnificent archive of press material. Javier Castro also helped us access press material. We also thank Pedro Cribari, Miguel Aguirre Bayley, Martín Ponce de León, Jorge Pasculli, Álvaro Padrón, and Luis Casal Beck for sharing their documents and their deep knowledge about the FA.

The project has been enriched by the generous and thoughtful comments of many colleagues. In 2016, Fernando Rosenblatt presented the pre-analysis plan of the project at Seminario ICSO of the Facultad de Ciencias Sociales e Historia of the Universidad Diego Portales. We are thankful to Maite de Cea for her help in this activity. In 2018, we organized a book workshop at the Universidad Diego Portales, Chile. We are deeply grateful for the time our colleagues took to read and discuss a very rough draft of the manuscript. David Altman, Santiago Anria, Rossana Castiglioni, Jorge Gordín, Alfredo Joignant, Patricio Navia, Lihuen Nocetto, Carolina Segovia, Sergio Toro, Gabriel Vommaro, Laura Wills-Otero, and Lisa Zanotti participated in the eight-hour workshop. Beyond these workshops, many other colleagues contributed at different stages of the project. Jake Bowers and Guadalupe Tuñón contributed significant methodological insights that helped us prepare our survey and survey experiments. We are also very grateful to Kurt Weyland, who gave us very important comments on Chapter 4. Juan Pablo Luna and Jorge Lanzaro offered very interesting comments and critiques that helped us improve the presentation of our argument. Jaime Yaffé read the entire manuscript in the final stage and raised very interesting points that enabled us to improve the final version of the book. We also had numerous conversations with Felipe Monestier, Cecilia Rossel, Germán Bidegain, Diego Hernández, Santiago López Cariboni, Juan Andrés Moraes, Diego Luján, Cecilia Rocha, Daniela Vairo, Sebastián Etchemendy, Daniel Buquet, Adolfo Garcé, Daniel Chasquetti, Juan Bogliaccini, and Rosario Queirolo. They were all very generous and offered valuable remarks on different issues at various stages of the project.

We have presented early versions of different chapters of this book at several conferences. We received thoughtful comments from Germán Lodola at the Latin American Congress of Political Science (ALACIP) in Montevideo in 2017. He also offered very interesting comments as a discussant at LASA 2017. At LASA 2018, we received very generous comments from Santiago Anria. Finally, we are very thankful to the three anonymous reviewers whose comments helped us to streamline the theory and improve the empirical analysis.

Finally, we are very thankful to our families and friends. Ricardo Bica contributed his talents in creating the cover photo. Rafael thanks Susana, José, Verónica, and Manuel for their unceasing support. Fernando thanks Rosario Destéffanis for all her support. He also thanks Yamhi and Lena for their love, patience, warmth, and enthusiasm that sustain him.

# Abbreviations

| | |
|---|---|
| ADEOM | Asociación de Empleados y Obreros Municipales (Mayoralty's Union Workers) |
| ANCAP | Administración Nacional de Combustibles, Alcohol y Portland (Oil, Alcohol, and Cement National Administration) |
| AU | Asamblea Uruguay (Uruguayan Assembly) |
| CAP-L | Corriente de Acción y Pensamiento-Libertad (Action and Thought Tendency-Freedom) |
| CNT | Convención Nacional de Trabajadores (National Workers Convention) |
| CPO | Causal Process Observation |
| DC | Partido Demócrata Cristiano (Chilean Christian Democratic Party) |
| DSV | Double Simultaneous Vote |
| EGAP | Evidence in Governance and Politics |
| EP | Encuentro Progresista (Progressive Encounter) |
| FA | Frente Amplio (Broad Front) |
| FIDEL | Frente de Izquierda de Liberación (Leftist Liberation Front) |
| FLS | Frente Líber Seregni (Líber Seregni Front) |
| FRAP | Frente de Acción Popular (Popular Action Front) |
| FREDEJUSO | Frente por la Democracia y Justicia Social (Social Justice and Democracy Front) |
| FREPASO | Frente País Solidario (Solidary Country Front) |
| FTA | Free Trade Agreement |

| | |
|---|---|
| GAU | Grupos de Acción Unificadora (Groups of Unified Action) |
| GDP | Gross Domestic Product |
| IDI | Izquierda Democrática Independiente (Independent Democratic Left) |
| ISI | Import Substitution Industry |
| JUP | Juventud Uruguaya de Pie (Uruguayan Standing Youth) |
| MAS | Movimiento al Socialismo (Movement toward Socialism) |
| MERCOSUR | Mercado Común del Sur (Common Market of the South) |
| MLN | Movimiento de Liberación Nacional-Tupamaros (National Liberation Movement) |
| MPG | Movimiento por el Gobierno del Pueblo (Movement for the Government of the People) |
| MPP | Movimiento de Participación Popular (Popular Participation Movement) |
| NGO | Nongovernmental Organization |
| ONI | Organización Nacional de Independientes (National Organization of Independents) |
| PAP-Q | Preanalysis Plan-Qualitative |
| PC | Partido Colorado (Colorado Party) |
| PCCh | Partido Comunista de Chile (Chilean Communist Party) |
| PCU | Partido Comunista del Uruguay (Communist Party of Uruguay) |
| PDC | Partido Demócrata Cristiano (Christian Democratic Party) |
| PIT-CNT | Plenario Intersindical de Trabajadores – Convención Nacional de Trabajadores (Interunion Workers Plenary – National Workers Convention) |
| PJ | Partido Justicialista (Justicialist Party) |
| PLUNA | Primeras Líneas Uruguayas de Navegación Aérea (First Uruguayan Airlines) |
| PN | Partido Nacional (National Party) |
| POR | Partido Obrero Revolucionario (Revolutionary Workers Party) |
| PPD | Partido por la Democracia (Party for Democracy) |
| PRSD | Partido Radical Social Demócrata (Radical Social Democratic Party) |
| PSCh | Partido Socialista de Chile (Chilean Socialist Party) |
| PSU | Partido Socialista del Uruguay (Socialist Party of Uruguay) |

| | |
|---|---|
| PT | Partido dos Trabalhadores (Workers Party) |
| PVP | Partido por la Victoria del Pueblo (Party for the Victory of the People) |
| TISA | Trade in Services Agreement |
| UCR | Unión Cívica Radical (Civil Radical Union) |
| UN | United Nations |
| UP | Unidad Popular (Popular Unity) |
| US | United States of America |
| USSR | Union of Soviet Socialist Republics |

I

# Introduction

How do party organizational structure and rules affect political engagement and its reproduction? To answer this question, you might take a walk in Montevideo, Uruguay on a Thursday evening, around 8 PM. It is likely that, at some point, you will find a locale where eight to fifteen people are discussing politics. They might be debating the Middle East conflict, free-trade agreements, labor policy, or the future of the neighborhood's public square. Among these people you might notice some young persons but, most likely, you will see middle-aged persons or retirees. You might find both men and women. These gatherings occur any time of the year, summer or winter, regardless of the electoral calendar. The locales are humble places that have only the essential furniture, usually old and often not in great condition. There are basic amenities, such as a gas or electric heater for warmth in the winter or a fan to provide relief from the summer heat. These items are usually donated by the same people who participate in the meetings. The interior walls are covered with political symbols and old campaign posters. The exterior walls are painted in red, blue, and white and usually have a blackboard announcing upcoming meetings or events. This is a Frente Amplio (Broad Front, FA) Comité de Base (Base Committee).

María Ema is typical of the attendees you might encounter at a Base Committee meeting. She is around seventy years old. After graduating from university, she worked as a teacher and principal in a school for children with disabilities and participated in the teacher's union. She has been a member of the FA since its founding. After her husband died in the 1990s, she decided to become active in a Base Committee. She initially participated in a Base Committee located in the western part of

Montevideo, the sector where the FA has its stronghold. She later moved to the center of the city and participated in another Base Committee. Over the years, she became familiar to her fellow FA activists and, in 1997, she began participating as a grassroots activist delegate to the National Plenary and the National Political Board (the highest decision-making bodies of the party). Since becoming a delegate, she has been participating both in her Base Committee and in the meetings of the highest decision-making bodies of the party.

Gabriel is another typical attendee. He is around thirty years old. He joined a Base Committee for the first time when he was twenty-seven, in November 2010, after the presidential elections of 2009. He holds a BA in Communications. Since 2012, he has been serving as a delegate to the National Plenary. José is another typical attendee. He is around sixty years old and is an independent bookseller, selling door-to-door. He has been in the FA since its founding in 1971, when he was fifteen years old. Since the 1990s, he has participated in different commissions and now serves on the FA's directorate. Verónica is another attendee. She is in her thirties, a biologist, and has participated in the FA since she was eighteen years old. She began by participating in one of the FA's factions and subsequently participated in a Base Committee. A few years later, she was selected as the organizational secretary of her zone. More recently, she has become the FA vice president, representing the FA's grassroots activists. After becoming vice president, she continued to participate in her Base Committee as an organizer.

As these histories illustrate, people who attend a Base Committee meeting might also act as delegates to different bodies of the party organization, including the top echelons of the party. However, these delegates are indistinguishable from the rest of the attendees. Anyone can be a delegate, and delegates neither hold a government position nor receive any compensation for their role. Moreover, neither the delegates nor the Base Committee have any resources to distribute, either to Committee members or to their neighbors. None of the delegates are professional politicians and none harbor aspirations of pursuing a political career that could lead them to a government position. As grassroots delegates, however, they sit face-to-face with the most important political leaders of the party.

Our data suggest that there are around 7,000 committed FA activists who participate in some type of political activity many times during the year. Across the country, the FA has over 300 Base Committees, which hold meetings at least once every two weeks and where activists gather and debate political issues. As elections approach, they start coordinating their campaign activities, such as intense face-to-face canvassing and meetings with national leaders. Many FA leaders question the role of the Base Committees within the party structure, arguing that they do not renew their membership, that they are essentially outdated, i.e., in their ideological preferences and their type of organization, or that they are controlled by the most leftist factions. Regardless of these arguments, the Base Committees are unequivocal proof of a party that has intense activism from voluntary grassroots members.

The FA has been successful in electoral terms, obtaining 18.3 percent of the votes in the first election in which it participated in 1971, and reaching 50.4 percent in the national election of 2004, the first time it won the presidency. It also retained the presidency and an absolute majority in both chambers of Congress in the two subsequent elections, garnering 49.3 percent and 49.4 percent of the popular vote in 2009 and 2014, respectively.

Yet, the history of the FA is not simply of electoral success. It also has an impressively large number of members: 502,930 according to FA administrative data (as of 2017). This number constitutes 19.3 percent of the Uruguayan electorate. As with every party registry, the FA's registry is outdated, and this number almost certainly overestimates the actual number of active members. However, the number of people who participate in internal elections (i.e., to elect the organization's officials) is significant. In 2006, 222,795 of these members, out of a national population of 2.5 million adults (i.e., sixteen years old and older), voted in the party's internal election. In 2012, participation declined to 170,770 and in 2016 only around 80,000 people voted. This level is still impressive, given the voluntary and strictly partisan nature of the election. If 80,000 is the actual number of active members, they represent 3 percent of the Uruguayan adult citizenry.

The 2016 internal election took place in winter, in every sense of the word. It was cold, it was windy; a typical dark, rainy, winter day in Uruguay. Also, elections occurred at a time of retrenchment of progressive and leftist forces in Latin America, of both populist and more institutionalized parties, after eleven years in government and at the lowest point in the government's popularity. If we add to these factors the fact that some members urged people not to vote, as a way of expressing the degree of their frustration and anger against the party, the expected level of turnout was very low; and, indeed, a lower number of *frenteamplistas* voted, compared to 2012. In fact, while the turnout for the 2016 internal FA election was indeed lower than in previous years, it is remarkable that the organization was able to organize 1,000 voting locales and mobilize 5,000 volunteers who prepared and organized everything.

Notwithstanding the number of members that distinguishes the FA from other parties, many political parties in the world have a membership that represents an equally high percentage of the electorate (Scarrow 2015). The distinctive trait of the FA lies in the number of its grassroots activists (not simply adherents) and, more significantly, the organizational structure and rules that grant these activists a direct political role.

The FA so far has exhibited a uniquely high level of organizational vitality. In fact, Levitsky and Roberts (2011) classified leftist parties in Latin America and categorized the FA as the only mass-organic leftist party. What facilitates the reproduction of party organization after forty-eight years of existence and fourteen years in government? What is the effect of the party's organizational traits on political engagement and its reproduction? Finally, how do party structure and a high level of activist participation influence party success? By employing multiple methods, which include process tracing, thick description, and experimental research, this volume seeks to develop a theory concerning the effects of vibrant party organization and democratic representation.[1]

Scholars widely accept that democratic representation requires the existence of political parties (Aldrich 1995, Fiorina 1980, Hagopian and Mainwaring 2005, Sartori 1976). Indeed, almost every book that analyzes parties or party systems quotes Schattschneider's (Schattschneider 1942) famous dictum that democracy is "unthinkable save in terms of parties" (1). Therefore, the study of party organizations is crucial to our understanding of the way democratic representation works in different contexts.

The party-politics literature has contributed significantly to our understanding of the evolution of types of political parties (Duverger 1954, Gunther and Diamond 2003, Katz and Mair 1995, Kirchheimer 1966,

---

[1] It is widely accepted that experimental designs ought to be registered (Dunning 2016). However, and in line with Evidence in Governance and Politics (EGAP) research standards, we argue that qualitative research should also be registered. Following Piñeiro and Rosenblatt (2016): "beyond reinforcing the connection between theory and evidence, and encouraging greater transparency in qualitative research, the PAP-Q supports and guides the work of the researcher by structuring the process and by pushing the researcher to carefully think of the design" (p. 794). The pre-analysis plan is posted to the study registry of the EGAP network. http://egap.org/registration/1989

Panebianco 1988). One of the dimensions along which parties are classified is the level of membership attachment. The cadre party comprises a small elite of members of parliament, while the mass-organic party includes a large number of citizens within the party ranks. There are compelling analyses concerning the structural (Mainwaring and Zoco 2007, Webb and White 2007a), institutional (Samuels and Shugart 2010), and organizational (Scarrow 2015, Scarrow and Gezgor 2010, Scarrow, Webb, and Poguntke 2017) determinants of the decay of party activism, especially in recent decades. Thus, the literature also highlights circumstances that make it difficult for parties to function properly in contemporary societies, even while it emphasizes the essential role parties play as the most critical agents of democratic representation.

Whether or not one agrees with this general claim, it is clear that the old mass-organic type of party, described by Duverger (1954), has disappeared. New technologies have significantly decreased the costs of disseminating a political message and to incorporate voters' needs in party platforms. Political parties in high- or middle-income societies no longer need activists to win elections (Hersh 2015, Issenberg 2012). Also, given that having a large and complex organization is costly and harder to manage and control, party leaders have no interest in maintaining activists and a large organizational structure.

The party-politics literature typically accounts for the evolution of parties and their organizational changes in terms of exogenous factors. That is, the organization is usually set as the dependent variable, influenced by societal changes or contextual conditions, exogenous factors that determine the organizational forms and the transformations that parties undergo. From this perspective, parties cannot avoid their supposed fate. By contrast, focusing on the dynamics that occur within parties – especially the institutions established within parties – might help elucidate the diverse ways in which parties adapt to exogenous challenges and overcome the determinism that characterizes the literature. This volume thus contributes to the literature studying the role organizational structure plays in determining the fate of a political party (Anria 2018, Bermeo and Yashar 2016, Burgess and Levitsky 2003, Calvo and Murillo 2019, Cyr 2017, Levitsky 2003, Levitsky et al. 2016, Panebianco 1988, Scarrow 2015).

In some cases, when organizations exist they are merely vehicles of party leaders who determine party strategies. In other cases, however, the organization is important and constrains leaders' preferences. In institutionalized party systems, where organizations have value, party organizations' characteristics influence both their ability to adapt to contextual challenges and secular changes and the form this adaptation takes (Huntington 1968, Piñeiro and Rosenblatt 2018).

The electoral success of the FA and its capacity to challenge the established Uruguayan foundational parties (Colorado and National Party, PC and PN) and its ability to be a pole of attraction for social movements was accompanied by the existence of institutionalized channels for *voice*, through which the party activists influence strategic decisions. These channels provide a means for activists to influence the party's agenda, and to exercise a veto over party leaders' objectives. Activists participate in the party's strategic discussions and party leaders, when making decisions, consider the potential problems they might face if they deviate far from activists' preferences. Thus, the party grassroots members constitute a potential (or actual) threat to incumbent party elites.

We claim that organizational attributes have historical causes (Stinchcombe 1968). In our case study, the FA was born as a coalition of left-of-center organizations. However, due to an explosion of bottom-up activism that coincided with the party's inception, the FA developed a common structure that privileged consensus and balance among members. This resulted in the gradual establishment of grassroots activists' institutionalized role in the decision making in every aspect of the party's life (e.g., programmatic discussion, presidential ticket nomination, among others). Moreover, the founding leaders conceived the FA both as a coalition and as a movement. Indeed, the party's founding proclamation expresses this notion. This implies, from the very beginning, the presence of strong bottom-up participation and clear organizational structures by which grassroots activists could directly influence party decisions. This well-structured organization with institutionalized opportunities for bottom-up voice inhibits radical changes and favors long-term political consistency of the party brand.

Throughout the FA's foundational stage, the party gradually ensured multiple veto points, and checks and balances between party structures. This, in turn, was consolidated and reproduced through feedback mechanisms (see Chapter 4). We claim that the early consolidation of a dense and complex organizational structure and rules that ensure activists a significant voice in the organization is the key to understanding the ability of a mass-organic party to reproduce activism, both while in opposition and while in government (see Chapter 5). The party acquired this characteristic during its foundational stage (1971–1986) and the FA continues to this day to be a party with activists. As a result of the production and reproduction of this structure and rules, the party organization limits the discretion of the government, a crucial way in which the FA differs from the norm of party organizations in presidential regimes (Samuels and Shugart 2010). This does not imply that one observes a constant confrontation between grassroots activists and national leaders; in fact, the general picture is one of support, of an army of volunteers who are willing to work for the organization and for the success of those leaders. However, the grassroots activists have been able to exercise veto power on both symbolic and substantive issues for a leftist party (see Chapter 6). Yet, the FA is not governed by this movement. Moreover, the activists do not necessarily facilitate the party's approach to the median voter. In terms of decision making, the activists' influence has the potential to block a particular government decision on a sensitive issue or they might simply reduce the government's decisiveness concerning a given course of action.

At its origin in 1971, the FA relied heavily on volunteer activism to advance its electoral goals. Nonetheless, as time went by, the FA ceased to depend exclusively on volunteer organizers to win elections. More critically, there are fewer people today willing to volunteer as party activists or to invest time in the organization. This weakening of organizational attachment is a general trait among other mass-organic parties. The critical difference is that the FA still reproduces activists. The FA reproduces its mass-organic nature in its grassroots structure, the movement of Base Committees.

In the context of the generalized decline of mass party organizations that were formed by significant numbers of activists, the FA is a deviant case, because the party still retains large numbers of engaged activists who are not a cadre of bureaucrats nor a part of a structure to deliver clientelistic goods (c.f. Levitsky 2003). Moreover, it is an intensely and permanently mobilized institutionalized party organization in Latin America. Thus, it provides an opportunity to test several hypotheses about the reproduction of activists' engagement beyond the impact of exogenous processes.

The crucial difference between the FA and other parties is the presence of activists throughout the territory who have an active role in the party's decision making. These activists differ from adherents or members, both in their willingness to engage in volunteer activism and in the elasticity of their engagement behavior based on individuals' perceptions of efficacy within the organization (see Chapter 5). While grassroots activism now plays a less important function for the party than it did during the foundational stage, grassroots activism still exists and is widespread in the territory.

This book analyzes the value of an organization-centered approach for understanding parties and their role in democratic representation. First, it sheds light on the evolution and challenges of intense engagement in political organizations. Second, it addresses the significance of bottom-up participation. Lastly, the study's findings illuminate the problems confronting declining, eroding political parties in democracies of the developed world. The study thereby addresses important current questions, such as whether parties remain efficacious vehicles of democratic representation, and, if so, what kinds of parties are most promising in this respect.

## THEORY

The case of the FA challenges general theories about party development. On the one hand, it challenges Michels' "iron" law of oligarchy (1999 [1911]). In the FA, the presence of grassroots activists in the decision-making structure, with veto power and autonomy from leadership, constrains elites' ability to pursue any given strategy. On the other hand, it challenges the idea that parties exhibit a uniform trajectory of development and decay in contemporary societies, especially in the Latin American context. The reproduction of activism in the FA challenges the idea of a linear trajectory of party development, especially in a region where all structural conditions hinder party development.

The case of the FA also challenges the dominant perspective in the party-politics literature that stresses that candidate selection is the cornerstone of a party's internal democracy. This dominant perspective typically equates internal democracy with the competition between elites or groups that seek to influence the candidate-selection processes. In the case of the FA, however, this dynamic is only observable in the faction structure (described below), while in the grassroots structure democracy is based on the existence of grassroots delegates who influence the direction of the party. Candidate selection thus is not critical for the party's internal democracy because it is built around the direct participation of grassroots activists throughout the party decision-making bodies. Moreover, the separation of the grassroots structure from the candidate-selection process and grassroots members' influence in the party's decision-making process helps the FA grassroots structure avoid oligarchization. That is, party leaders cannot exert direct influence over the grassroots structure by, for example, controlling candidate selection or material resources.

Michels (1999 [1911]) described what he termed the "iron" law of oligarchy, i.e., a natural process that all political organizations undergo. Parties, according to this view, oligarchize as a result of a natural force that closes the channels for effective *voice* within the organization. Hence, at the organizational level, parties proceed unavoidably down a path toward the concentration of power in the hands of a small, professional elite. As a result, agents (party elites) distance themselves from principals (party members) who do not constrain their decisions. On the one hand, professional politicians control information and generate asymmetries of information with members. On the other hand, elites control resources that are valuable for members, which helps elites control members. In Michels' account, oligarchization leads both to the exhaustion of activists' role in the decision making and to the moderation of parties. In this vein, for example, the party-in-government might trigger this process by strengthening a group of elite incumbents who control many resources, as happened with the Partido dos Trabalhadores (Workers Party, PT) in Brazil (Ribeiro 2014).

The literature has also claimed that party organizations are decreasingly relevant actors of interest aggregation and representation (Dalton and Wattenberg 2000). Numerous authors have suggested that modernization and globalization largely account for parties' increasing difficulties at remaining relevant institutions (Dalton and Wattenberg 2000, Inglehart and Welzel 2005, Mainwaring and Zoco 2007, Webb and White 2007a). The literature has described the general erosion of century-old voter and partisan loyalties (Dalton and Wattenberg 2000). Societal transformations in recent decades have put pressure on party organizations because contemporary parties must now share the representation function with more organizations than in the past. New means of communication have changed how collective action is organized (Bimber, Flanagin, and Stohl 2012). Parties now seem forced to transform themselves into smaller and more professional organizations that activate for electoral campaigns; as a result of societal changes, a new, more professionalized and cartelized party organization has emerged (Katz and Mair 1995). This literature tends to depict an unrealistic normal course that stresses homogeneity and mutes divergence in outcomes.

The literature concerning political parties and, more broadly, the literature on democratic representation capture a general trend of political party transformation in response to exogenous changes. For example,

Kitschelt (1994) studied the challenges of societal transformations in the organization of European social democracy. More recently, Scarrow (2015), in work concerning the transformations of party organizations, observed a reduction in number of activists and an increase in adherents. The FA also exhibits a smooth decline over time in level of activism, yet it retains an organizational structure and rules that challenge the general trend found in most of the literature.

In developing societies, parties are also subject to additional structural and contextual constraints that they find difficult to escape. The "dual transition" to democracy and to a market economy in Latin America was followed in some countries by the decomposition of party systems and, in other countries, by the inability to establish a stable system (Bogliaccini 2019 Coppedge 1998a,b, Roberts 2014). During the Third Wave of democratization that started around the end of the 1970s and continued during the 1980s, Latin American party systems showed high levels of electoral volatility (Jones 2005, Mainwaring 2018, Mainwaring and Scully 1995, Roberts and Wibbels 1999). The exhaustion of the ISI development model, the succession of deep economic and political crises (including hyperinflation, coup attempts, etc.) and the enactment of market reforms (Remmer 1991, Weyland 2002) undermined the representation function of political party systems (Roberts 2014). The abrupt transformation of the development model, from state-centered to market-oriented, was a critical juncture that, according to Roberts (2014), fundamentally changed the social bases of political parties. This affected party organizations. As the author notes, not all party systems, nor all party organizations, react similarly. Roberts provides an explanation for the party system level; he claims that divergent results depend on the intersection of three causal factors, which in turn correspond to different historical phases: 1. the nature of the party system during the ISI; 2. the depth and duration of the 1980s economic depression and the enactment of market reforms; and 3. the political characteristics of those who led the reforms. These factors determined whether the double transition resulted in an ideologically aligned party system or a dealigned (or even collapsed) party system.

The relationship between presidentialism and democratic instability has been extensively analyzed in the comparative politics literature (Linz 1994, Mainwaring and Shugart 1997, Przeworski et al. 2000). Presidentialism also affects the stability of party systems (Linz 1990, Samuels and Shugart 2010, Webb and White 2007b ). Presidents are directly elected for fixed periods, and parties in a presidential regime cannot control the chief executive as effectively as can parliamentary parties under parliamentarism. Presidentialism also endangers party organization through the personalization of politics (Linz 1994). Samuels and Shugart (2010) show that under presidentialism, parties are weaker and there are far more "policy switches" than under parliamentarism.

In Venezuela in the 1990s, and in the Chilean, Colombian and Costa Rican party systems in the 2000s, deinstitutionalization, or even collapse, has ensued (Dargent and Muñoz 2011, Luna and Altman 2011, Morgan 2011, Rovira Mas 2001, Seawright 2012). Public opinion also reveals the erosion of links between parties and societies (Lupu 2014). While we do not deny the causal effects of these factors – indeed, their importance is widely accepted based on considerable empirical evidence – we believe that other factors, especially parties' organizational structures and rules, can explain different party trajectories.

Some studies have identified causal factors that account for the ability of some party organizations in Latin America to adapt to exogenous challenges (Burgess and Levitsky 2003, Cyr 2017, Levitsky 2003, Levitsky et al. 2016, Wills Otero 2015). Hunter (2010), for example, focuses on the PT's gradual process of adaptation and its impressive electoral growth. Madrid (2012) and Anria (2016) explain the emergence of the Movimiento al Socialismo (Movement Toward Socialism, MAS) in Bolivia. Yet, the literature that emphasizes the causal role of organizational attributes is scant compared to the large body of work that focuses on societal and institutional variables.

## Historical Causation

The peculiar internal structure of the FA and the rules that ensure the direct participation of grassroots activists' delegates in the highest decision-making bodies of the party are a result of historical causes. As Stinchcombe (1968) stresses, for this type of causation, the outcome of interest reproduces itself over time regardless of whether the causes that ignited its occurrence in the first place continue to exist. We explain the historical causes of the FA's organizational structure and, more critically, we highlight the mechanism of reproduction (i.e., the feedback processes that reproduce the outcome). Our explanation resembles Panebianco's (1988, 50) argument about the importance of "genetic imprints" (50).

Despite the historical trends and structural conditions that allegedly hinder party activism, the FA did not become a professional–electoral party and did not oligarchize. The key to understanding the ability of the FA to reproduce activism and its grassroots structure is related to the early establishment of rules that gave a significant role to grassroots activists in the party's decision-making bodies. Moreover, the *frenteamplista* base movement, which grew explosively in a single year, from the end of 1970 to the national elections of 1971, was granted a direct, significant, and irreversible political role and a voice in the party's decision-making structure. Thus, since its inception, the party has maintained the political role of volunteer activists and has ensured space for engaging with new activists. This structure ensures that the grassroots activists have direct representation in the decision-making organs that is not tied to the will of the leaders or to competition between factions. Thus, the grassroots activists who gain access to the decision-making organs remain grassroots activists – they have neither access to material resources nor a decisive power of government appointments and candidate selection. With respect to their fellow grassroots activists, they act as delegates, not as trustees.

Once established, this organizational structure engendered a lock-in effect (Pierson 2004) and reproduced the party's grassroots structure. The literature that analyzes the effect on policy making and policy change of the existence of multiple actors with effective power has already emphasized that the existence of multiple actors with decision-making authority inhibits policy change and ensures policy stability – i.e., the existence of multiple players with veto power engenders policy resoluteness but inhibits policy decisiveness (Haggard and McCubbins 2001, Tsebelis 1995). Extrapolating this theory to the analysis of party organization, the institutional veto players in the FA structure set very high barriers to the introduction of changes to its basic rules. As previously noted, this does not imply that grassroots activists always act as veto players, reacting against party and government leaders, but they do retain the potential to block leaders' decisions.

The organizational structure of the FA, created during the initial stage of the party's development, engenders two avenues of engagement with the party – one that, as in every political party, channels the ambitions of prospective and incumbent professional politicians, and a second that gives voice only to grassroots activists. The former avenue comprises the allied political organizations that compete in national, regional, and local elections. The latter avenue is the common grassroots organizational structure (essentially the Base Committees). Each part of the organization selects, through internal elections, half of the party directorate, and each does so independently. The former avenue, associated with the participation at the faction level, is the one that leads to a professional–electoral party organization with an oligarchized elite. The latter avenue does not grant faction leaders tools to control the discussion and the selection of grassroots delegates. Also, grassroots members' delegates in the directorate lack status or the power to distribute positions or resources; thus, they are unlikely candidates for oligarchization.

The FA was born as a coalition of political organizations. The coalition was formed by traditional leftist parties, the Partido Socialista del Uruguay (Socialist Party of Uruguay, PSU), the Partido Comunista del Uruguay (Communist Party of Uruguay, PCU), other minor leftist groups, the Partido Demócrata Cristiano (Christian Democratic Party, PDC), and progressive factions that exited from the foundational National and Colorado parties. Even though the Communist and Socialist parties had deep roots in Uruguay, and despite the fact that the FA included well-known leaders from the traditional parties, no single leader or faction dominated the new FA structure. Yet, the social circumstances in Uruguay at the end of the 1960s, a period of economic stagnation and political polarization, triggered mass activism that was not channeled through the faction organizations. These grassroots activists, organized in Base Committees, became critical players in the coalition's early stages of development; they demanded participation in the decision-making structure and the coalition leaders granted it. The FA thus acquired its dual structure: one structure that pertains to the coalition of political organizations (the coalition), and the other – the Base Committees – that institutionalizes in the party the political role of the grassroots activists (what the FA calls the movement). The FA movement is essentially composed of organizers (Han 2014). These grassroots organizers are not paid and do not seek office; they thus have a rationale for participating in politics that is different from professional politicians or from those who also seek a career in government.

Professional politicians who, as in every political party, seek a career in government, satisfy their ambition in their respective political organizations within the FA – the coalition (Moraes 2008). The FA's shared structure, the movement, thus does not experience the pressure to oligarchize that is associated with the candidate-selection process and with having sufficient resources to influence political careers. Moreover, given the FA's organizational structure, the leaders of the coalition member organizations cannot control the process by which the grassroots representatives are selected. Thus, political elites cannot fully control the political process of the FA, and must share power with grassroots representatives. For grassroots members, the only available means to reproduce their political clout in the FA is by keeping their organization – the movement – alive.

At first sight, the fact that FA grassroots activists do not take part in the candidate-selection process might suggest that they are excluded from one of the most important decisions of the party and, because they do not participate in the candidate-selection process for the House and the Senate, cannot hold the party representatives accountable. However, and herein lies the FA's crucial difference, the grassroots activists' structure is relevant because it has power within the party's structure, which, in turn, controls and holds representatives and officials in government positions accountable. This grassroots structure, through its interaction with the members of the coalition (factions), helps to ensure that those who hold office in the executive and in the legislature maintain adherence to the party's programmatic principles.

The grassroots members' decision-making authority enables them to block changes to the organization's statutes, engendering a lock-in effect. These particular organizational rules explain the resistance to change. The intense activism during the early stage of the party, beyond the organizational structure of each faction, acts as a historical cause. The original rules engendered at a specific historical moment – i.e., at the birth of the party – then fostered a positive feedback; these rules produced a self-reinforcing trajectory (Mahoney and Thelen 2015) and a lock-in effect.

The lock-in effect is manifested in the institutionalization of quorums and qualified majorities that prevent changes to the statutes without the approval of grassroots activists. The positive feedback that reinforces this lock-in over time is grounded in grassroots activists' control of the socialization of new activists and their control of those who operate as delegates in the party's structure. At present, the FA does not depend exclusively on volunteer organizers to win elections. More critically, there are fewer people willing to engage as party activists or to invest time in the party. This is a general trait among other mass-based parties. However, the FA reproduces its mass-organic character. In contrast to the case of the PT (Ribeiro 2014), the power of FA activists within the organization did not wane.

## Constant Causation

Even though there are historical factors that account for the decision to establish this peculiar organizational structure and its reproduction over time, it is necessary to provide an explanation for the relationship between organizational-level structure and individual-level activism. All parties have adherents or members, i.e., people who identify with the party and eventually pay party dues and participate in party activities, mainly rallies. Football clubs that turn into business companies also retain loyal fans who are willing to buy a ticket to support their team. Nevertheless, only a few party organizations also have developed a structure of activists, that is, volunteers who are regularly involved in the organization – especially beyond electoral cycles. The crucial difference between the FA and other parties is the significant and permanent presence of activists throughout the territory who have an active role in the party organization and in the party's decision-making bodies.

Other studies that have examined the individual-level determinants of party activism focused on individuals' resources (e.g., education) or individuals' incentives – material or purposive – to join a party (Van Haute and Gauja 2015). Thus, the literature on political parties is essentially silent on the role organizational structural incentives play in the reproduction of activism, with the exception of Panebianco (1988), who discusses the role collective and selective incentives play in the reproduction of party organization. It is critically important to elucidate how organizational rules produce incentives, because sustaining an organization is the greatest challenge for a political party.

The literature on civic engagement that explains the reproduction of activism in civil-society organizations helps us build a theory about activism in party organizations (e.g., Baggetta, Han, and Andrews 2013, Bimber, Flanagin, and Stohl 2012, Han 2014, 2016, Verba, Schlozman, and Brady 1995). In this vein, Han (2014, 2016) develop multiple empirical strategies to analyze the determinants of individuals' decisions to participate in or donate money to a civic organization. More specifically, Han (2014, 5) analyzes the organizational settings of sustained activism in civic associations that make public claims, have voluntary membership, and have democratically elected leaders. High levels of engagement in these civic associations, she claims, arise when leaders seek to reach as many people as possible and also invest in forging intense attachment with new adherents, transforming them into activists. More recently, Han (2016, 296) seeks to answer how a "relational organizational context" breeds more activism in civic organizations. She stresses that a relational setting is one that ensures "responsiveness" and "openness," among other traits.

Political parties, however, are essentially different from civic associations. While civic associations are inherently oriented toward influencing or contending power, political parties are, crucially though not exclusively, oriented toward winning office (Aldrich 1995, Schlesinger 1994, Strom 1990). Thus, the role of political ambition and its satisfaction distinguishes parties from civil-society organizations and warrants a separate analysis to explain the reproduction of volunteer-member engagement, especially because political ambition might collide with a more altruistic basis for cooperation. The furtherance of a political career (and thus winning office) does not necessarily imply the construction of an organization with activists – as illustrated by the existence of "electoral–professional" parties. As suggested above, political parties have less and less need of activists to win elections. Moreover, activists are also a source of potential challengers who may seek to depose existing party elites.

In democracies, political parties fulfill other functions besides furthering individual political careers, such as, most prominently, the representation function. This function can be fulfilled even if the party only serves the career interest of one or a few ambitious leaders. Yet, to ensure the fulfillment of this function (which might otherwise be contingent on the will of a leader), parties must build a structure that operates and decides independently (based on institutionalized rules), limiting the will of the leaders. If the resulting structure institutionalizes multiple channels for voice, leaders are less likely to exert absolute control over the destiny of the organization and over the party's platform.

We argue that when a party has completed all of Panebianco's (1988) main developmental stages, the reproduction of widespread sustained party activism can be explained by an organization having an institutional design that promotes activists' voice (qua veto power). More specifically, if a party organization builds institutionalized channels to give activists a significant *voice* (Hirschman 1970), activists develop a strong sense of efficacy. When their participation is relevant for the definition of party strategies and positions, activists perceive that they exert real influence in party decision making. In this vein, rules generate both selective incentives (associated with individual's perceived efficacy) and collective incentives (associated with individuals' role in maintaining the party's identity and programmatic stance). The existence of these organizational structures generates the necessary incentives for those who participate in it to remain engaged and to maintain the organization's vitality. The only way that grassroots activists can retain their *voice* is by keeping the organization operative. This includes reproducing engagement with the organization, transforming adherents into activists. A party that lacks activists with a vested interest in transforming adherents into activists eventually would have only adherents. Activists work as organizers in the FA, keeping alive the party organization. As Han (2014) stresses, organizers transform adherents into activists by engaging with people who were attracted to the party by its leaders. For example, once a person shows interest in engaging with the party, FA activists keep these prospective activists informed of meetings, and invite them to work for the organization as volunteers. Therefore, the FA, like all parties, has leaders who mobilize voters, but it also has organizers. As Han (2014) has shown, this type of organization is the kind that reproduces activism.

One strand of the literature focuses on analyzing regime-level institutions to explain engagement. Rhodes-Purdy (2017) surveys the effects of perceived efficacy in the reproduction of participation in populist regimes. As another strand of the literature has shown, clientelistic parties maintain activists at the base level to build a clientelistic network where an organization with territorial penetration is needed to distribute goods and mobilize voters, especially in settings where TV propaganda is not necessarily the most efficient tool for mobilizing voters – e.g., Peronism in Argentina (Kitschelt and Wilkinson 2007, Levitsky 2003, Luna 2014, Nichter 2008, Stokes et al. 2013). However, our analysis focuses on the FA, a party that, in contrast to populist regimes or parties that build a clientelistic linkage between leaders and a party cadre, reproduces voluntary engagement in what is basically a programmatic context.

In the case of the FA, activists have an institutionalized role in the decision-making structure. They have institutionalized channels that facilitate participation; more crucially, these channels enable them to exert a significant *voice* (Hirschman 1970), which imbues activists' participation with a strong sense of *efficacy*. Building on Pizzorno (1970), Panebianco (1988) analyzed how selective and collective incentives affect individual's level of engagement with parties. The term *collective incentives* refers to how leaders reproduce a party's identity and satisfy party members' need to identify with ideas and values. Selective incentives, by contrast, concern leaders' ability to distribute positions within the party or in government, or other types of patronage. While collective incentives are crucial for voters, supporters, and members, activists' willingness to continue their activism depends on a combination of both collective and selective incentives. Activists will participate as long as the party leadership provides these two types of incentives. However, this exchange between leaders and activists, whereby activists provide their voluntary work in exchange for these incentives, implies, in Panebianco's terms, that such participation is functional to leaders' interests. In other words, activists delegate to leaders the authority to define the party's strategies. As a result, leaders are not restricted by activists' preferences but by the party's general identity, i.e., leaders need to satisfy collective incentives.

According to Panebianco, the terms of the relationship and exchange between activists[2] and leaders is influenced by exogenous conditions (Panebianco 1988). In this exchange, leaders will have more power vis-à-vis activists when the latter have no alternative (i.e., no ability to participate in other parties or organizations that represent their ideas and values). For Panebianco, party rules and their operation only set the party positions that leaders can use as selective incentives. In Panebianco's terms, these rules are completely manipulable by leaders and are only restricted by the decreasing marginal utility leaders derive from the creation of new positions and offices within the party. This point of view is also assumed by those who observe party rules and claim that formal rules are a façade that obscures the actual informal rules that are easily manipulated by leaders (Freidenberg and Levitsky 2007, Levitsky 2003).

Our point is that rules do, in fact, matter and can influence these exchanges between leaders and activists, and hence activists' relative power vis-à-vis leaders. In the case of the FA, formal rules matter. They ensure activists' voices in the definition of the party's positions and this efficacy operates as a selective incentive to participate. The efficacy operates as a selective incentive because FA rules empower individuals to influence party decision making. This is not an incentive controlled by party leaders, it is an incentive set by the rules that prevent leaders from exercising power over activists in the party's decision-making process. Even if activists lose their relevance for the party's day-to-day operation and electoral success, and are no longer relevant for leaders, these rules limit the power that leaders hold over them. Activists do not depend on leaders for selective incentives to participate.

We argue that perceived efficacy does not imply individual causal influence over party decisions but, rather, participation in a process that aggregates individual wills to produce collective decisions. As Przeworski (2010) states:

---

[2] Believers – only interested in collective incentives, and careerists – interested in selective incentives.

No rule, however, of collective decision making other than unanimity can render causal efficacy to individual participation. Collective self-government is achieved not when each voter has causal influence on the final result, but when collective choice is a result of aggregating individual wills.

(15)

Perceived efficacy is thus associated with understanding that the decision-making process is not captured by the party bureaucrats or the leadership. This does not imply that every person who engages in the party structure will have a strong sense of efficacy. In particular, those who hold policy positions that are systematically in the minority might feel alienated by the party rules and exit the organization.

The sense of efficacy stimulates activists' willingness to participate and reproduce such activism. In line with Han (2014), these activists need to be organizers (i.e., activists who reproduce the organization by transforming new adherents into activists). The reproduction of activism in the FA with an extensive network of permanent activists is facilitated by a specific institutional design that creates positive incentives for reproducing activism. As suggested by the historical causation, this organizational structure is locked-in; while it is possible to change this structure, there are very high thresholds for enacting a change in party rules. The extension of the "shadow of the future" due to the high costs associated with enacting institutional change elicits the reproduction of voluntary activists' political engagement (Axelrod 1984, Dal Bó 2005).

## METHODS

### Case Selection: Why the Frente Amplio?

The FA is a deviant case that enables us to focus on endogenous factors to explain the reproduction of activism. In the context of the generalized decline of mass party organizations that were formed by significant numbers of activists, the FA is a deviant case because the party still retains engaged activists who are neither a cadre of bureaucrats nor part of a structure to deliver clientelistic goods. It is a successful case of leftist party building and reproduction. Moreover, it is a permanently mobilized party organization. The FA has been successful in electoral terms, increasing its electoral share of the votes from 18.3 percent in its first election in 1971 to 50.4 percent in the national election of 2004, when it won the presidency. It retained the presidency and the absolute majority in both chambers of Congress for the next two elections (in 2009 and 2014). Also, thus far, the

FA has not become a cartel party; there is no complete "interpenetration of party and state" (Katz and Mair 1995, 16). Levitsky and Roberts (2011) categorizes the FA as the only institutionalized mass-organic leftist party in Latin America.

Why, then, is it relevant to analyze the FA's organizational characteristics? The FA is an excellent case from which to extract "ideas at close range" (Collier 1999). The study of the FA provides insights into the construction, institutionalization, and reproduction of vibrant political organization in contemporary democracies. The FA has escaped the global tendency toward professionalization and personalization of politics and structural factors that have pushed mass-organic parties to become electoral–professional organizations. The organizational structure of the FA, and its specific rules, activates the reproduction mechanism. These rules not only ensure the existence of a grassroots structure but also imbue the structure with efficacy, which is perceived by FA activists.

The performance of parties qua organizations is oftentimes missed. Stable and valued party organizations are still emerging or have recently emerged. Throughout democratic regimes at different degrees of consolidation, in societies at different levels of socioeconomic development, it is still possible to find parties operating as the most important political actors, leading the political process. The impressive resilience of Uruguayan parties, the continued centrality of parties in the USA and Great Britain, and recent examples of parties that emerged in Eastern Europe, East Asia, and Africa, should at least call into question the assumption that parties are increasingly irrelevant and unable to establish themselves as central and valued actors of the political process. In Eastern Europe, which underwent a very challenging transition, successful cases of democratic consolidation also have stable and vibrant political parties and, though less frequent, institutionalized party systems. Successful instances of democratic transition or the less frenzied instances of transition to a semi-democratic regime have at least one strong party organization as the central actor (Cavatorta and Merone 2013, Riedl 2008, 2014, Tavits 2008, 2013).

Yet, why should we bother studying a political party of a tiny country in South America? This is the kind of question a social scientist receives every time a phenomenon in Uruguay is put forward as a case study. Uruguay has a negligible impact on the global economy, world peace, or military power. On the other hand, it is an early polyarchy. Uruguay showed early significant levels of political incorporation and democratic competition. Moreover, its two traditional parties are among the oldest surviving parties in the world. Thus, in light of its historical trajectory, it merits consideration as a case study of the long-term dynamics of party organization. Nevertheless, Uruguay itself is not the case study; it is, rather, the context of our case study, the FA. Why, then, is it theoretically relevant to analyze an exceptional case in a small country, a case, moreover, of a type of party that is disappearing and whose birth conditions are not easily replicable?

An analogy from the natural sciences can help clarify the relevance of analyzing a case such as the FA. Medicinally useful chemical processes occur in nature and some are very difficult to replicate under laboratory conditions. Nevertheless, the only way to reproduce the useful compounds in laboratories, once the necessary technology is available, is to know the conditions under which these chemical processes occur, regardless of their rarity or of how hard they are to replicate in the laboratory. The New York Times, for example, published an article about the axolotl, a salamander found in Mexico. The story of the axolotl illustrates how studying deviant or exceptional cases can, in fact, help advance new knowledge to address recurring problems.

Scientists have decoded the genome of the axolotl, the Mexican amphibian with a Mona Lisa smile. It has 32 billion base pairs, which makes it ten times the size of the human genome, and the largest genome ever sequenced. The axolotl, endangered in the wild, has been bred in laboratories and studied for more than 150 years. It has the remarkable capacity to regrow amputated limbs complete with bones, muscles and nerves; to heal wounds without producing scar tissue; and even to regenerate damaged internal organs. This salamander can heal a crushed spinal cord and have it function just like it did before it was damaged. This ability, which exists to such an extent in no other animal, makes its genes of considerable interest (...) Now researchers, using one genetic sequencing technique to do their analysis and then another to "proof read" it, have provided researchers with the tools to study and manipulate the genes of the axolotl. Their study appears in Nature. The researchers have identified some of the genes involved in regeneration, and some genes that exist only in the axolotl, but there is much work still to be done."

(New York Times, February 1, 2018)[3]

In Biology, nobody questions the merit of research based on the size of the animal or plant, or on the size or distribution of its population. For some purposes, such as medicinal ones, the relevance is intrinsic to the case and not based on an organism's ecosystemic importance. Just as the

---

[3] The story is available in the online edition of the NY Times, www.nytimes.com/2018/02/01/science/axolotl-genes-limbs.html (accessed on March 23, 2018).

TABLE 1.1 *FA Brand Across Latin America*

| Name | Country | Date of Birth | Vote Share Last Election of Representatives |
|---|---|---|---|
| Frente Amplio | Chile | 2017 | 16.5% |
| Frente Amplio | Costa Rica | 2004 | 4.9% |
| Frente Amplio | Dominican Republic | 1992 | 1.1% |
| Frente Amplio por Justicia, Vida y Libertad | Peru | 2013 | 9.1% |
| Frente Amplio* | Paraguay | 2002 | 5.1% |
| Frente Amplio por la Democracia | Panama | 2013 | 1.0% |
| Frente Amplio Progresista | Argentina | 2011 | 16.8% |

* Includes Frente Guasu electoral coalition.
*Source*: National Electoral Commission of each country

study of the axolotl salamander may help biologists build the knowledge base needed to advance the potential of regenerative medicine, the thick study of the FA can help political science better understand the role organizational structure and rules play in promoting the reproduction of activism in political organizations.

While the FA has not captured the interest of academia,[4] over the last decade, many politicians in the region have looked to it as a model or at least as a valued brand. As a result, "Frente Amplio" parties have emerged in other Latin American countries, including Argentina, Costa Rica, Peru, and Chile (Table 1.1). All these new parties pointed to the Uruguayan FA as a successful example worthy of emulation. Its leaders, especially José Mujica and Tabaré Vázquez, are praised in the region.

In recent years, several authors have studied the causes and effects of the left turn in Latin America. Hunter (2010) and Ribeiro (2014), for example, provide a thick explanation for the impressive adaptation of Brazil's PT. Madrid (2012) and Anria (2016, 2018) provide an interesting account of the emergence of the Movement to Socialism (MAS) in Bolivia. Queirolo (2013) explains this left turn as the normal movement of the Latin American political pendulum, which experiences alternating

---

[4] The exceptions are Anria (2018), Lanzaro (2011), Luna (2007), and Pribble (2013).

periods of right and left ideological dominance. Finally, Levitsky et al. (2016), Lupu (2016), Mainwaring (2018), and Roberts (2014) provide compelling explanations for the determinants of party-system stability or instability in the context of the dramatic change that ensued following the transition from authoritarian to democratic regimes and the neoliberal wave (the so-called "dual transformation"). However, these studies, in general, do not focus on the crucial characteristics of party organizations that mediate between, on the one hand, electoral and social changes and, on the other, leaders' strategic decisions during elections and while in office (Anria 2016, 2018, Calvo and Murillo 2019 and Ribeiro 2014 are exceptions). Neither do they survey the relationship between organizational attributes, internal rules, and individual behavior, and the capacity to reproduce intense mobilization. Studying the FA provides a useful case with which to examine deeply the crucial questions raised by this literature. In contrast to Anria's study, we focus on a case in the context of an institutionalized party system and one that has persisted for more years than has the Bolivian MAS. In contrast to Ribeiro, who focuses on the "natural" process of oligarchization in the PT, our aim is instead to describe and explain how oligarchization was avoided in the FA.

In most of the literature, the organizational form and nature of political parties is overdetermined by context. In this vein, the literature has essentially described party organizations as a result of contextual changes, i.e., as an inevitable consequence of great societal, institutional, and economic contexts. The literature thus described the process of transformation from cadre to mass parties, then to catch-all and cartel parties. While we do not dispute the significance of these contextual factors, they obscure the value of the organization as an independent variable. Regardless of the type of challenge a party organization confronts, what enables a party organization to reproduce itself; i.e., to retain engaged activists? In-depth analysis of a single case facilitates the identification of endogenous sources of change as well as the interactions with institutional and structural context. More importantly, though, this case allows for an in-depth analysis of the mechanism by which parties reproduce organized, institutionalized, collective action.

The FA is a permanently mobilized party organization that emerged in the context of socioeconomic crisis and political polarization (Astori 2001, Nahum et al. 1993). Ever since – a period of more than 48 years – it has remained as a party with activists. Even though the party organization underwent a process of ideological transformation (see Chapter 6), it retains its leftist ideological identity, and is the only remaining institutionalized mass-organic party in South America (Levitsky and Roberts 2011). The two other comparable cases in the region, the Partido Socialista de Chile (Chilean Socialist Party, PSCh) and the PT in Brazil, have turned into professional electoral parties. Both have significantly reduced or even severed the relationship between the party grassroots – volunteers – and the party's decision-making apparatus. In the case of the PT, the party structure is still relevant, though significantly less so than in the past, and it is dominated by the party elite (Ribeiro 2014, Samuels 2004, Samuels and Zucco Jr 2016). The crucial difference between the FA and other parties is the presence of a cadre of autonomous activists, an army of volunteers, throughout the territory who have an active role in the party's decision making. The FA presents an excellent opportunity to analyze the theoretical significance of party organization per se for the performance of political parties. It is a successful case of party building and reproduction.

## Analytical Tools, Data Gathering and Sources

Recent advances in comparative historical analysis and case-study research have emphasized the need to better specify the connection between cause and effect (Collier, Brady, and Seawright 2010). In this book, we follow various scholars' recommendation to use process tracing to improve descriptive and causal inference (Bennett and Checkel 2015) – in our case, by applying the method to a study of the reproduction of a party organization.

To better trace the FA's trajectory over time, our research included an in-depth process tracing of the FA's formation and the mechanism of reproduction of its most important organizational attributes over time. We employed a systematic analysis to identify specific causal process observations (CPOs) to validate our descriptive and causal inferences. We followed Collier's (2011) approach to determine the inferential value of our CPOs. To this end, we used secondary sources, party documents (see Table 1.2 for a list of documents cited), party administrative data, and in-depth interviews.

We conducted thirty-nine in-depth semi-structured interviews with past and current party leaders from different generations, having different degrees of power within the organization, including ministers, senators, representatives, young prospective leaders, and party activists (see the Appendix for the complete list of interviewees). Finally, we conducted a

TABLE 1.2 *Cited FA Documents*

| Title | Date Issued | Amendments |
|---|---|---|
| Statement of the 7th of October | October 7, 1970 | |
| Organizational Rules | March 16, 1971 | 1984 |
| Political Commitment | February 9, 1972 | |
| Programmatic Bases of Unity | February 17, 1971 | August 9, 1984 |
| Constitutive Declaration of the FA | February 5, 1971 | |
| Party Statutes (substitutes Organizational Rules) | April 14, 1986 | 1993, 2004, 2006, 2008, 2011 |

thorough review of the local newspapers published during different relevant periods of our analysis.[5]

To complement the qualitative analysis and the analysis of causal mechanisms, we conducted an online survey to gather original data on the characteristics of FA activists and adherents. Also, to analyze the effect of this organizational structure and of perceived efficacy on people's willingness to participate, we included survey experiments. Our study is the largest survey of FA party activists conducted to date – and perhaps one of the largest surveys of party members in Latin America. We recruited survey participants via Facebook. Given that party adherents and activists are very difficult to reach, Jäger (2017) claims that this is a good strategy for collecting data from party members. Jäger also suggests that, to improve the representativeness of a survey, one can post-stratify using known population parameters. We designed a campaign with an advertisement that was targeted to people at least sixteen years old who stated in their Facebook profile that they lived in Uruguay and who indicated having an interest in the FA. The survey was distributed between June 6 and July 6, 2017. The advertisement had 306,198 prints and reached 89,732 Facebook users. The survey had 4,017 clicks, of which 2,487 were by people who declared themselves to be FA adherents. We post-stratified our sample with data on the sex and age

---

[5] See Online Appendix: http://partyactivism.net/.

TABLE 1.3 *Types of Engagement*

|  |  | Participate in Base Committees | |
|---|---|---|---|
|  |  | Yes | No |
| Participate in a party faction | Yes | 24.0 (1.0) | 22.1 (0.9) |
|  | No | 9.6 (0.7) | 44.3 (1.1) |

In parentheses we include the standard error for each measure.
*Source:* Online survey

of the people who voted in the most recent (August 2016) FA internal election.[6] Thus, we have reliable data about the population of active party adherents – to vote in the internal election, adherents must register as party members.

The survey included questions about different dimensions of the relationship between the respondent and the party. For example, it asked about the respondent's participation in the different organizational structures (factions and Base Committees), the frequency of the respondent's participation, his or her contact with party and government authorities, and whether the respondent pays party dues, among other issues.

The implementation of the survey through a Facebook advertisement was targeted to a broad population of people who stated an interest in the FA. The survey was designed to identify different types of people with different degrees of engagement with the FA – Base Committee activists, activists who exclusively participate in one of the factions of the FA, and party adherents who do not participate regularly in either the political factions of the FA or in the Base Committees. As Table 1.3 shows, more than one-third of the party adherents (33.6 percent of survey respondents) participate in Base Committees

---

[6] As a post-stratification technique, we used the *rake* function in the package "Survey" in R. As Lumley states, "Raking allows multiple grouping variables to be used without constructing a complete cross-classification. The process involves post-stratifying on each set of variables in turn, and repeating this process until the weights stop changing." (Lumley 2011, 139). All the estimations were calculated using the Survey package.

(24.0 percent in both Base Committees and in a faction and 9.6 exclusively in Base Committees). Twenty-two percent of the respondents are activists who only participate in a faction, while 44.3 percent do not participate in either the Base Committees or in a faction but identify themselves as a FA adherent. This distinction enabled us to conduct a heterogeneous-treatment-effect analysis. As stated in the pre-analysis plan, we expected that reducing the perceived political role assigned to the grassroots members would negatively impact activists' – but not adherents' – self-reported level of engagement (http://egap.org/registration/1989).

Finally, we built a database of "issues" discussed in the sessions of the two main party direction institutions, the National Plenary and the National Political Board. We had access to the minutes of all sessions from 2000 to 2016.[7] The database includes all "issues" that appear in the minutes. In total, we registered and classified 1,345 issues. Every row in our database represents an issue in a given minute. Issues were classified in five categories: "motions," which contain proposals of political issues to be debated at the directorate institutions of the party; "government appearances," which register the visit of ministers, undersecretaries, other government officials, etc. who attended a session to inform or discuss a government policy; "social organization appearances," which register the visit of a union, NGO, etc. who attended a session to formulate a problem or a need; and "others." Also, for the motions, we registered whether it was proposed by the grassroots' representative, the faction representatives, or both. Data from this database, as well as the in-depth interviews with government authorities, activists and the press, were used to analyze the internal life of the FA, to determine to what extent this organization limited or constrained the public-policy decisions of the FA while in government.

OVERVIEW

The party organization literature conceives the evolution of party organizations as a linear process, e.g., the mass party gives way to the catch-all (professional electoral) type of party, which then gives way to the cartel

---

[7] Specifically, we had access to the minutes of all sessions of The National Political Board from 2000 to 2016 and all sessions of the National Plenary from 2008 to 2016.

party (Katz and Mair 1995, Kirchheimer 1966). According to this model, the process of transformation occurs either through a natural-selection process or via imitation: parties that are efficient in their transformation persist, or parties transform themselves by imitating the most efficient. This theoretical expectation thus assumes that, at a given historical point in time, all parties have similar organizational structures and there is only one way to confront the contextual challenges that determine political action. Regardless of the extent to which this claim is true, there are parties that do not exhibit this linear transformation process but are nonetheless successful, because there are multiple ways to confront the challenges exerted by the changing contexts within which parties organize and mobilize to win elections. The FA case study provides an opportunity to rethink the theoretical expectation of unilinear party-organization change or transformation. Also, the case of the FA illustrates how internal rules and party structure can influence party reproduction and the reproduction of activism. Finally, this case also shows how internal democracy need not encompass candidate-selection processes and competition among factions; in the FA, internal democracy involves the way activists preferences' are taken into account in the party's decision-making process.

Chapter Two presents the party in context; it focuses on the Uruguayan party system (the oldest in the region), the institutional and socioeconomic setting that accompanied the FA's trajectory, and we review the main public policies of the FA's three governments. Chapter Three describes the case of the FA. It provides a thick description of the party's structure. The goal of this chapter is to show the relevance of activism in the FA and its interaction with leaders and factions in party life. It emphasizes the voluntary activism structure, describes the actual operation of the Base Committees, and provides a thorough description of the party's activists and their participation. Chapter Four delves deeper into the history of the FA to process-trace the construction of the organizational structures that account for the lock-in effect and the mechanisms that account for the positive feedback, which explains the reproduction of the activist structure. Chapter Five presents evidence of the role of perceived efficacy as a selective incentive for activists' willingness to cooperate with the party. The chapter presents the results of a survey experiment in which we manipulate activists' perceived efficacy. In Chapter 6, we present evidence of the role of the FA's organizational structure in limiting elites' ability to moderate or enact strategic decisions that conflict with some party statute or ideological position. Chapter Seven discusses the FA case in comparative perspective. The chapter reviews the case of the PT in Brazil and discusses some examples of leftist electoral coalitions in Latin America. The final chapter concludes by summarizing the argument and identifies major challenges for the reproduction of intense levels of attachment.

# 2

# Context Matters

## *The Political and Socioeconomic Setting*

### INTRODUCTION

Until 1971 the Uruguayan party system comprised two major parties: Partido Colorado (Colorado Party, PC) and Partido Nacional (National Party, PN).¹ Although there have always been other parties, especially leftist parties (e.g., Socialist and Communist), they were significantly smaller. The two major parties collectively obtained around 90 percent of the votes in every democratic election until that year. Thanks to the use of double simultaneous voting to elect the president, both parties had the opportunity to nominate more than one candidate.² As a result, the two major parties always had both a progressive and a conservative faction (Buquet, Chasquetti, and Moraes 1998).

A set of contextual factors help explain the emergence of the FA as the unification of the left in Uruguay: the economic stagnation of the 1960s; the political context of an increasingly authoritarian government (Jorge Pacheco Areco, 1968–1971); the unification in 1964 of the labor movement under the Convención Nacional de Trabajadores (National Workers Convention, CNT); the unification of grassroots-level popular organizations (in the Congreso del Pueblo – People's Congress – held in

---

¹ From 1931 until 1956 the PN was split in two different parties: the PN and the Partido Nacional Independiente (Independent National Party).
² The Double Simultaneous Vote (DSV) allows citizens to cast a ballot for the party and to select a candidate inside the party. As a result, parties could nominate more than one presidential ticket (until the 1997 electoral reform), more than one list for Senate and more than one list for the House of Representatives. Thus, electoral competition occurs both between parties and within parties between factions.

1965); as well as the political negotiations between five important leaders from the different preexisting parties or groups. In the following pages, we present the setting in which the FA was born and in which it developed over the years. We describe the political process and the socioeconomic context. The chapter also describes the political economy and the politics in Uruguay following the authoritarian regime (1973–1985) that accompanied the FA's development as a party organization. Finally, it describes the political economy of the FA in government.

## RISE AND DECAY OF THE POLYARCHY

Uruguay is classified as having been a polyarchy since 1919 and was a stable country during the first half of the twentieth century (Lanzaro 2012). With the exception of the period from 1934 to 1942, it was a healthy democracy until its decline in the end of the 1960s. Also, Uruguay has an institutionalized party system (González 1995). The two foundational parties (PC and PN) were created in 1836. Electoral volatility has been at healthy levels – neither low, with the risk of ossification, nor high enough to risk atomization and threaten the survival of the parties (Buquet and Piñeiro 2014). It is a party system where organizations matter and thus where brands matter; no political leadership can be successful if conceived outside party organizations. There is no real chance of building political leadership outside an organization (Caetano, Rilla, and Pérez 1987).

Uruguay shares the same dramatic structural challenges of other Latin American economies. This small South American nation has very little room to maneuver with respect to many critical economic issues, and thus the destiny of the Uruguayan economy depends on the global markets and, especially, on its larger neighbors, Argentina and Brazil. However, Uruguay does have room to implement its own version of a development model and, in this regard, it differs from these neighboring regional powerhouses.

In the first half of the twentieth century, the proponents of Batllismo constituted the PC's main faction. The Batllismo program expanded workers' social and economic rights in two waves, one which spanned from 1904 to 1913 and the second, which began after the Second World War and lasted until 1958 (Barrán and Nahum 1985, Collier and Collier 1991, Finch 1980, Vanger 1963). In this second wave, Uruguay developed highly interventionist economic policies based on the Import Substitution Industry (ISI) model, financed with the surplus of a prosperous export sector that was benefitting from high international prices as a consequence of the war (Bértola 1991, Cancela and Melgar 1985, D'Elía 1982, Finch 1980, Panizza 1990). During this stage, the state consolidated its role as a mediator between capital and labor. It achieved this by installing corporatist settings to negotiate salaries and the extension of social security (Finch 1980, Lanzaro 1986). Even though social spending had a strong clientelistic component (Filgueira and Filgueira 1994, Panizza 1990, Rama 1971, Solari 1991, Solari and Franco 1983), particularistic distribution was so extensive that it forged the image of a middle-class country and the notion of a "hyper-integrated" society (Filgueira and Filgueira 1994, Panizza 1990, Rama 1987, Real de Azúa 1964, Solari 1991).

After 1955, a long process of stagnation ensued. As in the rest of the region, the ISI economic model showed fissures that put the country under increasing fiscal strain. During this nearly twenty-year period, the Uruguayan economy was characterized by high levels of inflation, unemployment, and anemic growth, with periods of outright recession (Astori 2001, Cancela and Melgar 1985, Thorp 1998). During these years, GDP decreased or grew at a very low rate (e.g., the average rate of GDP growth between 1955 and 1970 was 0.9 percent) (Finch 1980, 235). Real wages fell 40 percent between 1957 and 1972, pensions fell 70 percent between 1963 and 1973 (Filgueira and Filgueira 1994, Real de Azúa 1964), and the country entered an unprecedented inflationary cycle. In 1968, annual inflation reached 1,395.9 percent. Poor economic performance led to the first change of government in the twentieth century: the PN won the national elections in 1958 and 1962.

Change of government did not improve the economic situation, but led to heightened political polarization. Street protests and strikes were more frequent, and armed groups emerged from the left and the right (Nahum et al. 1993, Panizza 1990, Real de Azúa 1964). From the left, the Movimiento de Liberación Nacional-Tupamaros (National Liberation Movement, MLN), an urban guerrilla organization that from 1962 to 1967 adopted a "friendly violence" policy, aimed more at unearthing systemic corruption than spreading terror, but in its final stage it directly confronted the police, the army, and paramilitary groups (Marchesi 2017). On the right, the Juventud Uruguaya de Pie (Uruguayan Standing Youth, JUP) or the Comando Caza Tupamaros (Tupamaros Hunting Commando) conducted attacks against labor unions, students, and leftist army members (Nahum et al. 1993). The critical generation of intellectuals emphasized the decadent environment of Uruguay's democracy and socioeconomic environment. Several social scientists elucidated the structural problems. The erosion at the socioeconomic level gradually hampered political organizations. Piñeiro (2014) explains that the economic and fiscal crisis affected clientelistic arrangements between established parties, and thus debilitated the cartelized competition between PN and PC.

The intensification of the crisis in the 1960s led to two types of realignment on the left. First, the union movement unified. In 1964, after a series of steps, the CNT – a unique central union – was formed, after which Uruguay overcame a history of fragmentation in its union movement (Lanzaro 1986, Padrón and Wachendorfer 2017). In 1965, the People's Congress took place, which brought together almost 1,400 delegates representing union organizations, cooperatives, rural producers, groups of retirees, and students. The Congress's platform contained solutions to the crisis, both immediate goals (e.g., wages, pensions, housing, education, etc.) and structural transformations (agrarian reform, nationalization of the central slaughterhouse, the banks, and foreign commerce, etc.). Different interviewees mentioned these two facts as significant antecedent conditions to the FA's foundation (Interview with Martín Ponce de León, Miguel Aguirre Bayley, and Óscar Bottinelli).

Second, there were attempts to unify the political left, led by the two historical leftist parties: the PSU and PCU (Yaffé 2016). The Socialist party was founded in 1910 and the PCU in 1920. Though Uruguay had organized leftist parties very early, compared to the rest of the region, the parties were unable to coordinate and mobilize significant numbers of voters (see Figure 2.1). Moreover, they repeatedly failed to construct successful electoral alliances. In 1962, the former PN leader Enrique Erro – who had defected from the PN, the PSU and several minor groups led the creation of the Unión Nacional y Popular (National Popular Union). The PCU was not included because the organizers felt that it engendered resistance among the electorate, especially in rural areas (Yaffé 2016). That year, the Frente de Izquierda de Liberación (Leftist Liberation Front, FIDEL) was formed. It was an alliance between the PCU, the Movimiento Revolucionario Oriental (Oriental Revolutionary Movement), other small leftist groups, and small groups from the PC and the PN. Both coalitions failed in the 1962 and 1966 national elections and the traditional parties together retained their 90 percent share of the votes cast.

In 1966, the PC won the presidential election with Óscar Gestido and Jorge Pacheco Areco on the ticket for president and vice president, respectively. Gestido died after only nine months in office and Pacheco's

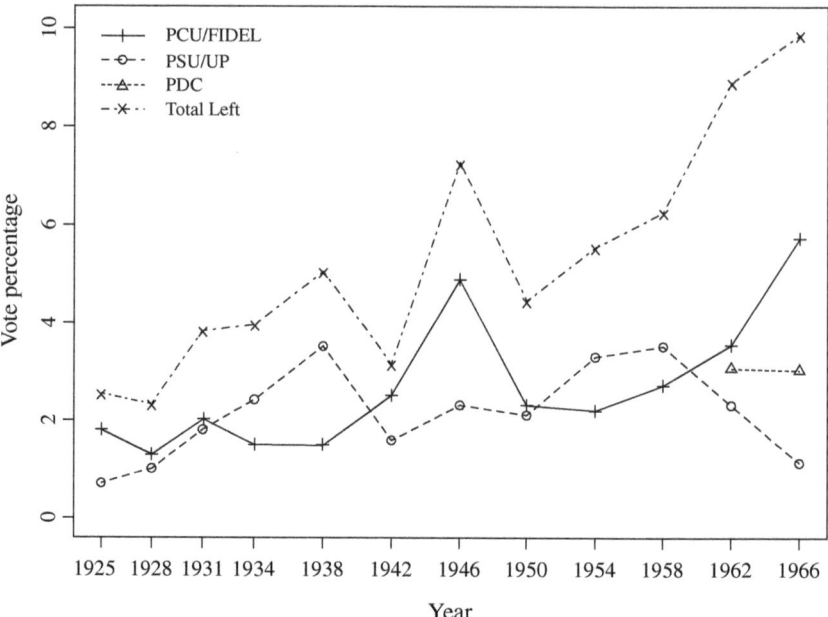

FIGURE 2.1 The electoral evolution of the left before 1971
Source: Data Bank of the Social Sciences School, University of the Republic, Uruguay

government (1967–1972) was marked by increasing restriction of civil rights and increasing authoritarianism (Nahum et al. 1993, Panizza 1990). A few days after Pacheco Areco took office, he outlawed leftist political parties, the PSU among them. Several media organizations were closed and the dissemination of news and information about strikes was forbidden.

In the context of an inflationary spiral, Pacheco Areco froze prices and wages. In response to increased labor unrest in public services and private banking, the government militarized civil servants and private banking employees,[3] an unprecedented measure for civil servants. The Pacheco Areco government also broke into university buildings to search for links to subversive activities and intervened in the autonomous councils of secondary-education governing bodies and other autonomous state institutions, such as the electric and phone companies. The president maintained

---

[3] For example, they received mandatory military training and union membership was forbidden.

the country in an official constitutional state of emergency and ignored Congress's prerogatives when the latter wanted to lift the state of emergency.

These authoritarian advances were contested with massive mobilizations and street protests. Students and union workers directly confronted the police. A high point in the student mobilization occurred in August 1968 when, after the police broke into a university building, a group of students took to the streets to protest against the police. One of them (Liber Arce) was intercepted and wounded, and he died the following day. A few days after, a new episode of student repression occurred in which two students were killed and around forty people were injured.

The unpopular measures of Pacheco's government, together with the deeply authoritarian nature of his administration, led some leaders from the most progressive sectors of the PC to leave the cabinet. Pacheco Areco had to look for support in the conservative factions of the PN, and he also relied on the support of the business associations that supported repression of unions. This context of violence in Uruguay, never before seen in the country in the twentieth century, together with an economic context that showed no signs of recovery, led some leaders of the center-left and the left to think that something had to be done. In the words of Juan Pablo Terra (leader of the Christian Democracy Party, PDC), it was necessary "to use a hose to put out the fire" (personal interview with Óscar Bottinelli).

It was during this critical period that the FA was founded. In Chapter 4, we describe in greater detail the specific political context prior to its foundation. On June 27, 1973 there occurred what the weekly magazine *Marcha* termed the "beginning of the end": Uruguayan democracy collapsed. The Uruguayan authoritarian regime was extremely repressive, resulting in the highest rate of political detention per capita in the region, as well as assassinations, torture, and disappeared detainees (Caetano and Rilla 1998). Also, thousands left the country to live in exile. These actions particularly affected activists and leaders from the left. In 1980, citizens rejected a constitutional reform proposed by the regime. A few years later, absolute administrative incapacity and economic crisis accelerated the transition to democracy. The year 1983 was marked by political negotiations between parties and the regime, political mobilization, and the gradual reestablishment of partisan activity.

## THE DUAL TRANSITION IN URUGUAY

In 1984, the first national elections since 1971 were held, and Julio Maria Sanguinetti of the PC was elected president. Democracy was reestablished when he took office on March 1, 1985. In terms of the distribution of votes between parties, the national elections of 1984 were impressively similar to those of 1971, the last democratic election before the dictatorship.

The Uruguayan party system began to realign itself in the late 1960s, as a consequence of the decline of the ISI model and the inability of the traditional two-party system to adapt. As Buquet and Piñeiro (2014) claim, this change implied the gradual incorporation of a third actor, the FA. After the authoritarian regime, and with the restoration of democracy, the two-party competition between the PC and PN gradually turned to a competition between blocks – one composed of the traditional parties and the other by the FA.

As with the process of electoral realignment, the process of structural reforms and the enactment of market reforms also occurred gradually. By the end of the 1950s, some tenuous liberalization efforts were enacted but were soon reversed. The Uruguayan authoritarian regime, as opposed to the Chilean case, did not significantly transform the country's economic model or its social policy regime (Castiglioni 2005). Nonetheless, the country started to undergo a process of financial and commercial liberalization (Bulmer-Thomas 2013, Morley, Machado, and Pettinato 1999). As occurred in the rest of the region, the pace of structural and market reforms increased after the so-called debt crisis of the 1980s (Morley, Machado, and Pettinato 1999, Weyland 2002).

In Uruguay, the process was led by the governments of the PN (1990–1995) and the PC (1995–2000 and 2000–2005). Lanzaro (2007) argues that the traditional parties underwent a process of "ideological convergence" (118) and "reconversion, turning away from Keynesian and welfare policies (...) toward state reform, liberalization, and market-oriented policies." (Lanzaro 2011, 355–356).[4] The FA, in alliance with the union movement, used the mechanisms of direct democracy and social mobilization to systematically oppose the reforms (Altman 2010, Monestier 2011, Moreira 2004). The FA's systematic opposition to the pro-market reform bills positioned the party as the single political actor on the center-left of the ideological spectrum, pushing both traditional parties – which historically had factions spanning from the left to the right – to right-of-center.

---

[4] Translation from Spanish by the authors.

TABLE 2.1 *Constitutional Plebiscites and Law Referenda since 1980*

| Issue | Year | Yes | No[a] | Outcome | FA Position |
|---|---|---|---|---|---|
| Constitutional Reform (under *de facto* regime) | 1980 | 36.4 | 48.6 | Overturn government | Against |
| Annulment of Amnesty for Human Rights Crimes Law | 1989 | 34.9 | 47.4 | Status Quo | For |
| Pensions indexed to salaries | 1989 | 72.5 | – | Overturn government | For |
| Annulment of Privatization of State Companies Law | 1992 | 55.1 | 20.9 | Overturn government | For |
| Social Security and Pensions Warranties | 1994 | 66.2 | – | Change | For |
| Education Fixed Budget | 1994 | 29.8 | – | Status Quo | For |
| Electoral Reform | 1994 | 24.6 | 54.4 | Status Quo | For |
| Judiciary Economic Autonomy | 1999 | 43.1 | – | Status Quo | For |
| Electoral Proscription for State Companies Directors | 1999 | 38.1 | – | Status Quo | Against |
| Reestablishment of State-owned Petroleum State Company Monopoly | 2003 | 59.5 | 33.9 | Overturn government | For |
| Water State Monopoly Initiative | 2004 | 64.6 | – | Change | For |
| Annulment of Amnesty to Human Rights Crimes Law (Second) | 2009 | 47.9 | – | Status Quo | For |
| Vote abroad Initiative | 2009 | 37.4 | | Status Quo | For |
| Criminal Responsibility Age Reducing Initiative | 2014 | 46.8 | – | Status Quo | Against |

*Source:* Data Bank, Social Sciences School, Universidad de la República, Uruguay and Corte Electoral de Uruguay

[a] Some initiatives require the Yes vote to achieve more than 50 percent of the turnout, thus a blank or null vote is, in effect, a No vote.

The opposition to market reforms materialized in the activation of several direct-democracy mechanisms (referenda and popular initiatives) – see Table 2.1. This strengthened the connections between social movements and the FA (Bidegain and Tricot 2017). The activation of direct-democracy mechanisms also illustrates the territorial penetration and organization of the FA, which was crucial to gathering the required signatures to launch these mechanisms (Altman 2010). This was manifested in the first referendum after democratic transition, on the Annulment of Amnesty for Human Rights Crimes Law in 1989. Organizers gathered the required signatures with a campaign "Yo firmo" (I sign). The campaign was carried out by the PIT-CNT, the FA, and Human Rights organizations. They organized a commission that gathered more than six hundred thousand signatures, 27 percent of the electorate above the 25 percent required by Law. The process was extremely complex. On the one hand, activists had to convince citizens who were still afraid of an authoritarian retaliation. On the other hand, the high threshold required to activate the direct-democracy mechanism was a major obstacle. Thus, it was a very labor-intensive campaign.

In the 1990s, as the market reform process advanced in Lacalle's term (1990–1995), direct-democracy mechanisms were intensively used, though with varying success. While the referendum on the Annulment of Privatization of State Companies Law successfully halted the privatization of state-owned companies, other referenda and popular initiatives did not fare as well. The success of a direct-democracy mechanism required the decisive support of the FA as a whole (Monestier 2011). Yet, given the uncertainty of the different referenda and popular initiatives, and that some of the proposals were not the preferred policies of FA leaders and main factions, on some occasions it was the FA grassroots activists who pushed for the activation of direct-democracy mechanisms. This was the case in at least two campaigns: the reestablishment of the state-owned Petroleum Company Monopoly, and the Annulment of Amnesty for Human Rights Crimes Law (second) – see Chapter 6 for a detailed description of FA's decision-making process to support this initiative.

As in other countries of the region, the neoliberal wave impacted the patterns of political mobilization. In countries that have had a highly developed ISI, there was a class cleavage; the popular sectors were mobilized as a class by mass labor, populist or leftist parties (Argentina, Brazil, Peru, Chile, Venezuela, and México). Structural adjustment and market reforms of the 1980s and 1990s produced a dealignment of class-based mobilization and the emergence of new and heterogeneous forms of political mobilization; more direct, tied to charismatic, outsider leaders, unrelated to established party organizations (Collier and Handlin 2009, Levitsky and Roberts 2011, Murillo 2001, 2009, Roberts 1998, 2002). In countries with weaker ISI, especially where popular sectors had been mobilized by old elitist parties, political competition was structured around segmented cleavages, multi-class alliances and essentially clientelistic linkages with voters, as in Colombia, Costa Rica, and Uruguay (Luna 2014,

Roberts 2014). Market reforms also affected the capacity of old, traditional parties in these countries to articulate interests as they did in the past.

The impact of market reforms on the party system also depended on the roles each party adopted during the juncture (Roberts 2014). When market reforms were championed by old left-of-center or populist parties, which had been responsible for extending social rights during the ISI, reforms created a vacuum in political representation, especially in the popular sectors. Old leftist or populist parties collapsed and dragged with them the rest (or almost all) of the party system, (the most extreme case being Venezuela, though Bolivia, Ecuador, or Argentina could be added to this category). In these cases, in the period after the reforms, new leftist parties emerged. In many cases, they achieved electoral success quickly– as a result of the dealignment crisis – without undergoing a process of accumulation and maturation. By contrast, when market reforms were implemented by conservative actors (right or center-right parties, the military, or an outsider) and a leftist party existed, exerting opposition to the reforms, the result was a programmatic realignment of the party system without an implosion. Citizens' malaise against neoliberal adjustment was channeled by a leftist party that was not contaminated by the policymaking process of reform. This explains the realignment and stability of these latter party systems. The typical cases were Brazil and Uruguay (Roberts 2014).

In this context of economic transformation, a number of different explanations have been offered to explain the FA's accumulation of political strength and its electoral gains over the years. One line of research focused on the process of programmatic moderation as a key source of electoral growth (Garcé and Yaffé 2005, Yaffé 2005). Lanzaro (2007) says that the FA's opposition to the neoliberal turn was accompanied by a systematic process of programmatic moderation:

The FA's political accumulation is based on a "two pronged" strategy. Its success is greatly due to its performance as a hegemonic opposition force, confrontational vis-á-vis the traditional parties, that rejects commitments and grows ever stronger as its electoral chances increase. But this strategy is articulated with the FA's political transformation and its development as a catch-all party, marked by ideological reconversion and competition for the center. Step-by-step, inter- and intraparty competition, political learning, and the experience of governing Montevideo have induced ideological moderation and pragmatic positions, in a movement that affirms a new political identity and at the same time conquers voters in the center.

(127)[5]

---

[5] Translation from Spanish by the authors.

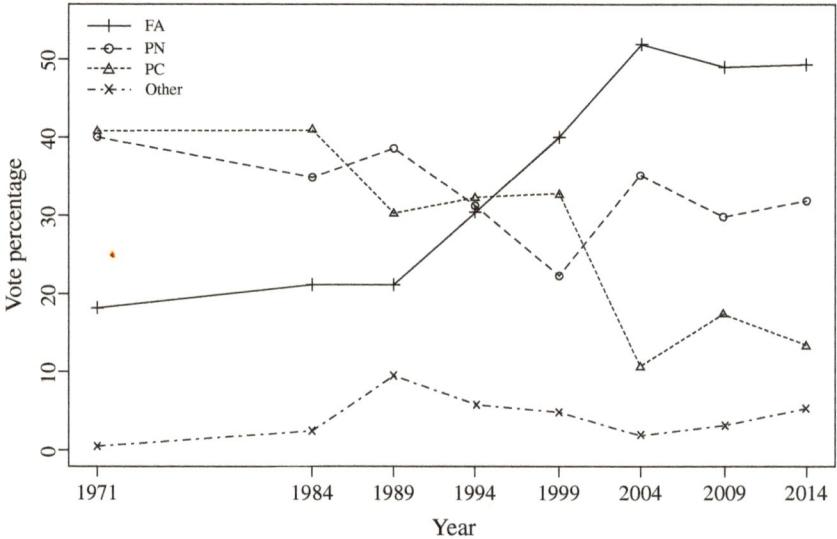

FIGURE 2.2 Electoral evolution in national elections, 1971–2014
*Source:* Own construction with data from the Corte Electoral

An alternative hypothesis explains the electoral growth of the FA (see Figure 2.2) as the result of a demographic shift and a generational turnover (Aguiar 2000, González and Queirolo 2000, Moreira 2004). Essentially, support for the FA was greater among young voters: "That vote [for the FA] systematically increases as age decreases; younger voters cast more votes for the challengers." (González and Queirolo 2000, 303). Buquet and De Armas (2005) challenge the idea that the demographic growth explanation is sufficient to account for the electoral success of the FA. The authors claim that it is also the result of political variables, especially the migration of PC and PN votes to the FA as a result of ideological moderation (130). The two processes are empirically observable and it is impossible to determine whether either or both is sufficient by itself to explain the electoral growth of the FA.

## THE POLITICAL ECONOMY OF THE FIRST THREE FA GOVERNMENTS

In 2005, the FA took office for the first time in its history. The FA initiated its first term in office in a country that was just overcoming the worst financial and economic crisis in its history (Paolillo 2004, Rosenblatt

2006). Its challenge was to consolidate the economic recovery that had been taking place since 2004, to achieve financial stability, and to address the societal effects of the crisis, what was referred to as the "social emergency." In this scenario, the FA not only addressed these challenges but also began a cycle of structural reforms that revitalized the role of the state. These reforms promoted redistribution of income and they contributed to the construction of a matrix of protections with universalistic appeals and attributes (Huber and Stephens 2012, Padrón and Wachendorfer 2017, Pribble 2013, Rossel 2016). During Vázquez's first term (2005–2010), social spending increased significantly (Caetano and De Armas 2011); a conditional cash-transfer program was implemented to address the social emergency that erupted as a consequence of the 1999–2003 economic depression. This program evolved into a universal, family-based transfer program (Pribble 2013). Also during this first FA government, collective bargaining at the sectoral level (i.e., within various sectors of economic activity) was reinstated, and was expanded to include previously excluded sectors, such as rural workers and housekeepers, and over forty bills on workers' rights were approved. Labor participation in the formal sector of the economy increased (Etchemendy 2019, Padrón and Wachendorfer 2017, Senatore and Méndez 2011). The government also implemented a progressive tax reform by adopting an income tax and a national, integrated health-care system was created, ensuring coverage to previously excluded sectors (Bergara 2015). Finally, the FA promoted the reduction of the "digital divide" through the implementation of the One Laptop Per Child program, "Plan Ceibal." José Mujica's government (2010–2015) continued these policies – even expanding the delivery of health-care services – and also advanced libertarian policies. For example, during Mujica's term, the Law of Voluntary Interruption of Pregnancy was approved, as were laws pertaining to self-cultivation and commercialization of cannabis and same-sex marriage (Bidegain Ponte 2013).

As opposed to other leftist governments in the region, the FA advanced with its redistributive and progressive agenda without endangering democratic norms (Weyland, Madrid, and Hunter 2010). This is manifested in having a political elite that is polarized in terms of attitudes though not in behavior. Thus, socioeconomic reforms undertaken by FA governments did not alter substantively the democratic structure of the country, as happened in other countries in the region. As a direct result of the policies implemented during these first two FA governments, the political economy of the country altered significantly in comparison to the neoliberal period. For example, unionization rates increased, especially among private-sector employees, and the number of workers in the formal sector also increased (Padrón and Wachendorfer 2017).

The first two FA governments were successful in macroeconomic terms; growth was systematically above historical rates. More importantly, though, is the favorable evolution of social and employment indicators. Unemployment reached the lowest levels in Uruguay's recorded history, informality decreased significantly, unionization increased along with a systematic increase in real income as a direct result of the reestablishment of collective bargaining in 2005 (Etchemendy 2019). Poverty levels, extreme poverty, and inequality were significantly reduced during the government's first ten years (Colafranceschi, Failache, and Vigorito 2013). According to the report of the Economic Commission for Latin America and the Caribbean (CEPAL 2016), Uruguay is the Latin American country that has achieved the greatest levels of poverty and income inequality reduction between 2010 and 2014 (Figure 2.3).

During the party's third consecutive term in office (2015–2020), the economic scene turned challenging again, and at that point the party did not have the energy that comes with fighting for access to office for the very first time, after having suffered political persecution, repression, and exclusion. Even though the financial setting was no longer the main problem, disappointing fiscal results, inflationary pressures, and the slowdown of the economy hindered the party's ability to consolidate structural economic transformations in light of severe fiscal restrictions. For the first time, the FA had to confront the challenge of administering a small, peripheral, developing country, heavily dependent upon global markets for its raw goods and access to foreign direct investment.

Compared to other moderate leftist governments in the region (especially the Concertación coalition governments in Chile), the FA did not abandon its mass-organic-based nature (Levitsky and Roberts 2011) and its clear leftist nature (Rosenblatt 2018). While a very small minority of extreme leftist groups eventually left the FA (manifested in the creation of the Unidad Popular – Popular Unity),[6] the FA, in contrast to other parties of the region (especially the Workers Party in Brazil), did not suffer opposition to its platform or real challenges from other sectors that could contest the political representation of the society's leftist and popular sectors (see Chapters 4 and 5). Moreover, far from being absorbed by

---

[6] In the 2014 national elections the Unidad Popular party elected its first representative.

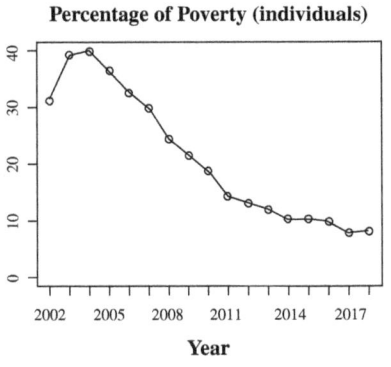
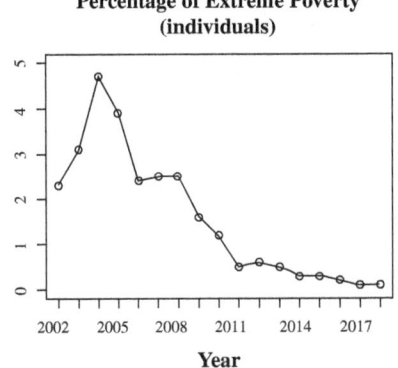
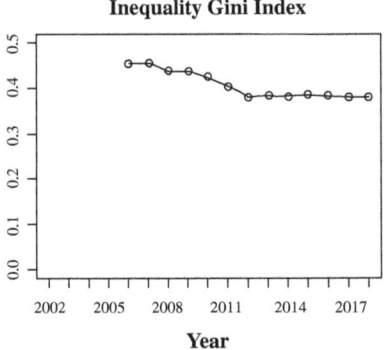

FIGURE 2.3 Poverty, extreme poverty, and Gini Index 2002–2017
*Source:* National Institute of Statistics, Uruguay

government, the FA continued manifesting an autonomous political life and electoral mobilization ability; the grassroots element of the FA both supported and was a counterweight to the party's political leadership (see Chapter 6).

The reforms carried out during the first two governments of the FA were produced in the context of favorable economic conditions, marked by the so-called commodity boom (Figure 2.4). For Uruguay, this boom meant high prices for soy, meat, rice, and wool, such that the country, a producer of food and raw goods, saw its economy grow exponentially during a decade. However, that context changed after 2014, affecting the country's future prospects. As a consequence, in terms of political economy, the FA's third government had to deal with the dilemma highlighted

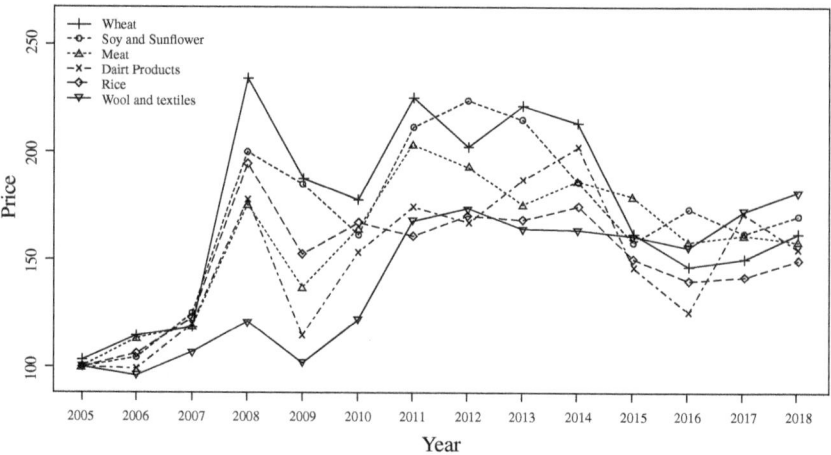

FIGURE 2.4 Main export items 2005–2018 (Paasche Index Prices in US Dollars 2005 = 100)
*Source:* Uruguayan Central Bank

in the literature on Latin American leftist governments that navigate junctures of economic stagnation or crisis(Pérez and Piñeiro 2016). On the one hand, the governments confront the need to answer the call for greater redistribution that emanates from their voters, especially unions, while, on the other, they need to protect the macroeconomic balance and encourage growth (Campello 2015, Murillo, Oliveros, and Vaishnav 2011).

The economic slowdown in China, the concomitant decline in the demand for raw goods, and the stagnation of the Brazilian economy put pressure on the Uruguayan economy and thus became a warning sign for the third FA government. Also, domestic consumption lost dynamism. The GDP growth rate was more in line with Uruguayan historic trends, between 1.5 and 2 percent per year. Unemployment increased, though it remained below average historical rates. Inflation also increased, above the 3–7 percent target band set by the government. Finally, the fiscal deficit in 2018 was 4 percent, while debt was 25 percent of GDP (Figure 2.5).

The economic slowdown interacted with allegations of wrongdoing by government officials, especially in the management of ANCAP, the state-owned oil company and one of the biggest companies in Uruguay. At the beginning of 2016, the government had to capitalize the company at a

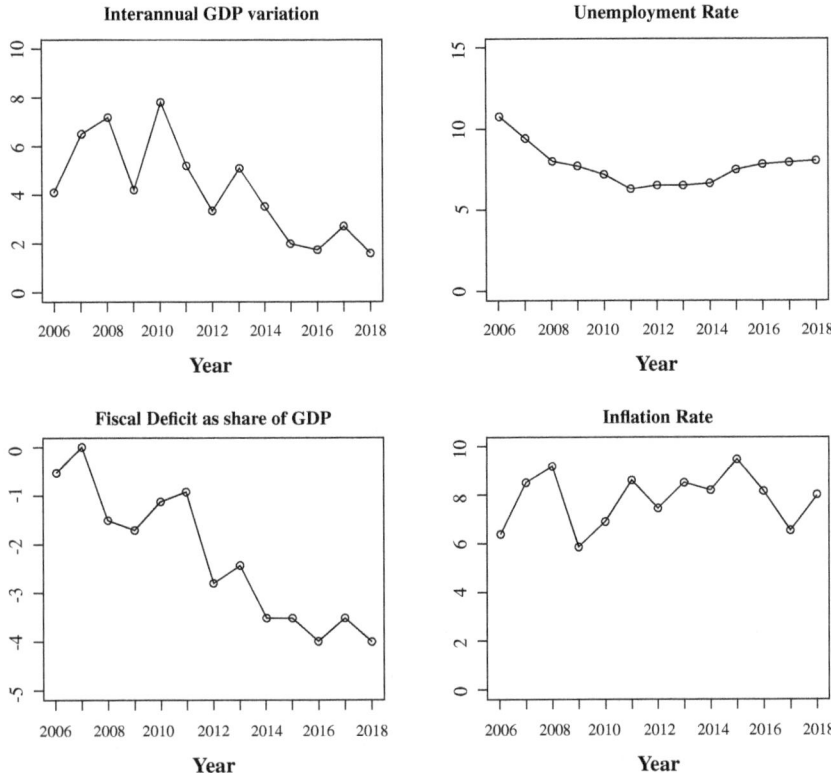

FIGURE 2.5 Evolution of GDP growth rate, unemployment, fiscal deficit, and inflation in Uruguay (2006–2018)
*Source:* Uruguayan Central Bank, Ministry of Economy and Finances, National Statistics Institute, Uruguay

cost of U$S 622 million because it was under serious financial strain.[7] Concurrently, Raúl Sendic, a former president of the company and, at the time, Vice President in Vázquez's government, faced accusations of mismanagement. Following several months of political scandal, he was forced by the FA to resign.[8] The economic slowdown, the need for a tax

---

[7] "Con votos del FA, se aprobó la capitalización de Ancap" (With the votes of the FA, the capitalization of ANCAP was approved), January 3, 2016 (available at www.elpais.com.uy/informacion/votos-fa-aprobo-capitalizacion-ancap.html last accessed March 14, 2019).
[8] There were other cases of alleged corruption or wrongdoing, most importantly one involving the bankruptcy process of PLUNA, the Uruguayan flagship airline, during Mujica's government.

increase to fund the growing fiscal deficit, and the accusations of wrongdoing led to a decline in support for the FA government (Carneiro and Traversa 2018).

## CONCLUSIONS

This chapter reviewed the socioeconomic and political context during the FA's birth and development. The FA was born in a context of socioeconomic decline, dramatic political polarization, political violence, and a repressive government that increasingly relied on authoritarian measures. A similar context occurred throughout almost all of Latin America during this period. The combination of the exhaustion of the ISI model, increasing political polarization, and the height of the Cold War dramatically determined the political dynamics of the late 1960s and 1970s. Interviewees claimed that this context heavily influenced the decision of the different leftist parties and factions from the traditional parties to forge a unified leftist movement. This is confirmed by a thorough review of the press of the time. The fight against the increasingly repressive government of Pacheco Areco was a significant incentive for the new party.

After the authoritarian government, the opposition to the neoliberal agenda of the different governments of the traditional parties also fostered activism within the FA. The FA promoted, in association with different social movements and unions, the repeal of different laws and the promotion of constitutional reforms through direct-democracy mechanisms.

In 2005, the FA gained office and won three consecutive national elections with an absolute majority in parliament. It was one of the most successful parties of the so-called "left turn" (Levitsky and Roberts 2011). The party in government enacted a series of structural reforms in different policy areas and also pursued a progressive agenda that was not necessarily part of the program of other leftist governments in the region. In terms of socioeconomic policy reforms, the FA was one of the two parties of the "left turn" that enacted deep labor- market reforms. The FA reinstated collective bargaining, regulated the minimum wage, and approved a series of laws that formalized many previously excluded popular sectors, including rural and domestic workers. In this process, the FA, in contrast to other leftist parties in the region, retained activism.

# 3

# Voluntary Activism in the FA

## INTRODUCTION

Both qualitative and quantitative research need a fully developed description of the dependent variable. In the case of qualitative research, and especially in case-study research, this is even more critical because the main goal is to trace the causes-of-effects (Goertz and Mahoney 2012). This chapter presents evidence of the "known" outcome: the FA is a party with intense grassroots activism and with a peculiar structure whereby grassroots activists have a substantial autonomous voice throughout the party decision-making bodies. All parties with members have some kind of structure that facilitates the participation of such members (Scarrow 2015), but the distinctive trait of the FA is that this participation is not mediated by the party leaders and factions that compete to nominate candidates.

Grassroots' participation in the FA occurs in Base Committees and in the factions, and the two avenues differ significantly. In the former, there is no direct control of factions, leaders, or party elites because Base Committees are not involved in the candidate-selection process. A Base Committee is essentially a humble room with some chairs and few other amenities (see Online Appendix for pictures of different Base Committees). Frenteamplista grassroots activists gather to discuss local, national, or international politics. They meet also with civil-society organizations from the neighborhood, channel demands to the decision-making structure of the FA, and organize the deployment of the electoral campaign in the field. Thus, it is volunteer grassroots activists who sustain the operation of a Base Committee.

Many political parties have adherents. Some parties have grassroots activists. In fact, some parties have a significant number of grassroots activists that are permanently involved. However, the FA exhibits the presence of a peculiar trait: the significant presence of grassroots activists throughout the structure of the party, even in the highest decision-making bodies.

This chapter focuses on one of the two avenues of engagement available within the party. The focus is on the grassroots avenue (essentially, the Base Committees), the locus of the most deviant aspect of the FA party structure. This avenue creates opportunities for altruistic cooperation. This chapter deepens the description of this avenue, which complements other forms of cooperation (e.g., tit-for-tat) that together account for the reproduction of a political organization. However, we will also pay attention to the other avenue of engagement, the factions. We will provide a general description of the type of factions that exist in the FA, and we will describe their interaction with the grassroots activists' structure.

The FA was born as a coalition of political organizations. Besides being a coalition of political organizations, the FA developed a movement of grassroots activists that organized from below. Thus, FA leaders and activists usually refer to the FA as a combination of "coalition and movement." These are the two different avenues of engagement. This structure was forged at the end of the 1960s, a period of economic depression and political polarization (see Chapters 2 and 4) that triggered mass activism, which was organized autonomously and channeled through a common label: Frente Amplio.

The FA coalition and movement structures are synthesized in a pyramidal organization with bodies at three levels: the grassroots level; the intermediate level; and the national level. This interaction between faction and grassroots activists is peculiar and stimulates checks and balances and power distribution. In this chapter, we describe and analyze in greater detail the intensity of the participation observed in the party, which is essentially located in the grassroots structure, i.e., the movement. The main goal is to provide a thick description of the activists' avenue of engagement. Also, we emphasize how this grassroots activist structure is connected with the highest decision-making structure of the party, and more crucially, grassroots activists' role in this structure.

## THE PARTICIPATION STRUCTURE: IN-DEPTH DESCRIPTION OF THE DEVIANT CASE

### Base Committees and Grassroots Activists

The Base Committees, at the grassroots level, are the local gatherings of party adherents. They have existed since the very beginning of the party (see Chapter 4 for further details on the historical process of the party's birth and development). There are two types of Base Committee: territorial units (the most common); and centers of functional activity (e.g., work place, student unions).

Grassroots activists became critical players in the party's early stages of development; they demanded participation in the decision-making structure and the coalition leaders granted it (see Chapter 4). The FA thus acquired its dual structure: one structure that pertains to the coalition of political organizations (the coalition); and the other, which institutionalizes the political role in the party of the grassroots members who are not necessarily affiliated with factions (what the FA calls the movement). The political organizations that formed the coalition oversee the candidate-selection process for elected and appointed positions in government. The grassroots activists do not participate in the nomination of candidates (except for the presidential ticket) or in the recruitment of government officials. It is essentially composed of voluntary organizers (Han 2014). Most activists work as volunteers. As our online survey shows, only 1 percent of grassroots activists hold a paid position. These grassroots organizers do not seek office, they are policy oriented (Kitschelt 1994); they thus have a rationale to participate in politics that differs from that of professional politicians or those who also seek a career in government. Also, the apparatus is neither based on clientelistic distribution nor functional to it. The following excerpt from an interview with a grassroots activist illustrates this point:

*So you say the grassroots structure is one where no positions are distributed.*[1]
No, no, which positions?!
*As a delegate to the National Plenary you have no resources to distribute and you do not charge for the things you do?*
We put [money], systematically.
(personal interview with Eduardo Alonso)

Activists' intense voluntary engagement is manifested in the organization of the internal elections, which rely almost entirely on Base Committee activists (personal interview with Mario Bergara, Mónica Xavier, and Manuel Mujico, among others). In the 2016 internal election, for example, there were 1,000 voting stations throughout the country, all covered by volunteer grassroots activists.

---

[1] The words in italics are the questions posed to the interviewee.

Finally, the Base Committees are not viewed as a necessary first step in a prospective political career (personal interview with José López and Manuel Ferrer) because recruitment and candidate selection are mainly carried out through the political factions. A grassroots activist said: "I believe they are not [a first step to a political career] I do not know many cases (...) The first thing you should do [to pursue a political career] is to join a faction. That is the first thing." (personal interview with Eduardo Alonso).

The political role of the Base Committees and of grassroots activists evolved over time. While they existed and were crucial to the FA's electoral organization and mobilization since its foundation, their political role was gradually institutionalized. In 1986, the Base Committees were granted a third of the total number of delegates in the national governing bodies of the FA; the National Plenary; and the National Political Board. In 1993, their presence increased to one-half of the delegates.[2] The Congress, which defines the programmatic platform and nominates the presidential candidate, is essentially composed of Base Committee delegates. All other commissions in the party also require representatives of grassroots activists. At present, the FA structure operates with an active and permanent participation of its grassroots activists.

The Base Committees meet regularly and frequently. Base Committees meet at least once a month. Yet most operate on a weekly basis or twice a month. In our online survey, 73 percent of Base Committee attendees claimed that their Base Committee holds a meeting at least once a month. Base Committees exist in all parts of the country, where activists engage in partisan activities (group interview with grassroots leaders, observation of Base Committee activities, and online survey). Forty percent of the Base Committees were in Montevideo and the others were located throughout the rest of the country. In 2015 in Montevideo, there were over 152 active Base Committees, which is equivalent to one Base Committee for every 10,000 people. In total, throughout the country, there were 352 Base Committees in 2015 (FA administrative data). The geographic distribution of Base Committees matches the population distribution within the country. Of all adherents, both those who participate in Base Committee

---

[2] At the local level of the party structure, plenaries and the executive boards were responsible for planning the party´s action in the department (the political, electoral and administrative subnational units in Uruguay), coordinating the initiatives of the Coordinating Groups and the Base Committees and serving as an appeal organ to resolve potential conflicts in the zone.

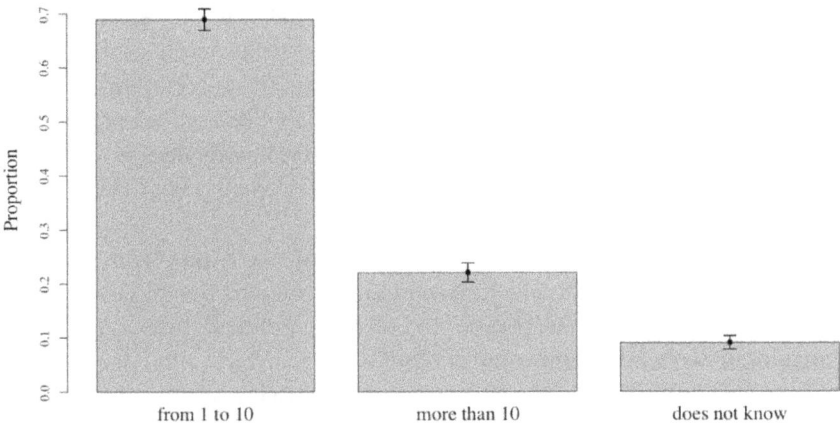

FIGURE 3.1 Self-reported distance from a Base Committee (in blocks)
* "Thinking about your neighborhood, and regardless whether or not you attend a FA Base Committee, how many blocks is your home from an FA Base Committee venue?"
*Source:* Online survey

activities and those who do not, 68.9 percent (std error 1.01) claim to have a Base Committee within walking distance (approximately less than 1 km away) and fewer than 10 percent do not know the location of a Base Committee (see Figure 3.1). The Base Committees are active in the everyday operation of the party, during elections and also between elections.

Our online survey allows us to estimate that around 7,000 activists regularly attend Base Committee meetings. Base Committee attendees are diverse in terms of age, sex, occupation, and educational attainment. The average age of Base Committees attendees is 51 years. Young persons, between 14 and 29 years, represent 15 percent of Base Committee attendees. Middle-aged adults and retirees account for between 27 and 29 percent, respectively. In terms of years of engagement with the organization, 55 percent have been involved for 26 or more years, thus extending back to the early stage of the party. This shows stability of engagement. Conversely, 18 percent have been involved for ten or fewer years, and 7 percent of the total have been involved for less than three years, showing that the organization continues to engage new activists – though in fewer numbers. Male and female activists participate in almost equal numbers; 46 percent are women. In terms of education attainment, Base Committee attendees are also diverse. A quarter of them have completed tertiary education, more than the proportion observed in Uruguay's general population (around 10 percent). At the same time, 26 percent have not completed secondary education. Another example of the diverse composition is the distribution of types of occupation (including retirees). Thirty percent of Base Committee attendees are retirees, 60 percent are active workers (36 percent of all Base Committee attendees work in the private sector[3] and 21 percent in the public sector), and 8 percent are students (Figure 3.2).

As part of our fieldwork, in the winter of 2016 (far from national elections), we visited Base Committees and witnessed the existence of the meetings, and saw that people engaged in political discussions. The agenda or some highlight topic is announced via the mailing list, WhatsApp group, or other media of communication that each Base Committee has. It is important to highlight that these networks are self-administered – there is no communication professional hired for this task at grassroots level.[4]

The issues they debate, deliberate, or decide range from neighborhood issues (e.g., garbage collection in a specific location, a conflict between a factory and the neighbors), to city problems (discussion of the design of the revitalized train line throughout Montevideo), as well as national (debate concerning the irrigation bill) or foreign policy issues (the Middle East conflict or the party's position toward a free trade agreement (FTA) with China). Mariano Bianchino, president of the Canelones Departmental,[5] shared the following anecdote, which illustrates the kind of political engagement that occurs at Base Committee meetings and the ability to channel a local concern:

> In a Base Committee a group of women gathered because they had a problem with bus stops, with the frequency of public transportation (...) I mean, San Luis is a Base Committee that works (...) They organized [the demand], they went to the Consultative [Coordinating Group of Canelones grassroots members] (...) and they requested the presence of the Transportation Ministry, and two weeks later [Víctor] Toto Rossi went, and they were together for three, four hours and the people asked him about everything.
> 
> (personal interview with Mariano Bianchino)

---

[3] This number results from summing the following categories: private sector employees; self-employed; entrepreneurs; business sector; and members of cooperatives.

[4] This does not rule out the possibility that there are activists who have expertise in some area that is valuable for the organization and who help the organization (voluntarily) in that area.

[5] Canelones is a department in the south of Uruguay, and northeast of Montevideo. It is the second largest department in terms of population, after Montevideo. Montevideo and the southern part of Canelones make up the Montevideo metropolitan area.

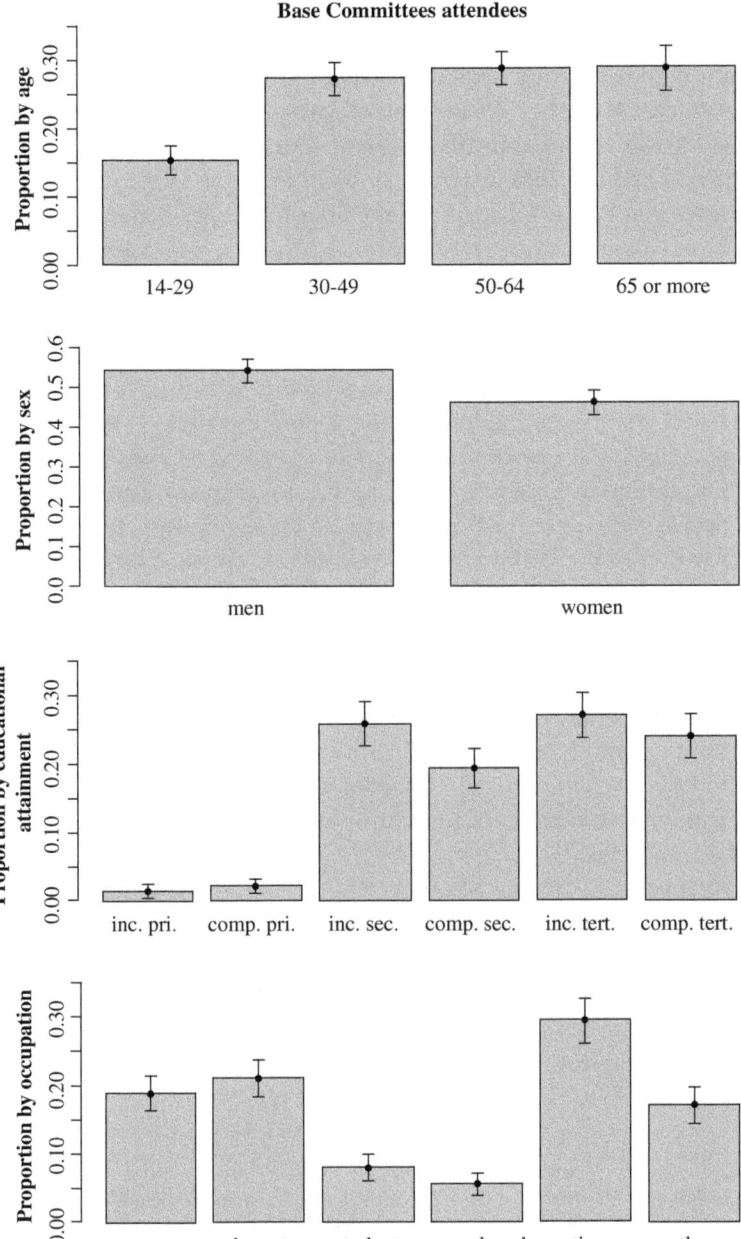

FIGURE 3.2 Sociodemographic characteristics of Base Committee attendees
*Source:* Online survey

Base Committees also discuss issues of national relevance: foreign policy, renewable energy, education, security, housing and environment, taxation, the irrigation regulation act, transformations in the global labor market, etc. Also, they debate general party strategies and organizational issues. In Calvo and Murillo's (2019) terms they act simultaneously as territorial and ideological activists. As an example of the diverse types of activities that occur, we surveyed the organized open activities in different FA Base Committees, where experts, academics, union leaders, or politicians were invited by the organizers to talk about different issues. As an example of the numerous activities organized by Base Committees and Coordinating Groups, we present a list of activities in one of the worst periods for the FA since taking office (this is not an exhaustive list). 2016 and 2017 were challenging for the organization. In different public opinion polls, the percentage of people intending to vote for the FA and the percentage who approved of the FA government were the lowest in the twelve years since the FA took office. Thus, this list is the best possible observation of the ability of the organizers to convene different meetings (in process-tracing terminology, it is a hard-descriptive test of the existence of an active organization in the territory):[6]

- On April 19, 2017 the Mario Benedetti Committee organized the meeting UPM: Transformation of the Neighborhood, a discussion about urban planning and infrastructure transformation.[7]
- On May 25, 2017 the "B" Coordinating Group organized a talk about memory testimonials of human-rights crimes during the last authoritarian regime.
- On June 22, 2017 the Mandela Base Committee organized the roundtable "ANCAP: truth and lies."[8]
- On June 24, 2017 the "M" Coordinating Group organized a talk at the Vanguardia Base Committee about "What happens in Venezuela?"
- On July 13, 2017 the Base Committees Primero de Mayo and 18 de Mayo organized the talk "A strong movement is a guarantee of our principles."

---

[6] Translation from Spanish of the titles of the listed activities by the authors.
[7] There was an intense debate about the refurbishment of train lines in Montevideo, as part of a request from the pulp mill paper factory, UPM, to install its second factory in the Uruguayan countryside, Durazno department.
[8] During 2015–2016, there was an intense political debate about the administration of the state gas and oil company during the former administration, presided over by the vice president at the time, Raúl Sendic.

- On July 18, 2017 the Base Committee thirty-three Orientales organized a talk about the public sector Budget for that year.
- On July 31, 2017, the Youth of the "Q" Coordinating Group organized the debate "We debate Education."
- On August 10, 2017, the Roberto Figueredo Base Committee from San Bautista in Canelones department organized a talk and roundtable about "Housing and Environment." It was held at the local bocce club in San Bautista.
- On August 26, 2017, the Toronto (Canada) Base Committee organized a talk and cultural event as a tribute to the intellectual writer José Enrique Rodó. It took place in 1280 Finch Ave. W # 204 "Casa Maíz."
- On September 9, 2017, the Comité Los Malvines organized a discussion about renewable energy and environment policy.
- On September 24, 2017, the "M" Coordinating Group organized the Ferifiesta with a talk about the "Education Congress" and "The Month of Diversity" at the Viera square in Montevideo.
- On November 20, 2017 the "L" Coordinating Group organized an activity at the Committee Marcha Venceremos about the FTA with Chile.
- On December 14, 2017 the Zelmar Michelini foundation organized the launch of a book about former FA leader Zelmar Michelini, who was assassinated by the dictatorship. It took place at the Zelmar Michelini Base Committee in Cardona, Department of Soriano.
- On December 16, 2017 the "O" Coordinating Group organized a talk about the irrigation regulation act. It took place at the H. Altesor Base Committee.

As illustrated by the interview excerpt above, where the grassroots activist described the visit of a government minister to his Base Committee, and the list of activities organized by the Base Committees, grassroots activists have regular access to government or party authorities. In our online survey, we asked Base Committee attendees about the visit of different national, local, and municipal government authorities to their respective Base Committee in the last six months.[9] All Base Committee attendees answered that at least one of these types of authorities visited their Base Committee. For example, 11 percent said a minister visited the Base Committee in the last six months, 21 percent received a visit from a Senator and 45 percent received a visit from a representative.

---

[9] This meant a period that did not include any electoral campaign.

Base Committee attendees are individuals who also participate in other civil-society organizations. Thirty-three percent of attendees participate in unions and 42 percent participate in neighborhood associations such as social or sport clubs, parent–teacher associations. In the group interview, a grassroots activist said:

> We want the Base Committee to be a sounding board of all that happens. We do not coordinate social actions from the Committee, but in our case, there is a natural dynamic because a number of our activists also participate in very different types of social organizations that support the Committee and that the Base Committee supports. And that is beneficial for both (...) The two largest committees of the area are a natural reflection of the neighborhood. When there is a concern, the neighborhood goes there [to the Committee].
> (personal interview with Manuel Ferrer)

There are many examples of the Base Committees' engagement with local community and civil-society organizations. For example, in October 2018, an Argentinean singer, who made misogynist remarks, planned to perform in an annual music festival that takes place at the beach of La Paloma (Rocha department in the East of Uruguay, far from the metropolitan area of Montevideo). Local social organizations and individual neighbors protested and tried to prevent his participation in the festival. To that end, they wrote a petition directed to the organizers of the event and to businesses and state institutions that sponsored the event. Among the signatories of the petition was the local FA Base Committee.[10]

During electoral cycles, Base Committees are a tool for the FA and its constituent factions to mobilize supporters in the neighborhoods. They have deep knowledge of the territory and thus help organize canvassing and provide detailed information about the problems and interests in each zone. They also make propaganda (e.g., paint walls, design and produce posters, set up stands in the local street markets). On election day, they cover many voting locales as party representatives. Thus, grassroots activists still play a role during the electoral campaigns. As has been mentioned before, all their work is voluntary.

> During the electoral cycle, the work of the Coordinating Groups and in the Base Committees is amazing. During the elections we systematically have

---

[10] "Entre las cuerdas: presentación de Gustavo Cordera en La Paloma genera revuelo," (On the ropes: Gustavo Cordera's perfomance in La Paloma ignites uproar), October 3, 2018 (available at http://lapalomahoy.uy/nota/3482/entre-las-cuerdas-presentacion-de-gustavo-cordera-en-la-paloma-genera-revuelo, last accessed March 15, 2019).

barriadas [canvassing] and we go to the street market on Saturdays, in that street market we deliver election materials, and, as a committee is supposed to do, we take the information of all the party lists, the ballots, of all factions. Moreover, when a faction did not give us its ballot we go and pick it up in order to have them all.

(personal interview with Manuel Mujico)

Base Committees are also functional to the electoral interests of factions. It is hard and costly for factions to maintain their own structure throughout the country. In this vein, Base Committees help factions in their electoral campaign in the territory. In the following excerpt, a faction activist describes her experience:

...we go out and deliver ballots in the neighborhood. We are a few activists [in the faction], that can [do it]. And if we go out to deliver in my area it is difficult. Even though they [in the Base Committee] do not vote Asamblea Uruguay [Uruguayan Assembly, AU, the interviewee faction], you have a structure [the Base Committees] and you can say 'I leave you the ballots'.

(personal interview with Daniela Stanisich)

Since its very inception, the participatory structure of Base Committees has rapidly expanded to areas of the urban periphery of the metropolitan area of Montevideo and gradually to the countryside, an area of the country traditionally hostile to the left. Our online survey and the administrative data show the intensity of participation in the Base Committees and their widespread presence in the territory. Figure 3.3 presents the distribution of Base Committees in Montevideo (capital city) in 1971. A few months after the foundation of the FA there were 250 Base Committees in Montevideo.[11] Figure 3.4 presents the distribution of Base Committees in Montevideo in 2015. In 2015 there were over 152 active Base Committees in Montevideo. According to FA administrative data there were 352 Base Committees in 2015; approximately 40 percent in Montevideo and the others throughout the rest of the country. Even

---

[11] This figure is based on data that the Grupos de Acción Unificadora (Groups of Unified Action, GAU) collected in 1971 for organizational purposes. The photos of the original registry were provided by Martín Ponce de León and are available in the Online Appendix. The original registry contains the name of the Base Committee, the address, the time and date of the meetings of their board and the plenary session. This registry contained the contact data of those in charge of each Base Committee and the representatives of the GAU who were engaged in each committee. This last piece of information was eliminated from the registries during the authoritarian regime to prevent the regime from gaining access to activists' personal data. The original registries are now in the FA's possession.

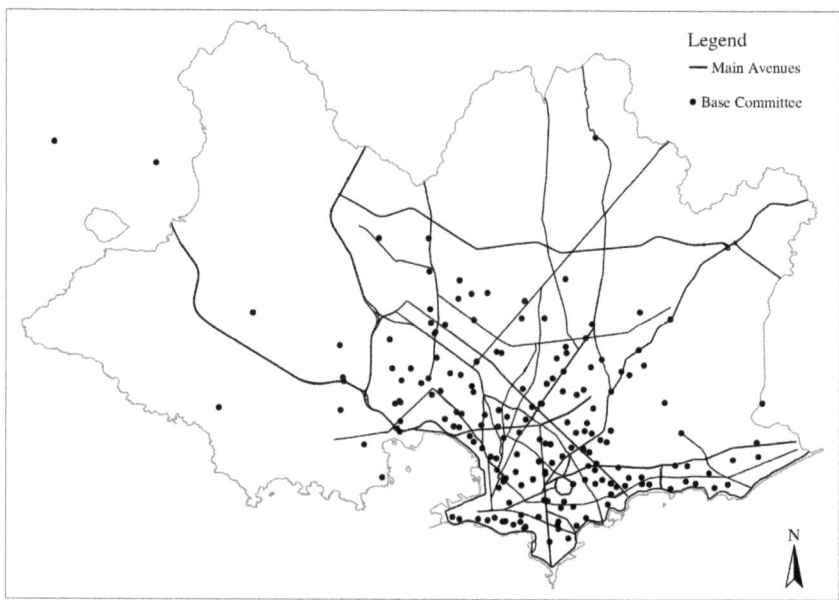

FIGURE 3.3 Active Base Committees in Montevideo in 1971
*Source:* Own construction using data from the FA

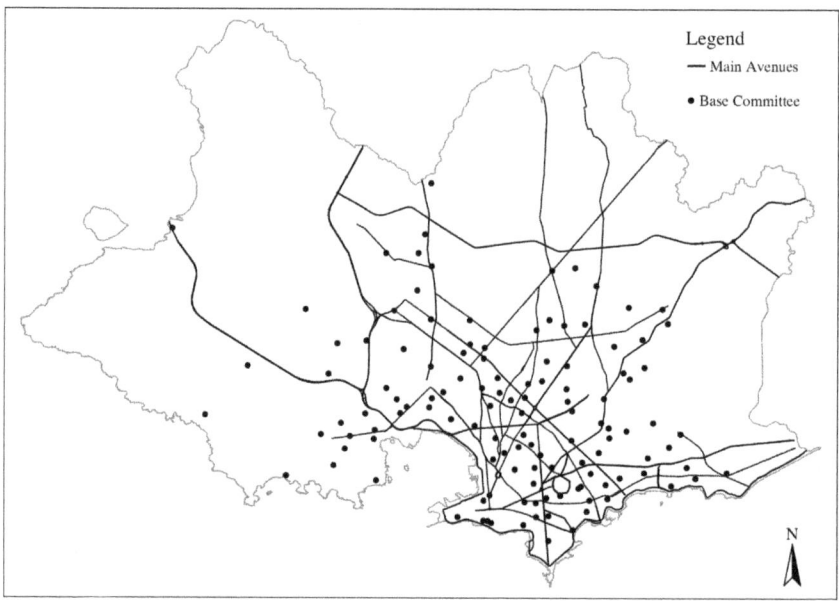

FIGURE 3.4 Active Base Committees in Montevideo in 2015
*Source:* Own construction using data from the FA

though there are currently one hundred fewer Base Committees in Montevideo than in 1971, they continue to exist throughout the city.

There is a set of requirements for forming a Base Committee. Those who want to form a new Base Committee have to gather at least fifty adherents and present an annual plan of work to the National Organizational Commission, which approves it. There is a commission in charge of analyzing the new Base Committee's needs in terms of infrastructure and this commission decides whether to provide resources to rent a venue. An example of the process of forming a new Base Committee is illustrated in the story of Mathias.

Mathias was twenty-five years old at the time of our fieldwork and was a student of medicine from Bella Unión (a small town in the north of Uruguay, 628 km from Montevideo) who participated in the students' union of the School of Medicine at the Universidad de la República (University of the Republic). He had been engaged with the party since 2016. With other fellow students, he considered there was a need to organize the FA at the School of Medicine. He first asked the Organizational Commission within the FA about the requirements to form a Base Committee. In 2017, Mathias and his friends started to gather signatures to organize a functional Base Committee. They gathered the necessary signatures from fifty adherents to formalize themselves as an FA Base Committee and held their first meeting on August 25, the Day of the Base Committee.[12] They named the Base Committee after Hugo Villar, a former FA leader, former Chair of the Hospital de Clínicas,[13] and former candidate for Montevideo's mayoralty in 1971. Mathias claimed that their idea was to support the FA government and generate a space to discuss and debate the process of the health-care reform that the government had been implementing since 2007 (personal interview with Mathias Robalez). Thus, the functional Base Committee at the School of Medicine of the University of the Republic was formally established. The Base Committee includes students, professors, and workers from that school. After they gathered the required support, the "C" Coordinating Group (which coordinates the activities of the Base Committees in that zone) gave them a meeting place. They meet every two weeks in the Base Committee's

---

[12] The launch of the new Base Committee took place on November 23, 2017. It took place at the FA's headquarters, in the "La Huella" room.

[13] The largest public hospital, which belongs to the School of Medicine of the University of the Republic.

"Allende/Cavani" locale at the intersection of Justicia and Nueva Palmira, in Montevideo, a few blocks from the School of Medicine. There are usually around fifteen activists at every meeting.

All Base Committees have names. Some are named after famous leaders, artists, etc. associated with the left (e.g., Nelson Mandela, Che Guevara, Uruguayan writer Mario Benedetti, Uruguayan singer Alfredo Zitarrosa). Others use the name of a historical social and political activist (e.g., Uruguayan union leader José Pepe D'Elía). Still others use the name of the neighborhood where they are located (e.g., Puerto del Buceo), or name the Base Committee after a significant event or date (e.g., 1° de Mayo, Labor Day). They usually operate in small locales or garages. They have chairs, a table, and many party emblems from the FA and the different factions, and posters from past elections cover the walls. They are humble places, without centralized heat or air conditioning or technological gadgetry. Outside the locale, there is a sign identifying the locale, and the exterior walls are usually painted with the colors of the FA (red, blue, and white). Thus, any bystander can easily identify a Base Committee from the outside.

Since 1986, the FA has celebrated the "Día del Comité de Base" (Day of the Base Committee) on August 25th.[14] On that day, every Base Committee holds an assembly to elect the Base Committee board. This is a celebratory occasion when grassroots activists organize activities in the neighborhood (e.g., talks, artistic performances) and the activists bring some food and beverages to share with participants. National political leaders, elected representatives and authorities visit different Base Committees.

One of the greatest challenges of this structure is how to finance the operation of the Base Committee. A significant proportion of it is covered by the dues grassroots activists pay, and some Base Committees receive financial support from the FA to cover the rent of the locale. Our online survey shows that 70 percent of Base Committee attendees regularly contribute money to the party.[15] In many cases the money is collected by the Base Committee itself, while in other cases the FA is in charge of this task. In the following excerpts, grassroots activists narrate their experience collecting party dues.

---

[14] The 25th of August is the Uruguayan national Independence Day.
[15] According to our online survey, 43.2 percent of FA adherents contribute money to the party.

I go out [to collect dues] on Saturday mornings, afternoons, Sunday mornings, and Sunday afternoons. During the week, in the morning, I go out to collect the dues from those adherents that I know are available in the morning. [I go out] in the afternoons, the days that I can, because sometimes I have to pick up my grandsons and take care of them before attending one of the meetings. And then I have Friday nights, on those days when [my wife] does not ask me out to go to the theater.

(personal interview with Manuel Mujico)

...I have an anecdote, they [a group of women from the San Luis Base Committee] once divided up the neighborhood blocks to collect the party dues and one block away from the Base Committee was the summer house of Tabaré Vázquez [President of the Republic at the time], with all the security apparatus and all that, and the old ladies did not move until he came out of the house and paid the 500 pesos [20 US dollars] party dues.

(personal interview with Mariano Bianchino)

According to data provided by the FA, there is no clear trend regarding the number of dues-paying members. The average number of dues-paying party members between 2006 and 2017 was 31,850. This number ranged between 24,544 (in 2006) and 41,410 (in 2007). The second largest number of dues-paying members occurred in 2012, and the third-largest number occurred in 2008 (Table 3.1). In 2017, 26,447 were dues-paying members.

The FA also provided the yearly number of new FA members: 502,930 people have registered since they began collecting the data in 1986. As stated in the Introduction, this number is likely inflated. As expected, the largest numbers of new members are observed during years when internal (FA) elections occur: 1997, 2002, 2006, 2012, and 2016. There has been

TABLE 3.1 *Number of FA Members Who Pay Dues (By Year)*

| Year | Number of Members Who Pay Party Dues |
| --- | --- |
| 2006 | 24,544 |
| 2007 | 41,410 |
| 2008 | 36,881 |
| 2009 | 32,713 |
| 2010 | 30,930 |
| 2011 | 28,606 |
| 2012 | 41,257 |
| 2013 | 34,455 |
| 2014 | 29,510 |
| 2015 | 27,896 |
| 2016 | 27,560 |
| 2017 | 26,447 |

*Source:* FA administrative data

TABLE 3.2 *New Party Members (By Year, 1986–2017)*

| Year | New Members | Year | New Members | Year | New Members | Year | New Members |
|---|---|---|---|---|---|---|---|
| 1986 | 13,077 | 1994 | 11,717 | 2002 | *131,652* | 2010 | 4,207 |
| 1987 | 942 | 1995 | 21,745 | 2003 | 2,427 | 2011 | 1,013 |
| 1988 | 659 | 1996 | 1,884 | 2004 | 1,902 | 2012 | *59,522* |
| 1989 | 568 | 1997 | *73,363* | 2005 | 10,368 | 2013 | 1,081 |
| 1990 | 199 | 1998 | 1,652 | 2006 | *107,189* | 2014 | 1,710 |
| 1991 | 160 | 1999 | 4,209 | 2007 | 668 | 2015 | 1,632 |
| 1992 | 52 | 2000 | 6,676 | 2008 | 2,282 | 2016 | *19,861* |
| 1993 | *16,179* | 2001 | 2,524 | 2009 | 1,322 | 2017 | 488 |
| Total | | | | | | | 502,930 |

*Source:* FA administrative data
*Note:* In italics are years when internal elections occurred.

a tendency since 2006 toward a decrease in the number of new members, and the current stability of population (i.e., minimal growth) makes it unlikely that the FA will be able to expand its membership in the short term (Table 3.2).[16]

There are no barriers to entry to the grassroots structure. Even though grassroots activists acknowledge that some Base Committees are more welcoming than others, there are no institutional barriers (formal or informal) to prevent the incorporation of new activists (group interview). In the group interview, a grassroots activist narrated the following situation:

> I was once at the Base Committee and there were two old ladies, historical activists of the "Nelson Mandela" Committee, and a neighbor entered and said "Hi, I am Frenteamplista, I have seen the Base Committee opened and decided to step in" [laughs][17] "We open on Thursdays at eight p.m., Where do you live?" [said the ladies]. "Colón" [street in Montevideo's old city] [replied the neighbor], "Ah, how long have you been in the neighborhood?" [the ladies inquired] "Around two years, approximately" [the neighbor answered] "Why didn't you come in before?" [said the ladies] [laughs] That is real people.
> (personal interview with Sergio Pratto)

The following excerpt from the interview with Daniela Stanisich, faction delegate to the Coordinating Group "J" in Montevideo, also illustrates this open access nature of the FA's Base Committee structure.

---

[16] While the electoral registry in Uruguay increased 9 percent between 1999 and 2015, the FA membership increased 230 percent over the same period.

[17] This story was told by grassroots representative Sergio Pratto during the group interview.

*When you participated at the Base Committee level, and you approached that Committee, how was your experience?*
Good, well, I was young and I also learned doing things at the organizational level, more than anything: for the internal elections, but it was very light. I was not that involved because I was 14 or 15 years old (...) it was an invitation, I remember the collector who went around the neighborhood to collect the party dues and said "you should come and join," and I went on Saturdays. It was nice because it is one of the few Committees that work on a Saturday. They are your neighbors, your friends, they are the people you know.
(personal interview with Daniela Stanisich)

The history of Gabriel Márquez, a young activist, illustrates how the grassroots structure of the FA is open to the entry of new activists. Gabriel was a FA voter. He attended the campaign rallies in 2004 with his family and he was a "network activist," but he wanted to deepen his activism in a FA locale. Also, he did not want to participate in a faction because, in his own words, he has never been "involved in a faction," and he did not see the faction as a place to participate. For Gabriel, the factions have the advantage of having clearer ideological definitions that help guide activists, though he considered himself frenteamplista: "frenteamplismo in itself deeply penetrated me." Even though Gabriel wanted to participate in the FA, he did not know how to do it, so he visited the FA web page and checked the Base Committees of the area:

...nothing clear came up so I sent an email, they answered and sent me to a locale that was two blocks from my house. I had not toured the neighborhood yet, it was my first week in this neighborhood, so I sent the email right away (...) it was [December] 2010 (...) and I arrived at a meeting that was actually one of a Coordinating Group, which was different from a Base Committee, then I understood the logic, but I entered and said "Hi," they greeted me, I said "can I come in?" and they replied "of course you can." I walked in, I participated, they briefly told me "look, this is a Coordinating Group, here a Base Committee operates, but it is on a different day and here what we do is to coordinate between Committees, stay in the meeting" (...) I remember that the discussion they were having was about a conflict that Ana Olivera [Montevideo mayor] was having with ADEOM [Mayoralty's union workers] and I perfectly recall it was about a strike of garbage collectors in 2010, it was a [conflict] over the budget (...) A guy there who also participated in the Base Committee that operated in the same locale told me "we gather every Thursday," "Ok I'll come on Thursday," and I went on Thursday, and in the Committee we were five or six people, it was a very low point (...) I kept engaged all through February, I was very excited, I wanted everybody to participate, but there was nobody, they were all on holidays, I was told. In March, we were seven or eight and there was a gang (...) it was interesting and we started to generate a plan of operation starting in 2011, that was cool, that also restructured the Committee.
(personal interview with Gabriel Márquez)

For Gabriel, Base Committees are open spaces for those who want to participate.

> My experience is that the Base Committee was prepared to receive people and we were of different ages. There was a group of young and a group of older people (...) We started to be excited that the Committee was very open to do a lot of things and we were given the room to do it as we pleased. Then, the 2012 election [FA's internal election] was a big excuse to mobilize frenteamplistas and people started to approach the Committee. We made a good effort in recruiting people in the neighborhood, [these people] saw that the Committee had young folks, it had people, it was alive. People who had not been attending returned and people who were attracted by personal connections, by friends (...) and in 2012 the Committee doubled the number of people that usually participated, and it started to grow. Then, it was the 2014 electoral campaign and it was out of control and it was impressive, and then it was a challenge all the time. What is the mystique, and how is it sustained...
>
> (personal interview with Gabriel Márquez)

Gabriel remembers that it was very easy to access the Committee, and now it sometimes is his turn to receive people "and the door is always open."

The last two excerpts above, especially the history of Gabriel's involvement, is a hoop descriptive test (necessary condition) of the existence of open access to the grassroots structure. We are not claiming that a large number of young activists are constantly seeking to access the FA, nor that it is universally open. However, both Gabriel and Daniela are young activists who were not involved in the foundational stages and thus do not have a connection to the founding epic. Thus, they are unlikely candidates to engage in the grassroots structure. Yet, they both decided to join it and they found it easy to do so. This supports the claim that, in order to join the grassroots structure of the FA, one simply needs to be willing to do it.

The two examples presented above do not imply that activists never exit the organization or that people who exhibit some interest in the organization are comfortable with the Base Committees' environment. Some party leaders and pundits argue that Base Committees do not provide a welcoming environment for new activists who want to join the party. However, our data show this criticism to be not generally valid; Base Committees do recruit new activists. Therefore, the negative experiences some activists may have had in Base Committees or the perceptions held by some party leaders are not explained by the Base Committee structure, rules, or by their operation. On the contrary, these experiences and perceptions are related to the fact that, as in every organization, the preferences of typical Base Committee participants, who tend to be more

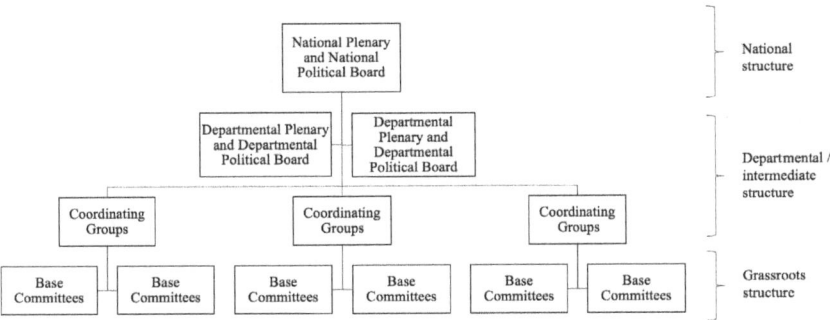

FIGURE 3.5 The organizational structure of the FA

committed activists, differ from the preferences of some of those who may be interested in joining the Base Committee. As a result, the policy positions and decisions of the Base Committees tend to alienate some people with different – usually more moderate – positions. The reduction in the number of Base Committee activists might reinforce this process of homogenization and radicalization of the Base Committee participants and make them less friendly to people with more moderate positions.

## From the Bottom to the Top: the Vertical Structure of the Party

The party has a complex organizational structure, with several collective decision-making structures (see Chapter 4 for a description and explanation of the origin and reproduction of this structure). Grassroots activists are granted the right to send delegates to these various decision-making bodies. Thus, beside the existence of grassroots activism, the FA has a vertical structure that connects base-level activism with the decision-making authorities and, even more crucially, grassroots activists have a significant presence in all organs of decision making within the party (see Figure 3.5), including the most important ones (Congress, National Plenary, and Political Board). Also, this vertical structure connects the grassroots structure with the factions (i.e., it connects the movement structure with the coalition structure), since both have representatives in the different bodies. Finally, grassroots activists have also developed informal institutions that complement the formal institutions and through which they coordinate their actions. This development is particularly important because factions' representatives have a structure that ensures their coordination at the faction level. Without these opportunities to coordinate, grassroots delegates would remain atomized and would lose relevance.

The intermediate level comprises the Coordinadoras Zonales (Zone Coordinators, henceforth "Coordinating Groups") in Montevideo and Mesas Ejecutivas Departamentales (Departmental Executive Boards) outside Montevideo. Both are part of the FA structure, where grassroots activists' and factions' delegates coordinate political positions and activities in the territory. Coordinating Groups in Montevideo are the first formal body where grassroots activists have delegates and meet faction representatives. Each Base Committee in Montevideo selects delegates to the Coordinating Group; the number of delegates depends on the number of attendees to the yearly assembly of the 25th of August. A Base Committee that gathers fifteen activists in its assembly – the minimum number required in order to be recognized as a Base Committee – is entitled to send one delegate to the Coordinating Group. A Base Committee that has twenty activists can send two delegates, and so on.[18] There are eighteen Coordinating Groups in Montevideo, each representing an area of the city. Beside the delegates from the Base Committees, faction representatives also participate, as do elected grassroots delegates to the National and Departmental Plenary. Coordinating Groups usually convene in the locale of one of the Base Committees of the zone. They meet on a weekly basis (every Tuesday). Their main task is to aggregate the political positions of the Base Committees and the factions' delegates of the area and provide guidance to the delegates that the Coordinating Groups send to the national and departmental bodies. The Coordinating Groups have a secretary of organization, as well as secretaries of finance and communications. These secretaries directly participate in the FA's national commissions of organization, finance, and communications. Thus, the Coordinating Groups not only influence the party's political discussions and strategic direction but also the party's operational decisions and actions. The Coordinating Groups also channel the information that flows from the decision-making bodies of the FA and the national commissions to the Base Committees. In our fieldwork, we visited several Coordinating Group meetings, and different interviewees described the structure of the Coordinating Groups and their role in the party's operation. In this vein, it is clear that Coordinating Groups depend heavily on the work of Base Committee delegates. Most factions, especially those with few activists, do not have the capacity to send delegates to

---

[18] The number of delegates per attendee is revised every year, through a bylaw defined by the National Organizational Commission.

participate regularly in the Coordinating Group meetings.[19] Discussions at the Coordinating Group meetings help to aggregate the positions and initiatives of the Base Committees of that area. Also, these debates help factions' and grassroots activists' delegates understand the issue positions of their respective groups. The discussions tend to moderate the more extreme positions that emanate from Base Committees. Therefore, Coordinating Group meetings are not simply a place to coordinate logistics and territorial actions but also provide a platform for discussing party positions. Because participation is voluntary and grassroots activists' engagement is volatile, a given Base Committee may or may not have a permanent activity. Coordinating Groups are more stable and thus provide a more permanent means by which the grassroots activists structure engages in the party's decision-making process.

The grassroots delegates to the FA's National Plenary, from each Coordinating Group in Montevideo, coordinate their positions through an informal institution, known as the Grupo de los 41 (Group of 41).[20] This group also selects from among the Coordinating Group delegates the grassroots delegates to the National Political Board. They also disseminate political discussion that emerges in the grassroots structure. In the rest of the country, this coordination is carried out by three Regionales (Regional Boards). The Group of 41 meets twice a week (Mondays and Wednesdays) in the FA's headquarters. On Mondays, they meet to analyze the report from the meeting of the National Political Board (the report is sent out every Friday). These reports are disseminated to the Coordinating Groups and Base Committees. On Wednesday, they meet again to articulate a position to be conveyed to the subsequent National Political Board meeting. This illustrates how the grassroots structure is connected on an on-going basis with the highest decision-making bodies of the party.

The highest directive body of the FA is the National Plenary. It comprises 170 delegates. Factions and Base Committees have the same number of delegates. All delegates are elected in open internal elections with secret voting. An FA adherent or sympathizer can affiliate at the moment of voting. In the 2016 internal election, 82,886 adherents voted.

---

[19] In the rest of the country, the departments are not divided into Coordinating Groups, though the grassroots activists meet faction delegates at the Mesa Política Departamental (Departmental Political Board).
[20] Forty-one is the number of grassroots activist delegates to the National Plenary from Montevideo.

The faction delegates are elected in closed and blocked lists in departmental districts. The Base Committee delegates are elected on a separate ballot that lists candidates by Coordinating Group in Montevideo or by department in the rest of the country. Adherents can mark two grassroots candidates for the National Plenary and two more candidates for the Departmental Plenary. The number of delegates each Coordinating Group zone can elect depends on the number of votes obtained by the candidates from that Coordinating Group zone (with a minimum of two). The National Plenary does not have a regular meeting day, but it convenes between three and four times a year and it discusses the main party guidelines and defines the most important political positions of the party. Grassroots delegates sit on the left side of the room where the National Plenary takes place, and the faction delegates sit on the right side.

The National Political Board is the permanent executive body. It convenes every Friday. It comprises the president and vice president of the party, fifteen representatives from the FA factions and eleven delegates from the Base Committees (six from Montevideo, two from Canelones, and three from the rest of the country). Even though the grassroots activists are not granted 50 percent of the seats on the National Political Board, the decisions are mostly arrived at by consensus. If there is no consensus, decisions can also be made by majority, as long as fewer than a third of the National Political Board members oppose (article 96, Party Statutes). This ensures the grassroots delegates a significant veto power because, for example, delegates from Montevideo can block a decision. Finally, the National Political Board has a Secretariat where Base Committee delegates also participate. The representatives of the Base Committees to the National Political Board and to the Secretariat are chosen in Montevideo by the Group of 41, in Canelones and in the rest of the country by the delegates that attend the regional Coordinating Group meeting. In general, Base Committee delegates to the National Political Board and to the Secretariat periodically rotate.

The FA Congress is the party's most important event, at which the party defines its ideological and programmatic positions. It convenes every thirty months, though occasionally the National Plenary will convene a congress outside of the normal schedule to address some significant issue. The Congress selects the candidates for the national presidential elections and, since the Constitutional reform of 1996 that established mandatory primary elections for all parties, the Congress authorizes the presidential candidates who compete in the primary. The Congress is presided over by the National Plenary, but it essentially comprises Base

Committee delegates. The members of the factions who act as delegates to the Congress are those who act as representatives to the National Plenary.[21] The FA congresses convene a large number of activists; more than 1,000 delegates participated in the 2016 "Rodney Arismendi" congress. The 2018 seventh FA Congress, "Compañero General Víctor Licandro y Compañera Susana Dalmás," gathered 1,143 delegates; 39 percent were women and 61 percent were men. It discussed the programmatic platform for the upcoming national election and authorized four candidates for the presidential primary. An FA activist and leader who was in charge of the 1986 discussion of the party constitution recalled in the in-depth interview:

The FA Congress remained as it was designed in the 1986 statute, and it has remained essentially the same [consisting almost exclusively of grassroot activists' delegates] (...) Doyenart [the Christian Democrat representative to the commission that discussed the statute] did not want the National Plenary to even preside over the Congress. He wanted to be a congress exclusively of Base Committees. Because [he thought] without representatives of the Political Board and the coalition, it was worthless.

(personal interview with Alberto Roselli)

Nevertheless, the Congress became a very significant event and its peculiar design, where grassroots activists are an overwhelming majority, engendered the unintended consequence of granting a very important role to grassroots activists in defining the programmatic platform and selecting the presidential ticket. Giving an important role to activists was an explicit design choice, but the goal of this design was to make the Congress politically irrelevant by depriving the Congress of the most influential party leaders.

Base Committee delegates to these national bodies are subjected to a strong vertical and horizontal accountability. If their vote or political position is not aligned with that of the Coordinating Group or of the Group of 41, for example, there is a strong social sanction by the delegates' peers and it can eventually lead to the request that the delegate resigns. Grassroots representatives are assumed to be delegates and not trustees. This is in line with the logic of operation and continuous discussion in the grassroots structure of the party. This is relevant because grassroots delegates might also identify or participate in a faction and they could participate in the decision-making bodies in accordance with

---

[21] The number of delegates of Base Committees is determined by a bylaw set by the National Organizational Commission for every Congress.

the position of their faction and not of their Base Committee. Even though many grassroots activists are also members or have some kind of participation in one of the FA factions, the Base Committee and faction structures are parallel. Grassroots delegates to the FA structure emphasize that if someone is acting as a grassroots delegate and the position he or she is supposed to take in that role differs or contradicts that of his or her faction, the grassroots delegate role will prevail. A grassroots delegate to the National Plenary, who is also an activist of the PCU, mentioned this issue in a personal interview:

*Did you ever have to vote differently than the position of your faction at the National Plenary?*
   Always, and sometimes there are disagreements. Your own faction tells you and you disagree, and your Coordinating Group is the sovereign. Many times we [the grassroots movement activists] are characterized as a party, the 41 (...) we meet twice a week, we coordinate, we take the position to the Executive Board...
(personal interview with Carmen Fernández).

If the faction has a different position from that of the Base Committee or the Coordinating Group and the delegate votes in line with the position of the delegate's faction and not that of the Coordinating Group the delegate is representing, the delegate's fellow fellow grassroots activists will complain and, as noted above, the delegate will find himself or herself facing a political problem. The following excerpt, also an interview with Carmen Fernández, illustrates this potential conflict.

...when I vote in the National Plenary, I have to tell [my peers] how I voted and what I said. [...] if you are from the grassroots you are from the grassroots. You are selected by the people from your neighborhood to be there. We don't emerge from a list of a faction.
(personal interview with Carmen Fernández).

Another activist also narrated the conflict that arises once a grassroots delegate takes a different position from that of his Base Committee:

I know Base Committee delegates that were removed. There is one concrete case, five years ago, here in the Buceo Port [an area in Montevideo], one delegate was removed. He came back to the Committee and the following week he was removed. His own faction reprimanded him for having gone to the Coordinating Group meeting and voting the opposite position to his Base Committee.
(personal interview with Eduardo Alonso)

Finally, the party has several national commissions. The most important are the Organization, Communications, Programmatic, and Finance commissions. On these commissions, party bureaucrats coexist with grassroots and faction delegates. Even though some hired individuals work on these commissions, they are essentially staffed by volunteers. The Coordinating Groups in Montevideo and grassroots delegates from the rest of the country actively participate on these commissions, each of which has its own coordinating body. The Group of 41 and other coordinating bodies are informal institutions, though all are permanent and active. This shows that the grassroots activists' political participation in the party structure is coordinated and not disorganized, which further enhances activists' significant *voice* and veto power.[22]

## The Coalition Structure and Its Relationship with the Grassroots

As stated elsewhere, the FA was born as a coalition. It was born in 1971 as a coalition of center and leftist parties (PSU, PCU, and PDC) and center-left factions from the foundational PC and PN parties. In the Uruguayan context, this implied the coalition of several preexisting factions from the traditional parties or leftist parties. Uruguayan parties are factionalized, and the main factions within each party are institutionalized. The Uruguayan electoral system facilitates the existence of factions by granting them an electoral expression; i.e., in Uruguay, voters cast a ballot for a party and for faction candidates within the party at the same time (see Online Oppendix for examples of ballots). Factions are usually national groups that present candidates for the Senate and the House of Representatives for each district.

Historically, there has never been a predominant faction in the FA. From 1971 until the 2004 national election, no faction received the most votes in two consecutive elections (Piñeiro and Yaffé 2004). More recently, in the national elections of 2004, 2009, and 2014, the Movimiento de Participación Popular (Popular Participation Movement, MPP) faction received the most votes, garnering around 30 percent of all FA votes. Four factions – the PCU, PSU, MPP, and AU – have tended to be the most important in organizational and electoral terms (see Table 3.3). Other factions have had a more volatile electoral expression and tend to form electoral alliances with other factions or groups. Party identification is stronger and more stable than faction identification. As a result, in the FA – as in the other Uruguayan parties – internal electoral volatility (between factions) is higher than that observed between parties.

---

[22] This political and organizational structure is somehow replicated in each department.

TABLE 3.3. *Electoral Evolution of FA Factions*

| Election / Faction | 1971 Vote Share | 1971 Sen.[1] | 1971 Rep.[2] | 1984 Vote Share | 1984 Sen. | 1984 Rep. | 1989 Vote Share | 1989 Sen. | 1989 Rep. | 1994 Vote Share | 1994 Sen. | 1994 Rep. | 1999 Vote Share | 1999 Sen. | 1999 Rep. | 2004 Vote Share | 2004 Sen. | 2004 Rep. | 2009 Vote Share | 2009 Sen. | 2009 Rep. | 2014 Vote Share | 2014 Sen. | 2014 Rep. |
|---|---|---|---|---|---|---|---|---|---|---|---|---|---|---|---|---|---|---|---|---|---|---|---|---|
| PCU | 32.9% | 2 | 4 | 28.2% | 2 | 5 | 46.9% | 4 | 11 | 9.4% | 1 | 2 | 8.2% | 1 | 1 | 6.2% | 1 | 1 | 6.4% | 1 | 1 | 6.6% | 1 | 1 |
| Patria Grande | 23.3% | 1 | 5 | | | | | | | | | | | | | | | | | | | | | |
| PDC | 20.1% | 1 | 7 | 10.6% | | | | | | | | | | | | | | | | | | | | |
| PSU | 11.8% | 1 | 1 | 15.3% | 1 | 2 | 22.4% | 2 | 5 | 18.1% | 2 | 6 | 28.5% | 4 | 14 | 14.9% | 2 | 11 | 14.6% | 2 | 9 | 12.3% | 2 | 5 |
| MPG | 10.3% | 1 | 1 | 39.0% | 3 | 12 | | | | | | | | | | | | | | | | | | |
| IDI | | | | 6.7% | | 1 | | | | | | | | | | | | | | | | | | |
| Vertiente Artiguista | | | | | | | 15.8% | 1 | 3 | 9.5% | 1 | 2 | 13.3% | 2 | 4 | 8.9% | 2 | 4 | 4.8% | 1 | 1 | | | |
| MPP | | | | | | | 10.8% | | 2 | 7.3% | 1 | 2 | 16.7% | 2 | 5 | 29.4% | 6 | 21 | 33.4% | 6 | 26 | 32.6% | 6 | 24 |
| AU | | | | | | | | | | 39.5% | 4 | 18 | 20.5% | 2 | 8 | 17.7% | 3 | 8 | 27.0% | 3 | 6 | 18.8% | 1 | 6 |
| Lista 78/738 | | | | | | | | | | 5.1% | | 1 | | | 6 | 7.8% | 2 | 4 | | 1 | 1 | | 1 | 1 |
| Unidad Frenteamplista | | | | | | | | | | | | | 2.8% | | 2 | | | | 2.1% | 1 | 1 | 4.8% | | 3 |
| Nuevo Espacio | | | | | | | | | | | | | | | | 7.7% | 1 | 3 | | 1 | 3 | | 1 | 2 |
| CAP-L | | | | | | | | | | | | | | | | | | | 6.9% | 1 | 2 | | | |
| Compromiso Frenteamplista | | | | | | | | | | | | | | | | | | | | | | 14.5% | 3 | 6 |
| IR | | | | | | | | | | | | | | | | | | | | | | 2.3% | | 1 |
| Casa Grande | | | | | | | | | | | | | | | | | | | | | | 3.8% | 1 | 1 |
| Other | 1.5% | | | 0.1% | | | 4.2% | | | 11.1% | | | 10.0% | | | 7.3% | | | 5.0% | | | 4.5% | | |

[1] Sen: Senators
[2] Rep: Representatives
*Source:* Own construction with data from Corte Electoral, Uruguay

FA factions have representatives in the different FA bodies and in the Coordinating Groups, the Departmental Executive Boards, Departmental Plenaries, National Plenary, and on the National Political Board. They also have representatives in the different FA permanent and ad hoc commissions.

Factions have different levels of internal organization and territorial presence. Some are highly organized, e.g., the PCU and the PSU. Others have a more flexible organization with less institutionalized processes of decision making, e.g., the MPP. Finally, others have little structure and their leaders exert greater influence in the decision-making process, e.g., the AU. Factions select candidates at the national level for the Senate and the House of Representatives and also candidates for the legislative bodies at the Departmental and Municipal levels. Thus, factions operate as the mainstream political-science literature conceives political parties to operate. In these political organizations, internal democracy is associated with the degree of openness and centralization of the candidate-selection process (Hazan and Rahat 2010).

The FA currently has twenty-nine factions. Some have existed since the FA's birth while others were formed later (see Chapter 4). Only ten of these factions won seats in the 2014 national election (see Table 3.4). Also, the most nationally relevant factions are the six that have won seats in the Senate. In ideological terms, there are three main groups of factions. The first group is the center-left Frente Líber Seregni (Líber Seregni Front, FLS), comprising the AU and other moderate factions. Danilo Astori is the most visible leader. He was Minister of Finance and Economy (2005–2010, 2015–2020) and vice president from 2010 to 2015. The second is a group of leftist factions, where the most important faction is the MPP. The leader of this faction is former president José Mujica (2010–2015). Within this group it is possible to locate the PCU, Partido por la Victoria del Pueblo (Party for the Victory of the People, PVP), Compromiso Frenteamplista (Frenteamplista Commitment, List 711), and Casa Grande (Big House). The third group is the PSU, which has operated as a buffer between these two main groups. This ideological distribution is not necessarily reflected in the electoral alliances or political positions that form on specific policy issues. Yet, it is possible to observe consistent alignment in terms of economic policy and international relations issues. The FLS, for example, tends to advocate less state intervention, a more moderate expansion of public spending, and it supports an international relations policy oriented toward signing trade agreements beyond the MERCOSUR. In contrast, the leftist factions

TABLE 3.4 *Electoral Strength of FA Factions (2014 National Election and 2016 FA Internal Election)*

| Faction | Senate | House | Vote Share in Internal Election | National Plenary | National Political Board |
|---|---|---|---|---|---|
| MPP | 37.5% (6) | 46% (23) | 21.2% | 21.2% (18) | 3 |
| FLS | 18.8% (3) | 18% (9) | 19.8% | 17.6% (15) | 3 |
| List 711 | 18.8% (3) | 12% (6) | 5.7% | 5.9% (5) | 2 |
| PSU | 12.5% (2) | 10% (5) | 12.5% | 11.8% (10) | 1 |
| PCU | 6.3% (1) | 2% (1) | 15.7% | 15.3% (13) | 2 |
| Big House | 6.3% (1) | – | 4.7% | 4.7% (4) | 1 |
| Frenteamplista Federation League | – | 4% (2) | 4.6% | 4.7% (4) | 1 |
| PVP | – | 2% (1) | 3.0% | 2.4% (2) | 1 |
| IR | – | 2% (1) | 1.5% | 1.2% (1) | – |
| Frenteamplista Congress | – | 2% (1) | – | – | – |
| Independent | – | 2% (1) | – | – | – |
| ther small factions | – | – | 11.1% | 15.3% (13) | 1 |

*Source:* Own construction with data from the Electoral Court and the FA Electoral Commission

favor developmentalist policies and a more decisive advocacy for regional integration in terms of international relations. However, these alignments are less clear in terms of public security, human rights, social policies, infrastructure and environmental issues, and the new agenda of progressive rights (especially concerning gender-based affirmative action policies). These differences do not undermine party discipline in Congress (Chasquetti 2014). Many of the differences are solved among the caucus members in Congress, though the most crucial, sensitive and conflictive issues are decided in the National Plenary of the FA. When the FA is in government, some of these debates are also resolved in the Council of Ministers.

Many political commentators and some FA leaders consider the grassroots activists to be an extension of the MPP and the PCU, especially of the latter. This gives rise to the idea that these two factions, and especially the PCU, are overrepresented in the FA's decision-making bodies.

The PCU's electoral strength is much weaker than its strength within the party decision-making bodies. In this vein, one FA leader said:

What happens is that in the end there is a debate, a questioning of the representativeness of the grassroots delegates that emerge from the [Base] Committees, because in reality the operation of [Base] Committees is less participatory and there is a prevailing role of the FA political groups [factions] that (...) does not reflect the votes and the relative distribution of [votes] (...). Somehow it is perceived that grassroots representatives [belong to] two or three groups, with a strength that differs from that given by the votes, in the National Board decisions, in the Secretariat, or in the [National] Plenary. Thus, I believe it is not a conceptual, ideological, philosophical issue about how much the grassroots have to participate as grassroots, but how life has led [to a situation in which] committees have a different composition, with a prevailing weight of groups...

(personal interview with Mario Bergara)

Another FA leader expressed a similar perspective, though he emphasized that this is not a new phenomenon.

*How is the relationship between the factions and the grassroots activists in the decision-making process?*
It has always been a close relationship, in some cases even promiscuous. The grassroots, that one pictures as something pure, of people from the neighborhood, evidently depends on the influence that the factions have, and they put people through the grassroots activists.

(personal interview with Álvaro García)

This perception, as illustrated in the two excerpts, is grounded in two ideas: first, that the grassroots structure tends to have political preferences and positions that resemble those of the MPP and PCU; second, it is believed that these two factions predominate among Base Committee activists and thus dominate the grassroots structure. Grassroots delegates have a different perspective, as illustrated elsewhere, and emphasize their independence when they are discussing and voting in the decision-making bodies of the party (see Chapter 6).

Faction activists have a significant role in the grassroots structure. As our survey shows, two-thirds of the grassroots activists in Base Committees participate in factions. Table 3.5 presents the distribution of Base Committee attendees by faction affiliation (all attendees and those who claim to attend frequently). Those who do not participate in a faction are the biggest group. No faction dominates the Base Committees, and no faction has more than 15 percent of Base Committee attendees. Even though only a relatively small number of Base Committee attendees are affiliated with the moderate faction (FLS), fewer than 30 percent of

TABLE 3.5 *Percentage of Base Committee Attendees by Faction*

| Faction | Base Committee | Base Committee Frequent attendees |
|---|---|---|
| No faction | 28.6% | 20.8% |
| MPP | 14.9% | 16.2% |
| PS | 14,6% | 15.8% |
| PCU | 12.6% | 14.9% |
| FLS | 8.4% | 7.0% |
| LIST 711 | 3.2% | 3.2% |
| Big House | 2.8% | 2.7% |
| VA | 2.7% | 4.1% |
| Federal League | 1.1% | 1.6% |
| IR | 0.4% | 0.6% |
| PVP | 0.3% | 0.5% |
| Other sectors | 8.6% | 10.2% |
| Do not answer | 2.0% | 2.3% |

*Source:* Online survey

attendees are affiliated with either the PCU and MPP (the leftist factions). Also, 15 percent of attendees are affiliated with the PS (a faction ideologically located between the FLS and the PCU and MPP).

Table 3.6 shows the percentage of Base Committee attendees who claim to also participate in each FA faction. It also shows the internal electoral strength of each faction and its performance in national elections. There exist differences between how well represented each faction is in the Base Committees, how well they perform in FA internal elections, and how well they perform in national elections. For example, the percentage of Base Committee attendees affiliated with the PCU and the percentage of votes the PCU received in the 2016 FA internal election is much greater than the percentage of the vote the faction received in the 2014 national election. Conversely, the percentage of Base Committee attendees affiliated with the moderate faction, the FLS, is less than the percentage of the vote the faction received in both the 2016 FA internal election and in the 2014 national election. The greatest absolute discrepancy occurs for the MPP, which received 32.6 percent of the vote in the national elections but accounts for only 20.9 percent of the Base Committee attendees affiliated with a faction. Th combined percentage of the votes received by the MPP and PCU in the national elections (39.2 percent) is similar to the combined percentage of Base Committee attendees (38.5 percent) affiliated with the two factions.

TABLE 3.6 *Faction Representation in Base Committees and Performance in a Recent FA Internal Election (2016) and National Legislative Election (2014)*

| Faction | Base Committee | Base Committee Frequent attendees | Internal Election | National Election |
|---|---|---|---|---|
| MPP | 20.9% | 20.4% | 21.2% | 32.6% |
| PS | 20.4% | 19.9% | 12.5% | 12.3% |
| PCU | 17.6% | 18.9% | 15.7% | 6.6% |
| FLS | 11.7% | 8.9% | 19.8% | 18.8% |
| List 711 | 4.4% | 4.1% | 5.7% | 14.5% |
| Big House | 3.9% | 3.4% | 4.7% | 3.8% |
| VA | 3.8% | 5.1% | 4.2% | - |
| Federal League | 1.5% | 2.1% | 4.6% | 4.8% |
| IR | 0.5% | 0.8% | 1.5% | 2.3% |
| PVP | 0.4% | 0.6% | 3.0% | - |
| Other sectors | 12.1% | 12.9% | 7.1% | 4.5% |
| Do not answer | 2.7% | 2.9% | - | - |

*Source*: Online survey. FA electoral data and Corte Electoral

Both tables illustrate that no faction accounts for a large majority of the activists in the FA grassroots structure. Power is distributed. A comparison of the percentage of votes the MPP and PCU factions received in the national elections with the percentage of Base Committee attendees affiliated with these factions indicates that the leftist factions are not overrepresented in the grassroots structure. Finally, independents (i.e., those not affiliated with any FA faction) are the largest group among the grassroots activists. They play a pivotal role in the FA discussions; they neither express extremist positions nor are they mechanically dominated by a given faction.

The discussion of the prospective approval of an FTA with Chile illustrates the pivotal role played by grassroots activists. In 2016, the FA government agreed to an FTA with Chile. However, the caucus in Congress was divided over its ratification. In the second semester of 2017 and the first semester of 2018 this was discussed within the organizational structure of the FA. In May 2018, the discussion reached the National Plenary and there was an intense debate and division. The majoritarian factions of the FA (MPP, FLS, and PSU) supported the FTA while the PCU, Big House, and other small factions opposed the agreement. In the National Plenary it was impossible to reach a final decision and the majoritarian factions suggested deciding this issue in the Congressional caucus, where they hold a significant majority. This motion was disputed by the factions opposing the FTA and by the grassroots activists (especially from Montevideo and Canelones) who did not want to give away the authority to decide this matter. One of the factions with more activists, the MPP, and especially its leader, José Mujica, was not able to impose its decision to push for the agreement or, more specifically, to delegate power to decide this matter to the caucus of FA Representatives and Senators in Congress. In June 2018, after the FA government produced a document with more information about the impact of the FTA on the Uruguayan economy, the grassroots activists changed their vote and approved the agreement. No faction that originally opposed the agreement changed its position, though. It was the change in the position of the grassroots activists that enabled the ratification of the agreement.[23] This illustrates the independence of the grassroots activists from the factions, especially their autonomy from the PCU and the MPP.

The preceding discussion regarding the FTA with Chile well illustrates the role of the grassroots structure in the FA's political decision making and the negotiations with the factions. Grassroots activists usually act as a buffer in the conflict between factions (see Chapter 6 for other examples). The FA institutional design that gives power to grassroots activists does not allow major factions, including leftist factions, to impose their will.

## CONCLUSIONS

In the FA, around 7,000 activists[24] meet every week in the Base Committees and in other available organizational structures. In the Base Committees, people discuss different political topics, from national and international affairs to local issues, and also discuss the party's political strategy and activities. The results of these discussions in each Base

---

[23] For further details see El Observador "Guía esencial para entender cómo el Plenario del FA trancó el TLC con Chile" (Essential guide to understand how the FA National Plenary blocked the FTA with Chile), May 8, 2018 (available at www.elobservador.com.uy/nota/guia-esencial-para-entender-como-el-plenario-del-fa-tranco-el-tlc-con-chile-201858500, last accessed September 28, 2018). Also, see La Diaria "FA dio luz verde a TLC con Chile" (The FA gave green light to the FTA with Chile), June 25, 2018 (available at https://ladiaria.com.uy/articulo/2018/6/fa-dio-luz-verde-a-tlc-con-chile/, last accessed September 28, 2018).

[24] To be an FA member, one has to be at least fourteen years old and sign a commitment to comply with the bylaws and the decisions of the authorities.

Committee are conveyed to the top of the FA's decision-making structure. At the same time, decisions and directives are conveyed from the top to the grassroots. This does not occur via professionals in charge of communications nor through the exclusive use of communication technologies; rather, delegates from the grassroots are a crucial part of all bodies within the FA structure and they coexist with delegates from the FA factions and party leaders.

Professional politicians who, as in every political party, seek a career in government, satisfy their ambition in their respective political organizations (factions). As described in this chapter, the FA has different factions with different organizational and ideological characteristics. They select candidates for the different levels of government and have representatives throughout the structure where they interact with grassroots activists' delegates.

The FA structure, especially the grassroots structure, does not select candidates and does not experience the tendency to oligarchize that is associated with the candidate-selection process, with the appointment of government positions, and with the distribution of other kinds of resources. No resources are distributed throughout the grassroots structure. Thus, leaders cannot use these resources to control the grassroots structure. Moreover, as stated above, given the FA's organizational structure, the leaders of the coalition member organizations (factions) cannot control the process by which the grassroots representatives are selected. Thus, political elites cannot fully control the political process of the FA, and must share power with grassroots delegates. For grassroots activists, the only available means to reproduce their political clout in the FA is by keeping their organization alive. As a result, the accountability of elected representatives and party leaders does not depend on the grassroots activists' participation in the candidate-selection process. Grassroots activists, through the party's common structure, exert control over the action of representatives and government officials.

Contrary to conventional wisdom, grassroots delegates and the grassroots structure are not coopted by the factions that have more activists who participate in this structure. Even though there can be a confluence of preferences between the grassroots activists and those factions with more activists in the grassroots structure, the latter is not a mere rubber stamp for these factions' preferences. In the process of discussion and decision making in the FA, grassroots activists operate autonomously. They act as a buffer in the conflicts and negotiations between factions. This institutional design prevents majoritarian factions from controlling the structure and also prevents minority groups from acquiring veto power, as illustrated by the discussion of the FTA with Chile presented above.

Beyond demonstrating the existence of a vertical structure, this chapter has described the existence of low barriers to engagement with the organization and the existence of known and relatively open channels for efficacious participation, which accords with Queirolo (2001) findings concerning the FA's structure during the late 1990s. If the hypotheses of Norris (1999) and Inglehart and Welzel (2005) are correct, i.e., that modern democracies must face the challenge of more demanding citizens, the FA organizational structure is well-suited to adapt to this challenge. We will return to this issue in the final chapter of the book.

The FA has developed an organization where activist delegates are the activists' peers; they do not transform themselves into political leaders, but, rather, remain as grassroots activists notwithstanding their close connection to the party elite and political leaders, with whom they sit face-to-face to discuss the most important issues of the party's political agenda.

# 4

# Origins and Reproduction of the Mass-Organic Structure

## INTRODUCTION

Beyond explaining the FA's electoral success, this volume emphasizes the production and reproduction mechanisms that explain the FA's organizational development qua a party with activists. This is the most striking aspect of the party in theoretical terms. The FA emerged in the context of severe political crisis (Astori 2001, Nahum et al. 1993) and throughout the more than forty-eight years since its birth, it has remained a party with activists (see Chapter 3). Although the FA underwent a process of ideological transformation (Garcé and Yaffé 2005, Yaffé 2005), it retains its leftist ideological identity and remains the only mass-organic institutionalized leftist party in Latin America (Levitsky and Roberts 2011).

The emergence of this structure in the Uruguayan institutional context is even more peculiar if we consider the incentives set by the electoral system. The DSV, which makes possible electoral alliances, such as that of the FA, enables each political organization in the coalition – each faction – to nominate candidates for the House and the Senate; this promotes both inter- and intra-party competition (Buquet, Chasquetti, and Moraes 1998, González 1991, Luján and Moraes 2017, Piñeiro and Yaffé 2004). In fact, until the constitutional reform of 1997, parties were allowed to nominate more than one presidential candidate. However, even though the coalition members were not forced to nominate a single common presidential candidate, because the electoral system did not impose this requirement, the FA coalition not only nominated one common candidate for the presidency, but also developed a common organizational structure, parallel to those of each faction. This type of organization is rare for electoral coalitions; typically, the amount of common structure is only the minimum necessary and each member retains organizational autonomy (see Chapter 7). As Líber Seregni, the presidential candidate for the 1971 national elections, and the main leader of the FA for more than twenty years, acknowledged in a public speech:

> The FA is an agreement, a coalition of factions and political parties. It rests upon mutual collaboration and respect of these parties and associations. But it is not an alignment of watertight compartments, a sum of closed groups, without doors or windows. If the different components of the FA had no doors or windows, there would not be an FA. And it would be of little help if the FA had windows and doors only at the leaders' level, while the people become atomized, alienated from their own organizations. Or that they go out to the public stage, just in public meetings to hear the speaker of the time. If the FA were to be limited to this, there would not exist a true FA. The Frente implies real communication among its components on every single level. Only as this [type of political organization] would it turn into a fruitful experience for itself and Uruguay. Only as such is a fertile dialogue between its components possible. Hence, this is why the Base Committees are the setting for interacting and integrating. From the interaction between its components and at the same time a visible face that the FA is a real popular unity and not a sum of remnants
>
> (In Caetano 2005, 152).[1]

The main task of this chapter is to present evidence concerning descriptive and causal inferences regarding the origin and reproduction of the FA and, more specifically, its structure. First, we show that the FA was a mass-organic party at the time of its birth[2] and reproduced this trait over the forty-eight years since its origin. We present evidence concerning each of the four attributes that characterize this type of organization: 1) strong local branches; 2) active grassroots membership; 3) close ties to labor unions and other organized social constituencies; and 4) labor-intensive activity with widespread mobilization of grassroots partisans and social networks (Levitsky and Roberts 2011, 13).

Second, the chapter shows that the FA was a mass party with direct involvement of its grassroots activists in the decision-making structure at its inception and during its first stage of development (1971–1986).

---

[1] Translation from Spanish by the authors.
[2] We consider that this stage spans from the foundation of the party in early 1971 to 1986, immediately after the authoritarian regime and the first democratic election, and the consolidation of different party rules that would become entrenched.

This is because, first, the factions were overwhelmed by the activists who autonomously organized themselves in Base Committees and demanded participation in the structure. This activism was important for the electoral mobilization of the FA. Also, Base Committees provided a tool to organize at the local-level grassroots activists from the different factions – organizations that antedated the FA – as well as independents. Second, the grassroots activists quickly gained a crucial political role and were seen by some leaders of the political factions (i.e., the preexisting parties or groups) as a guarantor of the continued unity of the left.

Finally, we show that the reproduction of this structure was consolidated and reproduced through feedback mechanisms (Mahoney and Thelen 2015, Thelen 1999). The FA did not oligarchize, as did other similar parties such as the PT in Brazil (see Chapter 7), because of the political role granted to grassroots activists. In the FA, grassroots activists have representatives at the decision-making levels of the organization. This was granted to a degree that ensured their ability to block changes in the organization's statutes, engendering a lock-in effect.

In this chapter, we present the results of a process-tracing approach that we previewed in the introduction to this volume. We have systematically collected CPOs to test the descriptive and causal inferences preregistered in our design (Piñeiro, Pérez, and Rosenblatt 2016), as well as inferences that inductively emerged during our fieldwork. In each case, we detail the nature of the different pieces of evidence and their weight for the descriptive and causal inferences.

## THE ORIGIN OF THE FA AS A MASS-ORGANIC LEFTIST PARTY

In 1970, the Grupo de los Cinco (Group of Five) was formed. It included the leaders of the FIDEL, the PCU, the PDC, the Movimiento por el Gobierno del Pueblo (Movement for the Government of the People, MGP) of the PC, and the Movimiento Blanco Popular y Progresista (Blanco Popular Progressive Movement) of the PN. The groups began to talk to each other with the goal of forming a broad front of the leftist political organizations, without excluding anyone (in reference to the PCU). In 1970, a group of citizens that included union leaders, intellectuals, and scholars with ties to progressive ideals and in opposition to Pacheco Areco, signed the Declaración del 7 de Octubre (Statement of the 7th of October) in which they voiced their emphatic support for the formation of:

... [an] agreement without exclusions, between all the political forces that oppose the undemocratic policies of the current government, with the goal of establishing a platform aimed at overcoming the structural crisis of the country, to restore its destiny as an independent nation and to full restore individual civil liberties and union rights.
(Statement of the 7th of October, from Aguirre Bayley 2005, 32–33)[3]

By the end of 1970, there began to appear the Comités de Apoyo al FA (Committees of Support for the FA). Though there are no formal records of their number and location, Aguirre Bayley (2005) reports the existence of two of them: one in the city of La Paz, in the department of Canelones (close to Montevideo) and another in Sayago, a working-class neighborhood in Montevideo. *El Popular*, a weekly publication of the PCU, reported the existence of a third location in Juan Lacaze, in the department of Colonia.[4] Representatives from the Group of Five attended the inauguration of the one in Sayago. According to Aguirre Bayley, the event brought together over 600 people, exceeding the capacity of the local cinema. One founding leader, interviewed for the study, says that there is a debate about which was the first Base Committee, but what matters is that "by February 5, [1971, FA's birth] they were all over the country and Montevideo, and after February 5 that multiplied." (personal interview with Martín Ponce de León). Other interviewees referred to the existence and early reproduction of these committees; the press also captured this.

In December 1970, two splits from the traditional parties finally materialized. The splinter groups were going to be critical to the process of forming the FA. On December 5, the Congress of the MGP, led by Zelmar Michelini, decided to abandon the PC. Days later, the Blanco Popular Progressive Movement, led by the Blanco leader Rodríguez Camusso, abandoned the PN.

On January 8, 1971, the leaders of the MGP and the PDC decided to unite their action through a common organ that they called Frente del Pueblo (Front of the People), inviting all forces that aspired to "build a Broad Front" to engage in dialogue, and to convene a meeting – that would take place on February 5, 1971 – "with the goal of adjusting the principles for the constitution of the Broad Front" (Aguirre Bayley 2005, 37).[5]

---

[3] Translation from Spanish by the authors.
[4] Published in the print edition of the newspaper El Popular on January 9, 1971, 9. In the Online Appendix the reader will find a systematic review of the press of the time.
[5] Translation from Spanish by the authors.

The FA, at its foundation, was an alliance of the PCU, PSU, the PDC, factions from the traditional parties (like the MGP from the PC and Herrerista Movement from the PN), and independent leaders. But from its inception, the FA was also a movement. This implied, from the very beginning, the presence of strong bottom-up participation. The event that marked the birth of the FA took place at the Uruguayan Congress building, on February 5, 1971. The session was chaired by Zelmar Michelini, though all leaders from the various factions and parties that coalesced to form the FA spoke, as did Arturo Baliñas, representing the citizens that signed the Call of October 7, 1970. Among the attendees was José D'Elía, president of the CNT at the time.

The FA's Constitutive Declaration stated that:

> ... the unity of the progressive currents that culminate in the formation of the FA ... was achieved in the people's fight against the fascist philosophy of force. And that union ... in which the general public played a key role, has enabled a fraternal alliance of Colorados and Blancos, Christian Democrats and Marxists, men and women of different ideologies, religious faiths and philosophies, workers, students, teachers, priests ... the legitimate spokesmen of the nation.
> (Constitutive Declaration of the FA, February 5, 1971)[6]

The Constitutive Declaration of the FA was signed by twelve groups: members of the Group of Five, plus the PSU, the Movimiento Socialista (Socialist Movement), Movimiento Herrerista (Herrerista Movement, List 58, a PN faction), GAU, the Partido Obrero Trotskista (Trotskyite Workers Party), Oriental Revolutionary Movement, and the Comité Ejecutivo Provisorio (Provisional Executive Committee) of the citizens that signed the Call of October 7.

The signatories of the declaration committed themselves to establishing a common program, to generate the "...organization of base nuclei and common authorities, imperative mandates, and other discipline mechanisms." (Constitutive Declaration of the FA, February 5, 1971).[7] Moreover, it was stated that the main goal of the FA was permanent political action. The FA was more than an electoral coalition. Lanzaro (2004) summarizes the original organizational nature of the FA as follows:

> From the beginning, the whole was more than the mere sum of its parts, giving room to a frenteamplista corpus, in terms of identity and in terms of structure ... At the margins of the groups that form it, the FA put together a peculiar network

---

[6] Translation from Spanish by the authors.
[7] Translation from Spanish by the authors.

of base organizations ... that operated as nuclei of integration and activism, forging its activism in the electoral campaign and through mass mobilizations.

(38–39).[8]

Immediately after the constitutive act of the FA, the Mesa Ejecutiva Provisoria (Provisional Executive Board) was formed along with four commissions: Juridical and Electoral, Program, Political Commitment, and Organization. These commissions produced three key documents: the Bases Programáticas de la Unidad (Programmatic Bases of Unity), approved on February 17, 1971; the Reglamento de Organización (Organizational Rules), approved on March 17, 1971; and the Compromiso Político (Political Commitment), approved on February 9, 1972 (Aguirre Bayley 2001). On March 22, 1971, the Executive Board nominated Líber Seregni as the presidential candidate, and he was later proclaimed as such at the mass rally of March 26. Even though the PCU and PSU had deep roots in Uruguay, and even though the FA included well-known leaders from the traditional parties, no single leader or faction dominated the new FA structure when it formed in 1971.

The foundational process was interrupted by the coup and the authoritarian regime that ensued (1973–1985). In the authoritarian years, the party operated only underground through minimal local organization and, as was the case for other Latin American leftist parties, exiled activists developed an organization abroad; many FA activists and leaders were imprisoned, tortured, or had to face exile. During the first measures of liberalization from the authoritarian regime (in negotiations with political parties from 1982 onwards), the FA began to resume its organization and activities. In 1986, the FA consolidated its organizational and decision-making structure in its first statutes.

Since its founding, the FA has been a mass-organic party. The Organizational Rules document stated that the FA would have a pyramidal structure with organs at three levels: the base level, the intermediate level, and the directive bodies. The grassroots level comprised the Base Committees, defined as a local gathering of party adherents. The Base Committee could be of two types: territorial units (the most common) or centers of functional activity (e.g., work place, student unions). The Organizational Rules specified that the Base Committees were advisory organs to the party's board. Beyond the advisory tasks, the Organizational Rules of 1971 established that the Base Committees had to: 1)

---

[8] Translation from Spanish by the authors.

disseminate the party's platform; 2) foster the integration of as many forces as possible; 3) participate in the central party activities; and 4) organize the activities of the Base Committees according to the immediate goals that they themselves determine.[9] The Political Commitment of 1972 established the promise to agree on "... rules that would ensure the effective participation of the Base Committees in the governance of the FA at the national, departmental, and local level." (disposición transitoria literal a).[10] From the statutes' reform of 1986 onwards, the Base Committees have had a third of the total number of delegates in the governing body of the FA – and in 1993 their share would increase to one-half of the delegates.

The intermediate or coordination organs were the Coordinadoras Zonales (Coordinating Groups) in Montevideo and Mesas Ejecutivas Departamentales (Departmental Executive Boards) outside Montevideo. The Coordinating Groups were in charge of coordinating the tasks of their respective zones' Base Committees and were responsible for channeling the initiatives emanating from the Committees. These Coordinating Groups included delegates of each Base Committee in the territory and other representatives from the area; these latter representatives were appointed by the departmental party organ (Organizational Rules, art. 19). This organizational structure remains essentially unchanged (see Chapter 3).

At the local level of the party structure, plenaries and the executive boards were responsible for planning the party's action in the department, implementing the initiatives of the Coordinating Groups and the Base Committees and serving as an appeal body to mediate potential conflicts in the zone. Finally, the governing bodies of the FA, at the national level, were the National Plenary and the National Political Board, including representatives of groups comprising the FA and, until 1986, the president of the party; in 1986, grassroots representatives were incorporated.

These observations of the party structure, which was engendered in 1971 and consolidated in 1986, constitute a Hoop Test of the descriptive inference for the existence of the first and second attributes of a mass-organic party, namely strong local branches and active grassroots

---

[9] According to the Organizational Rules, every Base Committee had to have a registry of adherents. Internally, each one was constituted by an assembly – the highest decision-making organ of the Committee – comprising all adherents, and an executive board designated by the Committees' assembly.
[10] Translation from Spanish by the authors.

membership. This evidence constitutes a Hoop Test because the attributes are necessary conditions but are not sufficient (because the existence of the structure is not proof of the structure's actual operation). However, evidence of the actual existence of strong local branches and active grassroots membership in the FA's early years is available based on in-depth interviews and secondary sources; these constitute a Smoking Gun test. For example, Ponce de León and Rubio (2018, 86) state that in 1971 there were 269 Base Committees in Montevideo.

The Base Committees were a means to institutionalize the Committees of Support for the FA (personal interview with Óscar Bottinelli). Ponce de León and Rubio (2018), different interviewees, and press from the time (see Online Appendix) emphasize that they multiplied spontaneously, from below.[11]

In 1971, the FA was created with a very special characteristic not found in any other Latin American political party, namely, it was a combination of a coalition and a movement ... And the inclusion of the movement was justified because in 1971 the Base Committees were popping up everywhere.

(personal interview with Alberto Couriel)

On the spontaneous generation of the Base Committees, Líber Seregni said during the 1971 Base Committees Congress:

... the neighborhood of Malvín [in Montevideo] today has thirteen Base Committees of the FA that perfectly coordinate their activism. Beyond fulfilling their specific political tasks, those Committees in Malvín are setting an example that is worth imitating. Those committees have organized childcare so that mothers can attend the frequent assemblies that are held. And they have done something even better: the Committees in Malvín, in times of scarcity, have collected dozens of liters of milk that their brigade members offered to neighborhood households where children live.

(Speech of Líber Seregni, June 19, 1971)[12]

Very early in the life of the party, in the national elections of 1971, an army of volunteers was responsible for a significant proportion of the time and money invested in the campaign. They played a key organizational and mobilization role for a party with scant resources and unequal access to the media. Bottinelli recounted that activists painted so many trees in Montevideo that "there was no single tree in Montevideo that did

---

[11] La Hora newspaper (December 20, 1971, 5) indicates that delegates from 1,500 Base Committees from all corners of the country participated in the first Base Committee Congress, which took place on December 18.
[12] In Wettstein (1980). Translation from Spanish by the authors.

## The Origin of the FA as Mass-Organic Leftist Party 89

not have the red, blue, and white colors and the offensive joke was [from the traditional parties] that 'Seregni, idiota, los árboles no votan' ('Seregni, you idiot, trees do not vote')" (personal interview with Óscar Bottinelli). Accompanying their propaganda activity, the Base Committees raised funds for the campaign. According to two founding members of the time, most of the campaign resources came from small donations from activists (personal interview with Pedro Cribari). Martín Ponce de León[13] claimed that 80 percent of the financial resources raised in the 1971 national election came from the grassroots movement. The Base Committees' role was also discursive, "... to internally discuss significant topics ... and to go house-by-house or have face-to-face discussions with the neighbors or deliver short documents." (personal interview with Óscar Bottinelli). Thus, very early in the organization's existence, it intensely mobilized many activists.

Grassroots activism also manifested itself in the massive electoral mobilization that the FA engendered and was reflected in the public rallies that took place at the foundational event: the rally of March 26, 1971 in the Explanada Municipal (Town Hall terrace) and in Montevideo's main avenue "18 de Julio" included around 60,000 people. The rally that closed the electoral campaign later that year brought together around 180,000 people. These were the largest mass rallies in the history of the country up until that time.

> ... something gigantic ... we drove ourselves crazy. And on Saturday, the day before the election ... the Pachequistas and Wilsonistas came out [sectors from the Colorado and Blanco Party, respectively] together to the streets ... against the FA. They were completely afraid ... We then realized that all the Frente voters had come to the rally. We did not have more supporters than that, all were mobilized.
> (personal interview with Alberto Couriel)

In the national election of 1971, the FA received around 212,000 votes in Montevideo. When compared with the number of people attending the final rally, one can see that the FA had few passive voters; most of them were also highly engaged in the campaign (personal interview with Óscar Bottinelli). Even though the FA was a coalition of preexisting political parties and factions from the PC and PN, its vote share in 1971 was far above the aggregate number of votes obtained by those parties and

---

[13] Martín Ponce de León made this statement to the authors during a conversation that took place after the in-depth interview conducted for this research. The GAU group, of which Ponce de León was an active member, played an important role in the organization and finances of the 1971 FA electoral campaign.

factions in previous elections. Yet the results were disappointing (personal interview with Alberto Couriel). Given the strong mobilization of the party adherents during the campaign, leaders expected a better result (some even speculated about the prospect of winning the election). Despite the defeat, the FA obtained a decent electoral result: 18.9 percent of the votes. Even though the PC won the election, the traditional two-party system broke and a third actor emerged.

These pieces of evidence support the existence of strong Base Committees and active grassroots membership (attributes 1 and 2) and labor-intensive campaign activities (attribute 4). The existence of Base Committees and the party's territorial organization constitutes Smoking Gun evidence for attributes 1 and 2. These observations constitute a Smoking Gun test because they are grounded in administrative data accessed through Ponce de León and Rubio (2018) and interviews with key actors of the time. They are sufficient, but not necessary, conditions because there may exist other evidence of the party's strong territorial penetration and labor-intensive activism. The CPOs concerning grassroots activists' significant political role constitute Hoop Test evidence for attributes 1 and 2 because the evidence comes from formal documents and from the expressed opinions and perceptions of interviewees (who did not provide data on the actual political role). Similarly, the CPOs concerning labor-intensive campaign activities constitute Hoop evidence of attribute 4, because the evidence is the statements (e.g., recollections, perceptions) made by the interviewees, who were key actors in the events under investigation.

Finally, the characterization of the FA as a mass party is evidenced by the link it developed from the very beginning with social organizations, especially with the labor union movement. There are at least three indicators of this phenomenon. The first indicator is the creation of multiple functional committees, i.e., non-territorial Base Committees, based in the workplace. These committees stimulated the organization of the workers. "They were parallel to unions and a channel for communicating their demands and needs to the governing body of the party." (personal interview with Martín Ponce de León). Second, the first political board included important union leaders, such as Héctor Rodríguez, who had unionized the textile workers and was one of the key leaders of the People's Congress. Third, according to Senatore, Doglio, and Yaffé (2004), 10 percent of the first slots on the party's senatorial lists and Montevideo representative lists for the 1971 and 1984 national elections were union leaders. Fourth, in the 1984 elections (the first after the transition from the authoritarian regime), the FA ticket included José D'Elía for vice-president, the most important leader of the CNT. These observations constitute a Smoking Gun test for the presence of the third attribute of a mass-organic party (close ties to unions and other social organizations), i.e., they are sufficient but unnecessary, because, although they show strong ties between the party and unions, we have not examined other potential forms of ties between the party and social organizations. Table 4.1 summarizes the evidence and CPOs discussed in this section. The table contains only the observations that are key for determining the nature of the evidence (i.e., the process-tracing test).

## THE DETERMINANTS OF THE CONSTRUCTION OF THE PARTICIPATORY STRUCTURE

The FA combines two properties that are rare in contemporary political parties: a highly open decision-making structure (i.e., multiple veto points) and a strong mass-organic movement of volunteers. Intense grassroots-level engagement existed from the very beginning and was quickly incorporated into the party structure and into the highest decision-making levels of the new party (Organizational Rules, 1971). The FA was born as a coalition of political parties and factions, and from its inception it developed a structure that privileged consensus and balance among members. This resulted in the early establishment of institutionalized channels for decision-making, channels where grassroots members also played a significant political role in every aspect of the party's life (e.g., programmatic discussion).

The FA built a structure peculiar among mass-organic parties. This peculiarity is even more pronounced when we include in the analysis the early and ongoing participation of the grassroots movement, the Base Committees. This participation is the result of two combined factors. First, the Base Committees were a source of mobilization effort; they served the electoral interests of the political organizations that formed the FA. Second, the Base Committees played a significant political role during the foundational period, especially for unifying the left.

The bottom-up nature of the party structure was not an organizational innovation of the FA, either in Uruguay or in the world at large. What is striking is that the rank and file gradually permeated the whole decision-making structure of the party. Grassroots activists were not represented

TABLE 4.1 *Descriptive Inference Concerning the Origin of the FA*

| Evidence | Observation/CPO | Test |
|---|---|---|
| An organizational structure that acknowledges the territorial organization of grassroots activists beyond those of the electoral factions composing the coalition (attributes 1 and 2). | Organizational Rules (1971) where the existence of the Base Committees and Coordinating Groups is acknowledged; Base Committees Congress (1971 and 1984); 1986 Statute where the base structure is acknowledged and organized. | Hoop (necessary but insufficient proof) |
| | Effective existence of the Base Committees and territorial organization (Interviews and data from Ponce and Rubio 2018). | Smoking Gun (sufficient but unnecessary proof) |
| The grassroots activists were granted a significant political role in the decision-making structure (attributes 1 and 2). | Political Commitment (1972) to incorporate the grassroots activists in the national political board of the party; 1986 Statute where one-third of the seats on the national political board are granted to grassroots activist representatives. | Hoop (necessary but insufficient proof) |
| | Effective participation of the grassroots activists in decision-making bodies (interviews). | |
| Dual (union and party) membership of leaders and activists (attribute 3). | Functional Base Committees existed between 1971 and 1986; José D' Elía (president of the CNT) participated in the foundational rally of 1971; Héctor Rodríguez (active union leader) is one of the founding leaders of the FA and participated in the first executive; Evidence of joint work with social organizations; | Smoking Gun (sufficient but unnecessary proof) |

## Determinants of Participatory Structure 93

| Evidence | Observation/CPO | Test |
|---|---|---|
| | José D' Elía was vice-presidential candidate in the national election of 1984; In the national elections of 1971 and 1984, 10 percent of the spots in Senatorial and Representatives lists were filled by union leaders. | |
| Labor-intensive campaign activities in the 1971 and 1984 election (attribute 4). | Campaign activities that rely almost entirely on Base Committees: finances, propaganda, and intensive canvassing (evidence from interviews). | Hoop (necessary but insufficient proof) |

on the political board in 1971.[14] Nevertheless, during the foundational period (1971–1986), the grassroots activists claimed, and gained, their place in the decision-making structure. The National Organizational Commission was created at the founding of the FA. According to Ponce de León and Rubio (2018), there was an intense debate among the commission members about the existence and role of the Base Committees:

The discussion was long, especially about the Base Committees. In the first session [of the commission] their institutionalization was supported only by the GAU and the Organización Nacional de Independientes [National Organization of Independents, ONI] represented by Óscar Bruschera. With the passage of days, Base Committees expanded and brought together greater support until unanimity [in the commission] was obtained. As is known, the alternative approach was to do as the Unidad Popular [Popular Unity, UP] in Chile did, that is, to be a member of the party a citizen had to join the base structure of one of the sectors, and there were no common committees. The life itself of the emerging Base Committees determined otherwise

(80–81).[15]

---

[14] However, independent citizens were elected to participate at the National Plenary ("The Plenary is the governing authority of the FA," Organizational Rules, 1971, art. 22).
[15] Translation from Spanish by the authors.

In 1972, the political organizations that coalesced as the FA signed a commitment to include the movement in the decision-making structure. As Ponce de León and Rubio (2018) note, after the 1971 national election Líber Seregni convened a National Assembly of Base Committees. For the authors, this meeting sought to counter FA supporters' general disappointment with the electoral outcome and confirm the FA's commitment to permanent political action. On December 18, 1971 this National Assembly took place and many grassroots activists participated. According to Ponce de León and Rubio (2018), this meeting accounted, in part, for the FA's 1972 Political Commitment to incorporate the Base Committees. The evidence from our fieldwork indicates that one reason for this was that the organizations acknowledged that the grassroots activist movement flourished in the first year of the FA and played a crucial role in the electoral mobilization for the 1971 national election. As shown above in the evidence for the descriptive inference concerning the mass-organic origin of the FA, the Base Committees demonstrated a great capacity to mobilize, as well as to organize. Thus, leaders believed it was necessary to acknowledge the high degree of mobilization that had occurred – "it was the reality," said an interviewee – and it could not be ignored.

The Base Committees were electorally functional for the interests of the political organizations that formed the coalition. Political parties and splinter factions from the traditional parties that coalesced into the FA saw in the national election of 1971 that the Base Committees provided a shortcut to expand their influence and territorial presence. The leaders of the political organizations had to consider the emergence of a movement that superseded their capacity to organize and mobilize voters. Many of these voters did not identify with any of the preexisting groups. This expanded the traditional reach of the left. As one interviewee posited:

There remained no area of the country, especially in the city … without a Committee. Not any. Although the Communist Party and the Socialists had organization, there was no organization with such a widespread reach, such capacity to generate and promote neighborhood engagement.
(personal interview with Pedro Cribari)

In the electoral moment, it was useful for all political groups that Base Committees were operating. For the political parties [that formed the FA], Base Committees were more useful than their own [party offices] because people went to the Base Committee offices to pick up ballots of the FA and all [the different ballots] were there [in Uruguay, the DSV allows each party to present several lists of candidates].
(personal interview with Óscar Bottinelli)

The interviewees' remarks above accord with those of the leaders of the time, for example, Juan Pablo Terra and Zelmar Michelini, the leaders of the PDC and of the split PC's faction, respectively.

Facts have overwhelmed expectations about the growth and consolidation of the FA. There is an enormous amount of activism, activism that is organized, structured, armed, and ready to fight to resist all attacks. It cannot go back.
(Juan Pablo Terra speech given at a rally organized by M Coordinating Group in Rivera and Soca, two avenues in Montevideo, October 29, 1971. Reported in Ahora newspaper, October 30, 1971, 6)[16]

Of the novelty the FA has brought to the political fight, beyond the clash of ideas, and that everyday activism, selfless, convinced, authentic, Base Committees have undoubtedly been meeting centers, places for discussion, a true place to raise the people's awareness and achieve the active participation of the people in politics ... We have constantly repeated that the FA is a mass political movement ... This Base Committee Congress is saying so.
(Zelmar Michelini speech at the Base Committee Congress, reported in Ahora newspaper, December 18, 1971, 3)[17]

Second, the Base Committees were a crucial base of support for the first leader of the party, Líber Seregni, who himself was an unaffiliated independent and was concerned about the unity of the left under the FA. The founding leaders emphasized during the interviews that the existence of the Base Committees was especially important for Líber Seregni. He was interested in their relevance because, as an independent, he needed a base of support and the existence of a structure different from those of the political organizations that formed the coalition.

Every FA activist is a politician, and this is how it should be. To eliminate the politicking ... we promote the politicization ... this is why it is so natural and so necessary that the institutional organization assent to this desire of the activists, and that the Base Committees become integrated as another guiding element of the Frentista activity.
(Líber Seregni, February 4, 1972, public speech during the celebration meeting of the FA's first anniversary)[18]

The Base Committees also endowed the FA with a symbol of unity and gave meaning to the unity as a separate and different entity from the political organizations that formed the coalition. The movement was quickly seen as the realization of the unified political left, transcending

---

[16] Translation from Spanish by the authors.
[17] Translation from Spanish by the authors.
[18] Translation from Spanish by the authors.

the identities of the preexisting political organizations. "[They enabled] the creation of elements that solidified in the FA, which initially had been an alliance of political elites" (personal interview with Óscar Bottinelli). The Base Committees were not in the service of any leader nor was it their purpose to inform or "educate the masses" in a top-down fashion. As the following excerpt from Seregni's speech illustrates, the organization very early on insisted that the bottom-up political participation of the Base Committees played a political role:

> The Base Committees are essential to the FA. They are the visible expression of their fraternal reality. A place where parties and factions nourish reciprocally, without threatening each other. The Base Committees are a joint activism where everyone will be able to deliberate, participate, comment, discuss and organize.
> (Líber Seregni, speech given at a rally in June 19, 1971)[19]

In the final years of the dictatorship (1982–1985), the FA's identity quickly reemerged from below (personal interview with Óscar Bottinelli, Miriam Rodríguez, Jorge Pasculli). Between 1984 and 1986, the FA rethought its internal structure and statutes. The leaders of different political factions acknowledged in interviews that the party's grassroots members were crucial during the early days of the democratic transition, as gatherings in private houses were the main form of political meeting. As a result of the pressure from the grassroots activists, and as a consequence of the Base Committees' central role in the elections of 1971 and their capacity to spring up quickly during 1982–1983, the leaders simply felt it was natural to fulfill the promise of the Political Commitment of 1972 – i.e., to incorporate the party grassroots activists within the highest decision-making structures of the FA. This was realized in the first statute of 1986.

> On December 15, 1984, the Second Base Committees' Congress took place ... it was an impressive event ... In that Congress there was first a call to adjust the FA statutes to the new reality emerging from the dictatorship. This is an instance where the role of the Base Committees was important. And beyond that, there was Seregni's commitment to include the Base Committees on the board of directors. It was a very strong demand from the Base Committees.
> (personal interview with Alberto Roselli)

Alberto Roselli's opinion is supported by the statements of one of the main leaders of the FA, in the foundational year, about the need to institutionalize the Base Committees in the party's structure.

---

[19] In Wettstein (1980, 110). Translation from Spanish by the authors.

These people do not want to be mere spectators anymore; they demand, in turn, to be actors in the political fight for the country. The Base Committee gives it. It is necessary to reinvigorate this phenomenon, institutionalize it, to also give the FA the chance to intervene in the formation of the final will of the FA. And this does not at all mean conflict with the political parties [that form the coalition], on the contrary, it is the reaffirmation of what the FA is. For us the FA has two legs, two bases: one is the political parties ... that participate in the electoral competition, that have parliamentary representation. And the other leg is the Base Committees, that is where the people are, people who often do not manifest for a given political faction, but who can discuss, contribute with their experience and who contribute to [the party's] vitality and permanence.

(Zelmar Michelini speech at the Base Committee Congress, reported in Ahora newspaper, December 18, 1971, 3)[20]

Even though the process of incorporating grassroots activists into the decision-making bodies of the FA was seen as a natural consequence of their political role, the process was the subject of intense debate. The commission that drafted the proposed new statutes intensely debated this and other issues regarding the new structure of the party (personal interview with Alberto Roselli, member of this commission).

The first five CPOs listed in Table 4.2 – the existence of Organizational Rules; the perceived importance of the grassroots members' mobilizational role; Líber Seregni's speeches that acknowledge the grassroots activists' demands for participation in the decision-making processes; the Base Committees Congress of 1984; and the interviewees' claims concerning activists' demands for participation on the party's board – are a Hoop Test of the high-level of activism that played a crucial role for the new party.[21] They are insufficient proof because the interviewees provided only their perceptions or opinions and factual statements that we were not able to cross-check with other sources. These pieces constitute a weak Hoop Test (and not a Straw in the Wind test) because of the important role the interviewees and the quoted leaders played in the FA's initial stages (Collier 2011). The evidence presented regarding the importance of the Base Committees for the unity of the left constitutes a Straw in the Wind test of the claim that activists played a crucial political role. It is neither necessary nor sufficient because it consists only of the perceptions

---

[20] Translation from Spanish by the authors.
[21] The table contains only the observations that are key for determining the nature of the evidence (i.e., the process-tracing test).

TABLE 4.2 *Causal Inference of the Origin of the FA*

| Evidence | Observation/CPO | Test |
|---|---|---|
| Proof of the link between the high-level of activism during the party's initial stages and the political role granted to grassroots activists | Organizational Rules that set the functions and tasks of Base Committees | Hoop (necessary but insufficient proof) |
| | Interviewees' perceptions of the grassroots members' important mobilizational role and of the difficulty of excluding the activists from the decision-making structure | |
| | Líber Seregni's speeches on 4/2/1972 and 19/4/1986 acknowledge the role of the grassroots' demands for participation in the decision-making processes | |
| | Base Committees Congress of 1984 demand a place on the party's board (interview.) | |
| | Bases' demand for participation on the party's board (interviews) | |
| | Leader's speech and interviews about the role of the bases as guarantors of the FA unity | Straw in the Wind (unnecessary and insufficient, circumstantial proof) |

of actors and speeches from the leader. However, different interviewees converged on the same impression (see Online Appendix). This evidence connects the importance played in the unity of the left by the intense autonomous activism (from factions) and the grassroots activists' shared structure with the role granted to grassroots activists in the FA decision-making structure.

## THE REPRODUCTION OF THE MASS-ORGANIC NATURE

The FA sheds light on the relevance of organizational structure for reproducing activism over time. Historical causes explain the origin of this structure in which leaders have no control over the reproduction of the political role granted to activists or the organizational setting where the activists participate. Thus, the historical cause triggered positive feedback that produced a self-reinforcing trajectory and a lock-in effect (Mahoney and Thelen 2015, Thelen 1999). The lock-in effect operates in two dimensions: in the organizational dimension, it maintains space for activists to participate; and, in the political dimension, it ensures the political role of volunteer activists. The complex organization persisted, expanded, and became entrenched over the years.

Very early on, the party had multiple access points for grassroots activists' voices. The party granted grassroots activists a political role to a level that ensured their ability to block changes in the organization's statutes, engendering a lock-in effect. The 1986 statutes granted grassroots activists a share of the representatives to the National Plenary (a third of the representatives in 1986, and half since 1993) and, at the same time, required a super majority (9/10, i.e., almost unanimity) to reform those statutes. Therefore, the only way to change the role of the grassroots activists in the decision-making structure is with grassroots members' majoritarian support. This is the dimension of the lock-in-effect that consolidated the party bases' power within the organization (Pierson 2004). This phenomenon was raised in different interviews by leaders with very dissimilar trajectories, e.g., "there is no going back from this party structure," "questioning the bases' role is too costly," "no one shoots his own feet," "they have problems, and they have always had problems, though they are still the true guarantors of party unity."

The other dimension of the lock-in effect is the existence of multiple access to participatory structures (Base Committees). The existence of local-level entry venues is the necessary condition for individuals who have an interest in joining the organization; local-level venues make it possible for individuals to join the organization, making participation broadly accessible. Without such spaces, adherents who are willing to perform volunteer work would not be able to become activists.

After the authoritarian regime, organizational development of the FA, which had been stymied during the authoritarian period, resumed. In the period 1984–1986, during the democratic transition, the FA introduced rules to institutionalize the participation of the rank and file within the party's highest decision-making bodies. After thirty years of having been formally incorporated in the party's decision-making structure, the grassroots activist structure shows no signs of oligarchization or bureaucratization; e.g., none of the base level positions are paid. Moreover, most activists are voluntary adherents. Only 2 percent of grassroots activists hold a position for which they receive payment (online survey). Also, the apparatus is neither based on clientelistic distribution nor is the apparatus functional to it. Finally, the Base Committees are not viewed as a necessary first step in a prospective political career, because recruitment and candidate selection are mainly carried out through the political factions. According to our online survey, fewer than 23 percent of Base Committee activists hold or have held an elective or appointed office.

The 1986 Statute granted one-third of the National Plenary (highest governing body) delegate slots to representatives of the activists. The Congress, which defines the programmatic platform and nominates the presidential candidate, is essentially composed of representatives of the grassroots activists. All Commissions and the Political Board have representatives of the grassroots activists. The subsequent reform further consolidated the power of the activists. In 1993, a new statute took a new step forward toward the consolidation of the lock-in-effect: the activists would now comprise 50 percent of the party's decision-making structure. The combination of this level of penetration of grassroots activists and the quorum required to change the party's statues (almost unanimity) makes it almost impossible to eliminate this role or the associated spaces for grassroots participation. Also, the party and party leaders were not able to change the volunteer nature of the organization because it is not entirely under their control. Thus, the grassroots members not only remained crucial veto agents within the organization, they even gained more power, in contrast to the situation in other leftist parties in the region (e.g., PSCh in Chile or the PT in Brazil).

Table 4.3 presents evidence concerning the institutional rules that grant a political role to the grassroots activists, the volunteer nature of the activists' engagement in such institutions, and the fact that this engagement is not conceived as part of a political career. This constitutes a conclusive test (Doubly Decisive) concerning the reproduction of the party's open participatory structure and of grassroots activists' ability to influence decision making in the FA. These observations are necessary and sufficient CPOs of the reproduction of the party structure.

The process of organizational expansion, in electoral and territorial terms and in the composition of its social bases, was conflictive. The

# The Reproduction of the Mass-Organic Nature 101

TABLE 4.3 *Causal Reproduction*

| Evidence | Observation/CPO | Test |
|---|---|---|
| In the period 1984–1986, during the democratic transition and in the early 1990s, the FA introduced rules to institutionalize the participation of grassroots within the party's highest decision-making bodies | The 1986 Statute granted one-third of the National Plenary (highest governing body) delegate slots to the representatives of the grassroots activists. The Congress, which defines the programmatic platform and nominates the presidential candidate, consists entirely of representatives of the bases. All Commissions and the Political Board have representatives of the grassroots activists. In 1993, a new statute contributed toward the consolidation of the lock-in-effect: the bases would now represent 50 percent of the party's leadership structure and 100 percent of the delegates in the party's ideological and programmatic congresses. All these statutes have been enforced. | Doubly Decisive (necessary and sufficient, conclusive proof) |
| The base structure shows no signs of oligarchization and is not an apparatus based on clientelistic distribution | The grassroots activists are not paid. Only 2 percent of grassroots activists hold a position and are paid for it (online survey). Grassroots activists and faction leaders indicate | Doubly Decisive (necessary and sufficient, conclusive proof) |

*(continued)*

TABLE 4.3 (continued)

| Evidence | Observation/CPO | Test |
|---|---|---|
| | that neither the Base Committees nor the base representatives who influence the party's board are oligarchized (interviews). Base Committees are not part of a clientelistic structure (interviews and fieldwork observations). The Base Committees are not seen as a necessary first step in a prospective political career (interviews). Recruitment and candidate selection are mainly done through factions (interviews and online survey). | |
| Instances in which groups of leaders or factions sought, but failed, to change the role of the bases in the decision-making process. More specifically, failed attempts to change the nature of the FA as an organic mass party toward a coalition of political factions | Failure of the EP as a substitute organization for the FA; in the EP, the grassroots members had had no political representation in the political board. Any change to the statute needs to be negotiated with the Base Committees because they represent 50 percent of the National Plenary of the party and four-fifths of the National Plenary is needed to reform the statutes. | Straw in the Wind (unnecessary and insufficient, circumstantial proof) |

internal struggles to determine the party's ideological and programmatic commitments were intense. These struggles precipitated the resignations of several established party leaders and the exit of entire factions or groups. In 1989, for example, the MGP (the most important faction at the time in terms of its legislative caucus) and the PDC exited the FA. They felt that they did not have enough representation in the decision-making structures of the FA and did not agree with the role granted to grassroots activists. They also wanted their leader, Hugo Batalla, to be the FA's presidential candidate for the upcoming national elections.

During the 1990s, there were attempts to reduce the political power of the grassroots activists. In 1994, the formation of the Encuentro Progresista (Progressive Encounter, EP) as a political coalition that included the FA and other small moderate left-of-center groups was meant, in part, to circumvent the structure of the FA. This attempt lasted for eleven years. The basic rationale was to present a more moderate platform with a new, more modern identity, to win voters who had never supported the FA (see Chapter 6). It was also in line with the more gradual process of programmatic moderation of the FA (Garcé and Yaffé 2005, Yaffé 2005). However, during that period, the structural organization of the FA retained its activities, its complexity, and diversity. In the end, the FA structure prevailed and the EP vanished. In 2005, the groups that coalesced in the EP, but were not part of the FA structure, asked to join the party (source: decision of the FA Plenary in November 19, 2005). Thus, the proponents of the EP were successful, in the sense that it was a tool to foster an electoral strategy, but it was unsuccessful as an alternative organizational structure to the FA. This evidence is a Straw in the Wind test, because it is neither necessary nor sufficient to prove that the FA's decision-making structure inhibited the success of the EP as structure that could bypass the FA.

Despite variations in the grassroots activists' level of engagement, and despite the fact that the party's 2015–2017 level of intensity and penetration is below that which occurred in the 1971 election and during the transition in the early 1980s, the FA still retains the participatory structure. It not only has reproduced its identity over the years, even overcoming a long and very repressive authoritarian regime, but has also retained its grassroots structure. Union leaders are publicly identified with the FA, and many of them also participate in the organization. Also, since the FA took office in 2005, many union leaders have been appointed as ministers or other high-level officials.

At present, the FA organization not only retains its structure but also retains the way it operates with an active and permanent participation of its grassroots activists (see Chapter 3 for further details). The grassroots organization operates on a weekly basis all over the country, where around 7,000 activists engage in partisan activities (group interview with grassroots leaders, observation of Base Committee activities, and online survey). Even though the FA's campaign management is more professional when compared to the essentially voluntary structure of the 1971 campaign, activists still play a role.

Since its formation, the organization has expanded to areas traditionally unreceptive to the political left. Contrary to arguments emphasizing that party activists are only interested in defending more extreme positions, in the case of the FA, the organizational structure did not prevent the incorporation and representation of new sectors of society, and was not detrimental (and in fact was functional) to the successful development of electoral campaigns.

A series of CPOs regarding the reproduction of the FA as a party with activists has already been extensively discussed in Chapter 3 (i.e., number of Base Committees, frequency of Base Committee meetings, the territorial distribution of Base Committees, etc.). Table 4.4 summarizes the CPOs that are most relevant for substantiating the claim that the FA is at present a party with activists. The FA still exhibits high levels of party affiliation and large numbers of volunteers who contribute money to the party.

TABLE 4.4 *Evidence of Descriptive Inference – Reproduction*

| Evidence | Observation/CPO | Test |
|---|---|---|
| A large number of party locales distributed throughout the territory and an intense degree of activity at the Base Committees | 352 Base Committees in 2015 held a meeting during the Day of the Base Committee (*Acta* 39, *Mesa Política*, November 20, 2015) Base Committees convene at least twice a month (fieldwork observation) The eighteen Montevideo Coordinators and the nineteen departmental units convene on a weekly basis and actively participate in the | Doubly Decisive (necessary and sufficient, conclusive proof) |

## The Reproduction of the Mass-Organic Nature 105

| Evidence | Observation/CPO | Test |
|---|---|---|
| | governing structures and in the organization of the party (fieldwork observation) | |
| | According to our survey estimate, after post-stratification, 7,347 activists regularly attend Base Committee meetings (online survey) | |
| | 68.9 percent (std. error 1.01) claim to have a Base Committee within walking distance (approximately less than 1 km away) and fewer than 10 percent do not know the location of a Base Committee (online survey) | |
| | 73 percent of Base Committee attendees claim that their Base Committee holds a meeting at least once a month (online survey) | |
| Sustained high levels of party affiliation | 82,887 adherents voted in the 2016 internal election | Hoop (necessary but insufficient proof) |
| High proportion of activists regularly pay the party dues | 70 percent of Base Committee attendees regularly contribute money to the party (online survey) | Hoop (necessary but insufficient proof) |
| | 26,447 members paid the party dues in 2017 (FA administrative data, see Table 3.1) | |
| Labor-intensive campaign activities | Campaign activities that rely almost entirely on Base Committees: finances, propaganda, and intensive canvassing (evidence from interviews) | Smoking Gun (sufficient but unnecessary proof) |

CONCLUSIONS

From its very inception, the FA exhibited the characteristics of a strong political organization: it had a strong identity, a thriving presence throughout the territory, an army of volunteers, and historically unprecedented electoral results for the left. The FA's origin and its mass-organic nature offer two interesting conclusions that help explain mass-organic party organization.

First, as Panebianco (1988) originally stated, the origins of an organization leave a significant imprint. In the case of the FA, the origin is characterized by high levels of engagement in a polarized society. Very early, the party institutionalized the role of grassroots members in the structure. This happened because of grassroots members' role in mobilizing and forging the unity of the left.

Second, given this institutionalization, a strong lock-in effect ensued. This facilitated the FA's reproduction as a mass-organic party with a participatory structure. Once the grassroots activists were included in the party's decision-making structure, it became increasingly costly to weaken their power and in turn made activism matter. Hence, the FA case helps elucidate the conditions necessary for the reproduction of a mass-organic organization. To reproduce this type of organization, a party needs to have a democratic structure that allows grassroots activists opportunities to participate in the decision-making structure. This structure also needs to be independent from politicians' career paths to public offices; otherwise, the party will oligarchize.

The PT in Brazil and the PSCh in Chile became institutionalized professional-electoral parties (Levitsky and Roberts 2011), and thus are negative cases, that is, examples of the failure to reproduce mass-organic party organization. Although both had deep roots in their respective societies, they gradually lost their territorial penetration because they did not have grassroots-level activists in the decision-making structures of their parties (see Chapter 7). At present, grassroots members are not crucial for the persistence of the FA, because the party has enough resources to enable it to operate without volunteers, yet leaders cannot "kill the grassroots." Still, as part of the "causes-of-effect" logic of case-study research, we are not necessarily predicting that the reproduction of this mass-organic and participatory structure characteristic will continue into the future.

The historical context in which the FA developed as a mass-organic party is hardly replicable. It was a period of heightened political engagement. However, societies undergo different cycles of engagement in politics (Hirschman 1982). Thus, we should not expect similar levels of intensity in terms of engagement. Putting the issue of replication aside, the reproduction of strong commitment and engagement on the part of adherents is heavily influenced by the specific organizational channels for expressing *voice*. Our argument is essentially focused on the reproduction of the structure of the party. As one leader put it during an interview: "... if no decision-making influence is granted to the grassroots members, it is unlikely that they would be willing to keep cooperating" (personal interview with Mariano Bianchino).

# 5

# Party Structure, Efficacy, and Activism

## INTRODUCTION

A party organization can integrate its activists essentially in two different ways: activists either can be conceived as non-leaders who work for the success of the party leaders and expect to be recruited to become members of the party elite or activists can be integrated as stakeholders (Scarrow 2015). The latter implies that there is an organizational structure where the activists have significant *voice* (Hirschman 1970). In this type of organization, activists do not depend on the leaders' interest in including activists' opinions; the organizational structure ensures that role, through established procedures that forge careers that are less dependent upon the leaders' will. Political parties in both developed and developing – i.e., not yet established – democracies have reacted to the observed trend of membership decline by seeking to integrate activists. For example, as Scarrow (2015) has highlighted, different parties in the developed world have opened their decision-making processes to include their members and activists' voices. Yet, beyond this descriptive account, what is the impact of such decisions on the reproduction of party activism and on levels of engagement from partisan activists?

Political parties can retain or even gain adherents at given junctures (e.g., when they win an election or when a candidate becomes popular). These adherents may contribute money to the party organization and may eventually participate in some activities or regularly vote in internal elections. Nevertheless, these adherents will never participate in the party structure permanently, spending time and being involved in the party debates or being part of the decision-making process. Indeed, the professionalization of parties is related to the loss of volunteers' effective participation in the organization. Bureaucrats and political organization and campaign professionals substitute for activists. Adherents are mere consumers of party decisions, not stakeholders of the party (Scarrow 2015).

The substantive theoretical question, then, is what explains the reproduction of activism in party organizations? What type of organizational arrangements account for activists' greater engagement with parties? The path by which mass-organic parties transform themselves into professional–electoral parties, and by which the number of activists engaged with those parties, declines has two dimensions. The first dimension implies some organizational transformation that reduces the channels for influencing the decision-making process and limits it to the election of authorities. The second dimension refers to the loss of individual incentives to participate. Both dimensions converge in active members' perception of efficacy. In other words, as activists become less crucial to a party's success because other campaign tools can substitute for them, leaders become more willing to reduce the space left for activists to participate and to influence decision-making. In the same vein, activists who are sensitive to a reduction in their perceived efficacy will feel inclined to exit parties.

In the previous chapters, we have emphasized the construction of the organizational setting that engendered intense grassroots-level activism and why it did not oligarchize over time. We explained why the FA leaders at the birth of the new coalition created space for grassroots involvement in the decision-making process. We also explained why they subsequently were not able – and did not even attempt – to change this organizational structure after the foundational stage, when mass mobilization and grassroots volunteers were no longer required in order for the party to be competitive in national elections.

In this chapter, we turn to the individual level; i.e., the effects of the organizational setting on individuals' willingness to commit to the organization. A party organization that creates institutionalized channels to give activists a significant role in the decision-making fosters activists who feel a strong sense of efficacy. When their participation is relevant, activists perceive that they exert real influence in the life of the party. Rules generate both selective incentives (associated with individual's perceived efficacy) and collective incentives (associated with individuals' role in maintaining the party's identity and programmatic stance). The existence of these organizational structures generates the necessary incentives for those who participate in it to remain engaged and keep the organization alive. Thus, we ask whether or not time spent by activists in the organization is inelastic to changes in their perception of efficacy. We also survey whether those who already participate in the organization have incentives to engage in the recruitment of new activists to keep their source of power alive. The only way that grassroots activists can retain their *voice* is by reproducing activism, transforming adherents into activists. A party that lacks activists who have a vested interest in transforming adherents into new activists will eventually have only adherents, individuals who are not involved in the day-to-day life of the party and its operations. Without a network of grassroots activists, individuals have no way to engage with the party as an activist; one can only be an adherent with no regular contact with the organization.

Our theory yields three observable implications. First, activists should be different from adherents in terms of their willingness to participate and their actual levels of participation. Second, institutional factors that negatively affect *voice*, or, more precisely, individuals' degree of perceived efficacy, should reduce activists' willingness to cooperate with the organization but should not affect the willingness of adherents to do so. However, the manipulation of a collective incentive (programmatic coherence of the FA), should affect both groups willingness to cooperate with the party. Third, activists should work as organizers (á la Han (2014)), transforming adherents who show some willingness to participate into activists, which explains the reproduction of the grassroots structure. The chapter sequentially reviews each of these predictions.

## ACTIVISTS ARE DIFFERENT FROM ADHERENTS

People who engage with political party organizations have different levels of commitment. Several authors have emphasized the difference between types of members in a party organization (Heidar 1994, Selle and Svasand 1991,). The most conventional distinction was set forth by Duverger (1954), who distinguished between voters, adherents, members, and activists, according to the degree of involvement with the political party. Analyzing civic organizations, Han (2014) developed an "activist ladder," distinguishing between affiliates and activists. Affiliates are just members who explicitly support the organization or pay the affiliation's dues. Activists spend time and are committed to outcomes and to the organization's leadership development (34).

The evidence from our online survey shows a party with a structure that supports the existence of both adherents and activists. Even though these two groups generally do not differ in terms of age, sex, and ideological position, they systematically differ in their level of participation and in their willingness to invest time and effort in the party organization and in civil society associations more generally (Table 5.1).[1]

Compared to adherents, activists are more willing to participate in different forms of collaboration with the party organization. In the survey, we asked respondents about their willingness to engage in party-related work. For all the surveyed activities, FA activists – Base Committee attendees as well as those who only participate in a faction – are more prone to participate than are FA adherents. Also, compared to adherents, a greater proportion of activists think they will participate in the FA in the future (Table 5.2). Those who participate in Base Committees also show a greater willingness to engage in voluntary work than do activists who only participate in a FA faction.

In terms of reported behavior, activists dedicate significantly more hours to participating in FA meetings than do adherents. Also, a greater proportion of activists, compared to adherents, contribute money to the FA. Finally, a greater proportion of activists are involved in civil society organizations (Table 5.3). As in the case of reported willingness to participate, Base Committee activists devote more hours to the organization than activists who only participate in an FA faction. Also, Base Committee activists are significantly more engaged in neighborhood organizations.

Base Committee activists are different from faction activists, and both are different from those who are simply adherents; they exhibit a different degree of willingness to engage in party activities and they devote different amounts of time to the organization. Base Committee activists are more willing to engage with the organization, and they devote significantly more time to cooperating with the organization than do faction activists. Activists associated with FA factions are more willing than adherents to engage with the organization and they devote more time than adherents. However, they are more similar to Base Committee activists in that they maintain permanent contact with the party organization.

We have complemented our analysis with a linear-regression-model estimation of an individual's willingness to participate and self-reported

---

[1] The percentage of public employees is greater among Base Committee activists and faction participants than among the adherents.

TABLE 5.1 *Socioeconomic, Sociodemographic Characteristics, and Ideology*

| | Base Committee | Faction | Adherents | All |
|---|---|---|---|---|
| Age[a] | 51.0 | 51.7 | 52.5 | 51.8 |
| | (49.9–52.1) | (50.2–53.2) | (51.7–53.3) | (51.6–52.0) |
| Women[b] | 45.9 | 40.6 | 47.7 | 45.6[§] |
| Public employee[b] | 21.1 | 21.5 | 16.5 | 18.9 |
| | (42.9–49.0) | (36.4–44.7) | (45.4–50.1) | |
| | (18.3–23.9) | (18.1–24.9) | (14.2–18.1) | (17.5–20.3) |
| Homeownership[b] | 55.1 | 57.1 | 54.6 | 55.3 |
| | (51.4–58.7) | (52.6–61.6) | (51.6–57.8) | (53.2–57.4) |
| Ideological position[c] | 3.7 | 3.9 | 4.0 | 3.9 |
| | (3.6–3.8) | (3.8–4.1) | (3.9–4.1) | (3.8–4.0) |

[a] Measured in years.
[b] Measured in percentage.
[c] Average self-identified ideological position measured on a scale from 1 to 10, where "1" is extreme left and "10" is extreme right. 95 percent confidence intervals are given in parentheses.
[§] We cannot calculate confidence intervals for the percentage of women because we used sex to post-stratify our sample.
*Source:* Online survey

TABLE 5.2 Willingness to Participate in Different Activities by Type of Adherent

| Willingness to... | Base Committee | Faction | Adherents | All |
|---|---|---|---|---|
| Do voluntary work[a] | 7.10 | 5.86 | 4.24 | 5.52 |
|  | (6.90–7.29) | (5.58–6.14) | (4.05–4.42) | (5.38–5.65) |
| Make phone calls[b] | 5.73 | 4.47 | 3.22 | 4.31 |
|  | (5.48–5.98) | (4.17–4.78) | (3.05–3.40) | (4.17–4.46) |
| Integrate the local-level direction[b] | 4.77 | 3.87 | 2.88 | 3.71 |
|  | (4.51–5.02) | (3.58–4.15) | (2.71–3.04) | (3.58–3.84) |
| Attend a political education course[b] | 6.57 | 5.65 | 4.40 | 5.37 |
|  | (6.31–6.83) | (5.32–5.99) | (4.18–4.61) | (5.23–5.52) |
| Collaborate with a representative[b] | 5.67 | 5.12 | 3.87 | 4.73 |
|  | (5.41–5.93) | (4.79–5.45) | (3.67–4.07) | (4.58–4.87) |
| Distribute Propaganda[b] | 6.21 | 4.55 | 3.04 | 4.40 |
|  | (5.96–6.47) | (4.24–4.86) | (2.86–3.21) | (4.26–4.55) |
| Contribute funds[b] | 4.58 | 3.25 | 2.48 | 3.34 |
|  | (4.33–4.83) | (2.97–3.52) | (2.33–2.64) | (3.21–3.47) |
| Participate in the future[c] | 84.8% | 71.7% | 39.6% | 61.2% |
|  | (82.0–87.6) | (63.3–76.0) | (36.6–42.7) | (59.1–63.3) |

[a] "On a scale from 1 to 10, where 1 is 'not at all willing' and 10 is 'very willing,' how willing are you to do voluntary work as an FA activist?" Here we report the average and, in parentheses, the 95 percent confidence interval.
[b] "On a scale from 1 to 10 where 1 is 'not at all willing' and 10 is 'very willing,' how willing are you to dedicate at least four hours a week to do the following activities for the party?" Here we report the average and, in parentheses, the 95 percent confidence interval.
[c] "In the coming years, do you think you will participate in the FA?" This was a Yes/No question. Here we report the proportion and the 95 percent confidence interval (in parentheses) of respondents who answered "Yes."
Source: Online survey

TABLE 5.3 *Reported Behavior by Type of Adherents*

| | Base Committee | Faction | Adherents | All |
|---|---|---|---|---|
| Monthly hours dedicated to FA activities[a] | 23.2 (21.5–24.8) | 12.7 (11.0–14.4) | 4.2 (3.5–4.8) | 12.2 (11.4–13.0) |
| Regular monetary contributions[b] | 70.1% (66.6–73.6) | 47.2% (42.3–52.0) | 22.5% (19.7–25.3) | 43.2% (41.0–45.4) |
| Unions[c] | 33.2% (29.8–36.5) | 28.2% (24.2–32.1) | 21.3% (18.9–23.6) | 26.7% (24.9–28.4) |
| Neighborhood Commissions[c] | 41.9% (38.2–5.6) | 25.4% (21.4–29.5) | 19.1% (16.7–21.5) | 28.0% (26.0–29.9) |
| Cooperatives[c] | 16.4% (13.6–19.2) | 15.3% (12.2–18.4) | 8.7% (7.0–10.4) | 12.6% (11.2–14.0) |
| NGO[c] | 12.9% (10.4–15.3) | 10.9% (8.0–13.7) | 8.7% (6.9–10.5) | 10.5% (9.2–11.8) |

[a] "How many hours a month, on average, do you dedicate to FA activities?" Here we report the average and, in parentheses, the 95 percent confidence interval.
[b] "Do you regularly contribute money to the party?" This was a Yes/No question. Here we report the percentage and 95 percent confidence interval (in parentheses) of respondents who answered "Yes."
[c] "At present, do you participate in…?" This was a Yes/No question. Here we report the percentage and 95 percent confidence interval (in parentheses) of respondents who answered "Yes."
*Source:* Online survey

TABLE 5.4 *Linear-Regression Model: Willingness to Participate and Reported Participation*

|  | Reported Participation | Willingness to Participate |
|---|---|---|
| Base Committee | 13.287*** | 1.782*** |
|  | (0.973) | (0.137) |
| Faction | 9.761*** | 1.638*** |
|  | (0.801) | (0.139) |
| Ideological position | 0.056 | −0.106** |
|  | (0.224) | (0.039) |
| Education | −0.436 | −0.040 |
|  | (0.333) | (0.050) |
| Age | −0.004 | −0.015*** |
|  | (0.026) | (0.004) |
| Female | −0.500 | 0.011 |
|  | (0.762) | (0.128) |
| Constant | 5.700* | 5.580*** |
|  | (2.382) | (0.378) |

Standard errors in parentheses. *$p < 0.10$, **$p < 0.05$, ***$p < 0.01$.

participation. We constructed two multivariate regression models that take ideological self-placement, education level, and age, as control variables. Participation in a Base Committee is positively associated with both greater willingness to participate as well as with self-reported participation. The same holds true for participation in a faction. Ideological self-placement and age also show significant association with willingness to participate. Individuals who are younger and who identify with the political left are more willing to participate, though they do not report higher levels of actual participation in different activities (Table 5.4).

## VOICE REDUCTION AFFECTS ACTIVISTS

As stated in previous chapters, over the years, the FA grassroots structure became less and less important for the party. The organization has other campaign resources, and fewer people are willing to dedicate time to the party. The FA has access to financial and human capital resources to stage a modern electoral campaign – in fact, the FA campaigns have traditionally been regarded as creative and have professionalized the electoral campaign (e.g., well-known publicists identified with the FA have worked on electoral campaigns, as have experts in survey sampling and statisticians). Thus, the grassroots structure is less necessary as a mobilization tool. This resembles the observed trajectory of other mass-organic parties worldwide. However, the organization is still active and relevant (see Chapters 3 and 4). Why does this occur? The answer to this question involves two factors that work together to produce the outcome. On the one hand, activists have entrenched veto power over the organization's rules (as described and explained in Chapter 4); on the other hand, because the FA, through the direct representation of the grassroots members in the party's decision-making structure (especially in the National Plenary and the National Political Board), imbues grassroots activism with a sense of efficacy. This stimulates organizers to reproduce their engagement and to reproduce channels for *voice*.

In the following excerpt from an interview with an FA grassroots activist, the interviewee reflects on whether there have been attempts to change the FA's organizational structure. Beyond the actual attempts, it is interesting that he argues that what motivated the reproduction of a "FA mystique," i.e., the unity, is, among other related issues, the chance to participate in the party's decision-making.

*Why do you think they cannot do it?* [to change the role of the grassroots activists in the FA's decision-making structure]
  The Frenteamplista mystique was not made by party leaders who form the FA ... those leaders that back then in 71 ... they saw the way and pointed it, but the mystique began to be built and was built by regular people. And that strange story that you are nobody, but support an idea that is the FA, is not called Socialist Party ... it is called the FA, and you can endeavor to participate in the decision-making, is part of the Frenteamplista mystique, that does not occur in any other party...
  (personal interview Gonzalo Zuvela)

We move now beyond discussion of the differences between activists and adherents with respect to levels of engagement with the organization to discuss the effect of perceived efficacy (voice) as a selective incentive. These types of incentives, as Panebianco (1988) describes, are usually associated with individual rewards that members receive from the party – especially those members who are more involved (e.g., positions, goods, and privileged access to services associated with patronage and clientelism). We claim that perceived efficacy works as a selective incentive related to the individual reward of influencing in the party's direction. This type of incentive is different from collective incentives, i.e., those associated with how leaders reproduce a party's identity and satisfy party members' need to identify with ideas and values. As Panebianco (1988) emphasizes, selective incentives affect activists' willingness to participate, while collective incentives affect the identification of activists and members alike.

We present below the results of our test of the hypothesis concerning the role organizational settings play in explaining the reproduction of engagement. Because we cannot manipulate actual levels of efficacy that the organization grants to its activists, and given that we are studying a party that has institutionalized mechanisms that ensure activists' voice, our survey experiment sought to vary perceived efficacy. Our intervention is relevant (c.f Dunning 2012), both because the survey was conducted among different types of FA adherents (simple adherents, Base Committee activists, and faction participants) and because the nature of the organizational structure and the role granted to grassroots activists has been a matter of debate in the party. The latter, thus, increases the realism of the intervention.

The treatment prompt (Box 5.1) describes a situation where the FA decides to enact an organizational reform responding to the demands of

---

**Box 5.1** Survey Experiment[2]

Treatment Prompt: Imagine that the FA conducts an organizational restructuring to adapt to a new social and political context. These reforms involve professionalizing the party and reducing the role rank-and-file members play in determining the political strategies and political stances of the FA. On a scale from 1 to 10, where 1 is "not at all willing" and 10 is "very willing," how willing would you be to perform any of the following party activities in the next election?

Placebo-Control: Imagine that the FA conducts an organizational restructuring to adapt to a new social and political context. On a scale from 1 to 10, where 1 is "not at all willing" and 10 is "very willing," how willing would you be to perform any of the following party activities in the next election?

- Participate in campaign rallies
- Distribute campaign literature
- Volunteer as a party delegate at a voting station
- Canvass door-to-door
- Distribute party lists in the neighborhood
- Organize meetings with neighbors and candidates
- Donate money

---

[2] Translation from Spanish by the authors.

TABLE 5.5 t-test Results Comparing Means on Treatment (Selective Incentive) and Control[3]

| Group | Treatment (t1) | Control (t0) | t | Df | p-value[a] |
|---|---|---|---|---|---|
| All | 4.03 (0.075) | 4.42 (0.075) | −3.659 | 2,485 | 0.0010 |
| Base Committee | 5.28 (0.137) | 5.77 (0.121) | −2.699 | 808 | 0.0284 |
| Faction | 4.14 (0.158) | 4.70 (0.156) | −2.538 | 517 | 0.0457 |
| Adherents | 3.09 (0.087) | 3.30 (0.094) | −1.617 | 1,156 | 0.4248 |

Standard error in parentheses.
[a] These are Bonferroni corrected p-values for multiple comparisons.
Source: Online survey

the social and political context. This reform aims to professionalize the structure of the organization and reduces the role of the grassroots activists in the decision-making. We intended this prompt to affect – i.e., to reduce – the perceived efficacy of party members.

The outcome variable measures willingness to engage in voluntary activities in the next national election. We took the average of the reported willingness to engage in all these activities (see Box 5.1 for the list of activities). As registered in our pre-analysis plan (Piñeiro, Pérez, and Rosenblatt 2016), taking advantage of the nature of the survey, we analyzed heterogeneous treatment effects by type of engagement with the party (Base Committee activists, faction activists, and adherents who do not participate in either a Base Committee or a faction).

Table 5.5 presents the results of the survey experiment expressed as differences of means ($t$-tests). First, the treatment had a significant effect for all FA members ("All"), i.e., the organizational restructuring that reduced the role, and thus the perceived efficacy of rank-and-file members, reduced respondents' willingness to engage in voluntary work. Nevertheless, the analysis of heterogeneous treatment effects shows that this effect is statistically significant only for Base Committee and faction activists and not for adherents. This shows, in accord with our hypothesis, that those who develop a commitment to the organization in

---

[3] The $t$-test reported in this table is calculated from the post-stratified sample (see above). Nonetheless, the $t$-test using the sample without post-stratification, not reported here, shows similar results.

terms of activism are more sensitive to changes in their perceived efficacy. This perception of efficacy seems to work as a selective incentive. Therefore, in the FA, the entrenched institutional rules prevent the elites from changing the role of the grassroots members, and the latter's perceived efficacy ensures the reproduction of activism.

Unfortunately, we cannot know whether activists are different from adherents before engaging with the organization; i.e., whether they have personal traits that predispose them to engage more intensively in social and political activities. Whether or not the party organization transforms adherents into activists, the results show that activists are more sensitive to changes in their perceived efficacy. Therefore, the crucial issue is that the FA grants these activists the necessary room to channel their political commitment.

To show the difference between selective and collective incentives, we now present the results of another survey experiment we conducted in which we manipulated a collective incentive, the ideological and programmatic identity of the party. The goal of this comparison is to illustrate that treatments associated with different types of incentives affect different types of members in a different manner; while selective incentives essentially affect activists, collective incentives affect all members similarly.

The treatment prompt (Box 5.2) describes a situation where the FA decides to change its platform and ideology in light of contextual changes

---

Box 5.2 Survey Experiment 2[4]

Treatment Prompt: Parties regularly need to update their platforms and their ideological positions to move with the changes in their country and the world. Imagine that, in this scenario, your party abandons its historical ideological and programmatic positions to reach more voters or to facilitate its ability to become part of a governing coalition

Placebo-Control: Parties regularly need to update their platforms and their ideological positions to move with the changes in their country and the world. Imagine that, in this scenario, your party updates its historical ideological and programmatic positions.

In this scenario, would you be more, equally, or less willing to dedicate time to the party?

---

[4] Translation from Spanish by the authors.

TABLE 5.6 t-*test Results Comparing Means on Treatment (Collective Incentive) and Control*[5]

| Group | Treatment (t1) | Control (t0) | t | Df | p-value[a] |
|---|---|---|---|---|---|
| All | −0.40 (0.021) | 0.31 (0.020) | −24.186 | 2,485 | 0.0000 |
| Base Committee | −0.42 (0.039) | 0.26 (0.033) | −13.447 | 808 | 0.0000 |
| Faction | −0.36 (0.049) | 0.35 (0.042) | −11.042 | 517 | 0.0000 |
| Adherents | −0.40 (0.030) | 0.32 (0.030) | −16.811 | 1,156 | 0.0000 |

Standard error in parentheses
[a] These are Bonferroni corrected *p*-values for multiple comparisons.
*Source:* Online survey

and in order to improve its electoral performance or access to power. We intended this prompt to affect – i.e., to reduce – members' identification with the party's ideas and values.

The outcome variable measures willingness to dedicate time to the party. The outcome was measured as "less" (−1), "equal" (0), and "more" (1) willing to dedicate time to the party. To compare the results with the first survey experiment described above, we analyzed heterogeneous treatment effects by type of engagement with the party. This treatment is clearly associated with a collective incentive and thus there should not exist a difference in the effect of this treatment between types of members. Table 5.6 presents the results of the survey experiment expressed as differences of means (*t*-tests). The treatment had a significant effect for all FA members and this effect is similar across Base Committee activists, faction activists, and adherents.

## ORGANIZERS TRANSFORM ADHERENTS INTO ACTIVISTS

How is perceived efficacy reproduced over time? The entrenched institutional rules prevent elites from changing the role of the grassroots members

---

[5] The *t*-test reported in this table is calculated from the post-stratified sample (see above). Nonetheless, the *t*-test using the sample without post-stratification, not reported here, shows similar results.

## Organizers Transform Adherents into Activists

and from reducing the latter's perceived efficacy. Nonetheless, grassroots engagement keeps this structure running to allow the reproduction of activism. Adherents who are prone to become activists can meet with other activists who will incorporate them into the party structure. Thus, the channels for grassroots engagement are open and this structure facilitates activists' role in the transformation of adherents into activists.

After forty-eight years and three terms in government, the FA has preserved spaces for neighborhood-level activism, the Base Committees. We noted above the large number of Base Committees (see Chapter 3). As also mentioned in Chapter 3, 68.9 percent of all respondents in the online survey claimed to have a Base Committee within walking distance of their home. Thus, Base Committees are visible among FA members, both those who actually participate in a Base Committee and those who do not.

There are local-level entry venues, where individuals who have an interest in joining the organization can approach. As described extensively in Chapter 3, the numerous party locales, especially the Base Committees, are open to any adherent who wants to join. Without such spaces, adherents who are willing to perform volunteer work would not be able to do so and would simply remain adherents. Yet, Base Committees not only enable grassroots-level activism, they enable organizers to engage in transformative action by transforming adherents who join the organization into activists. The excerpts below from the group interview illustrate the role organizers play in engendering activism and, more specifically, in transforming adherents into activists. Beyond contextual processes, there is an open organizational mechanism that activates the reproduction of FA activists, though this does not imply that the reproduction of grassroots activists is immune to contextual challenges.

I am convinced that most of the activists are recruited at the Base Committees ... And I also believe that those are the important things of the movement ... If you ask who gathers more votes, the grassroots activists or the factions, perhaps the factions. Perhaps a speech of Pepe [Mujica], or Astori, or Vázquez, whoever is the referent, perhaps at one point captures more votes than the grassroots activists. Now, in terms of activists, in people who work [for the organization] I think the Committee ... I believe we have FA factions who are close to feeling as a [professional–electoral] party ... But I believe there are two major profiles, the one who bets on activism and the one who bets on major media.
(personal interview with Andrés Domínguez)

I believe that today there is much less activism everywhere ... Base Committees are smaller than those of when I was a child ... But there is a reconstructive history. And the truth is that, the compañeros who join, those to whom we extend the relationship ... are life-long compañeros. And then we start training with discussions and that is a form of social capital that I am convinced the FA has, no other party in the country has it.

(personal interview with Manuel Ferrer)

Activists transform adherents into activists and reproduce activism. This occurs in a relational setting where activists become part of the organization and develop close ties with fellow activists (Han 2016). The organizational structure not only stimulates activism through voice in a relational context, but also sets the incentives appropriately; i.e., the relevance of activists' voice is dependent upon their success at engaging new adherents and transforming them into activists. This ensures that the institutional decision-making positions granted to grassroots activists continue operating as real channels for voice. Without Base Committees and activists, those with positions in the FA decision-making structure qua representatives of the grassroots members would not be relevant since they would lack a clear base of support.

## CONCLUSIONS

Our theory claims that the organizational structure affects the reproduction of activists' engagement with party. The FA was born in 1971 with intense local-level activism and reproduced itself as a party with activists. This does not imply that at present the number of FA activists is the same as in the 1970s or early 1980s. In fact, since the early 1990s, the number of activists has declined. Moreover, given the electoral success of the FA, the party's relevance in national politics and general trends in technology and communications, activists are less needed. Yet, they still exist and the organizational structure that facilitates their reproduction is still in place. Even though there are undeniable historical factors that account for the decision to establish this peculiar organizational structure (see Chapter 4), the case of the FA also challenges the idea that parties based on volunteer activism are dead. If organizational settings can foster activism, there is a chance for policy interventions to reverse the declining role of party activists and adherents in contemporary democracies we return to this in Chapter 8. This case shows that a democratic party is not an organization that merely asks adherents about their preferences. It is, rather, an organization that provides open and accessible channels through which individuals can become activists, and grants activists *voice*. In this vein, this chapter has presented evidence concerning the effects of organizational traits on individual behavior.

The reproduction of party activism occurs at the grassroots level. Activism is located in each faction's organizational structure but, above all, at the Base Committees. This activism is powered by perceived efficacy, which in turn reproduces activists in a relational context. These Base Committees transform adherents into activists. At the same time, given the organizational structure, activists' efficacy is solely tied to their role as organizers.

It is reasonable to think that not all adherents have the same degree of interest in becoming activists, and a particular individual's interest in engaging in political activism waxes and wanes over time (Hirschman 1982). Therefore, the role of activists in transforming adherents into new activists only operates among those adherents who have the desire to become an activist. Thus, having organizers in the party structure is a necessary but not sufficient condition for the reproduction of activism, as Han (2014) seems to imply. Nevertheless, it is irrelevant whether it is sufficient or necessary to reproduce activism. That is, without this kind of organizational structure, those adherents who are prone to engage would not have the opportunity to become activists.

Beyond conducting a survey that yielded significant data on FA activists and adherents, we have conducted in-depth case study research about the FA for more than two years. This research has yielded a large number of pieces of evidence showing intense current engagement of grassroots activists (see Online Appendix). This evidence includes an image registry that depicts activists' meetings in winter, far from an electoral cycle, to discuss, for example, health-care policies. We have gathered flyers and email invitations to party activities organized by volunteers from Base Committees and Coordinating Groups.

This chapter sheds light on the potential effect of policy reforms aimed at improving the link between parties and society. If parties are to be effective channels of democratic representation, they should promote open access for prospective activists who want to contribute to the organization. Above all, however, they should make the costly decision to share power and ensure that the new activists who engage with the organization feel empowered by a sense of efficacy.

6

# The Limits to Strategic Adaptation

### INTRODUCTION

In previous chapters we have described and explained the origins and reproduction of the FA's peculiar party organization. We have also explained the behavioral effects of this organizational structure, which grants significant *voice* to grassroots activists. In this chapter, we explore the effects of the FA's organization on one of the main dimensions discussed in the party literature – i.e., the party-in-government (Aldrich 1995, Shefter 1994, Strom 2000).

Usually, political parties have directors, MPs (or representatives), and Prime Ministers (or Presidents) who are more centrist than are party members. Moreover, activists are always considered more radical than other types of members of party organizations and are considered to have more extreme preferences than do the party, its representatives, and its leaders in office. As stressed in the literature on the selectorate (Bueno de Mesquita et al. 2003), the more restrictive the pool of those who select and support candidates for office and government (outside the inner circle of leaders), the greater the likelihood of choosing policies far from the preferences of the median voter. In the candidate selection literature (Hazan and Rahat 2010), when activists have more power, more extreme candidates are more likely to be nominated. The FA, like every political party organization in a democratic context, has a tension between choosing policies and candidates who are closer to the median voter versus those who are closer to members or activists' preferences.

Table 6.1 shows this phenomenon in the case of the FA. Base Committee activists and other party members perceive themselves as more leftist

TABLE 6.1 *Members Perceptions of Ideological Positions*

| Position of...[a] | Base Committee | Faction | Adherents | All |
|---|---|---|---|---|
| Yourself | 3.7 | 3.9 | 4.0 | 3.9 |
| | (3.6–3.8) | (3.8–4.1) | (3.9–4.1) | (3.8–4.0) |
| Party Direction | 4.8 | 4.8 | 4.9 | 4.9 |
| | (4.6–4.9) | (4.7–5.0) | (4.8–5.1) | (4.8–4.9) |
| FA Parliamentary Caucus | 4.9 | 4.9 | 5.0 | 5.0 |
| | (4.8–5.0) | (4.8–5.1) | (4.9–5.1) | (4.9–5.0) |
| FA Government | 5.2 | 5.2 | 5.3 | 5.3 |
| | (5.1–5.3) | (5.1–5.4) | (5.2–5.4) | (5.2–5.3) |
| President Tabaré Vázquez | 5.4 | 5.4 | 5.6 | 5.5 |
| | (5.3–5.5) | (5.2–5.6) | (5.5–5.7) | (5.4–5.6) |

[a] Interviewee's ideological position, on a scale from 1 to 10, and the position of different authorities. "1" denotes extreme left and "10" denotes extreme right. Here we report the average and, in parentheses, the 95 percent confidence interval.
*Source:* Online survey

than the FA's party direction, the FA's parliamentary caucus, the government, and President Vázquez.

This distance between the preferences of the party members and the party's elected authorities engenders tensions and, in general, the tensions are resolved in favor of the position of the party elites. Yet, party leaders and government officials do not always have the power to impose their preferences. In what follows, we show how the tensions derived from the differences in the preferences between the party grassroots members and the government are processed in the FA.

The FA organizational structure limits the leaders' and government's room to maneuver. It limits the party leaders' incentives to moderate their positions, because major decisions need to have the organization's explicit support or, at least, an absence of opposition. When the FA is in government, the party organization – the combination of the coalitional nature of the FA and its grassroots activist structure – also limits the most substantive and crucial issues of government policies. In this party with activists and powerful (institutionalized) factional leaders, the party's decisions and the policy orientation do not depend on a leader, as in other parties with activists, such as the Partido Justicialista (Justicialist Party, PJ) (Levitsky 2003). This gives more stability to the party's positions and reduces the likelihood of a dramatic policy switch.

In government, parties can materialize their programmatic positions, and they can project new leaders. However, the exercise of government also tends to inhibit partisan activity because it strips the organization of its best leaders and cadre as these leaders assume government positions. This distances these leaders from the party and puts the organizational leadership in a secondary role vis-à-vis government authorities – who have to act on critical issues of national relevance (Pribble 2013). This holds for any party that accesses government, but it is even more critical in presidential regimes (Samuels and Shugart 2010).

The relationship between presidentialism and democratic instability has become conventional wisdom in the comparative politics literature (Linz 1994, Mainwaring and Shugart 1997, Przeworski et al. 2000) and this general relationship has also now been extended to explain instability in party systems (Samuels and Shugart 2010, Webb and White 2007b). Presidents are directly elected by voters for fixed periods, hence parties have no ability to control their president. Once in government, parties cannot dismiss or deauthorize their leaders or force them to quit, as they can in parliamentary regimes. According to this argument, presidentialism also personalizes political competition, thus endangering party organization. Samuels and Shugart (2010) analyze the relationship between separation of origin and survival under presidentialism. More specifically, they measure the effect of presidential regime rules on party organization and behavior. They show that under presidentialism there are far more "policy switches" than under parliamentarism.

The party politics literature has analyzed the impact of the party-in-government and the professionalization of politics in contemporary democracy. Katz and Mair (1995) refer to the "cartel party" to describe the transformation of party organizations as a result of the professionalization of their structures and their relationship with the party-in-government. Parties want to gain office – which is why they offer increasingly similar policies (cartelization) – but party elites also use public resources to control the party organization, gaining autonomy from grassroots activists. As we review in Chapter 7, this process is observable in the case of the PT in Brazil.

In the institutional setting in which the FA is immersed, the major challenge in the relationship between the party and the government is that the former might control the latter. Even though the party does not have institutional rules, as in parliamentary regimes, to restrict government policies, the FA has been able, directly or indirectly, to limit the FA in government. Most of the time, as expected, the party has supported the government and has taken responsibility for its actions – in theoretical terms, the exception should be the opposite. Yet, on several significant occasions, the FA structure, especially the grassroots structure in combination with the factions that participate in the FA's vertical structure, has clashed with government positions. These controversies engendered changes in government positions and prevented the government from turning to more centrist positions on these policies, positions that could eventually distance the government from the party's platform. Vetoes coming from the organization (and its parliamentary caucus), prevented the implementation of these policies but did not imply a general blockade of the FA's government agenda, nor did they create long-term conflicts between the organization and the government authorities. The ability of the FA to obstruct the government highlights the organizational strength of the party. This distances the FA from other left-of-center parties in Latin America, even from other well-organized parties like the Brazilian PT or the Chilean PSCh. Thus, as opposed to the cases of other parties in Latin America, FA party elites do not have the leverage to take the party in any direction they desire. In the case of the FA, activists have a significant influence over policy decisions, especially policies to which the left is particularly sensitive.

In this chapter, we present observational evidence of the influence of the party on crucial policy issues and on the government's decision making. Also, we briefly detail the process of ideological transformation of the FA as a Smoking Gun descriptive inference regarding the impossibility of major transformations controlled by a single leader.

To analyze the effect of the organizational structure of the FA on government policy and decision making, we used the following evidence. First, as detailed in Chapter 1, we constructed an original database of party decisions (from 2000 to 2016) in two of the party's main directive bodies, the National Plenary and National Political Board. Our purpose in creating this database is to present systematic observational evidence of the role the grassroots structure plays in determining the party's direction and the role the organization plays in influencing the FA government's decision making. We complement this description with interview material. Second, using secondary sources, we review the ideological transformation of the FA. This case is interesting because it illustrates the persistent relevance of the party organization's activist structure. This section is also complemented by qualitative primary evidence. Third, we discuss instances in which a significant government announcement was overturned by the organization. We present cases of important government policies or policy initiatives that, because of the FA's intervention, were significantly changed.

### EMPIRICAL ANALYSIS OF PARTY DECISIONS

In this section, we present evidence concerning the decisions made by the two most important bodies within the FA – the National Political Board and the National Plenary. As detailed in the Introduction, we had access to the complete set of minutes of all sessions from 2000 to 2016.[1] In total, we classified 1,345 issues. Issues were classified in four categories: "motions" (proposals to decide on certain political issues at the directive institutions of the party); "government appearance" (noting the visit of a government official who attended a session to present or discuss a government policy); "social organization appearance" (noting the visit of a representative from a union, NGO, etc. who attended a session to discuss a problem or a need); and "others." In the case of the motions, we recorded whether it was proposed by grassroots activists, faction representatives, or both.

An in-depth analysis of the database shows that both bodies met on a regular basis.[2] The Political Board met every Friday. From 2000 to 2016 the Political Board met 761 times (~44 times a year), and the National Plenary, between 2008 and 2016, met 30 times (~3 meetings a year). Thus, as expected, both bodies are very active and, as already described in Chapter 3, they are institutionalized bodies where the grassroots delegates, faction representatives, and party leaders interact. In both bodies, members discuss and decide various issues, spanning from organizational issues and strategies to national policy guidelines that signal the position of the party to the FA in government.[3] For example, in minute 10 of the April 8, 2016 National Political Board meeting, the grassroots delegates from Montevideo "reiterate their view that this [National] Political Board should incorporate an analysis of the systematic increase in prices. They

---

[1] Our evidence corpus begins with material from the year 2000 because it is the first year for which there are digitized records. The corpus covers the years before the FA was in government as well as the first three FA national governments. Also, the time span includes periods of heightened conflict in the context of a severe economic crisis and the period of economic expansion.

[2] In the case of the National Plenary, it is important to emphasize that there is no set schedule for the meetings.

[3] A systematic analysis of the database shows that the motions include various topics. See Online Appendix.

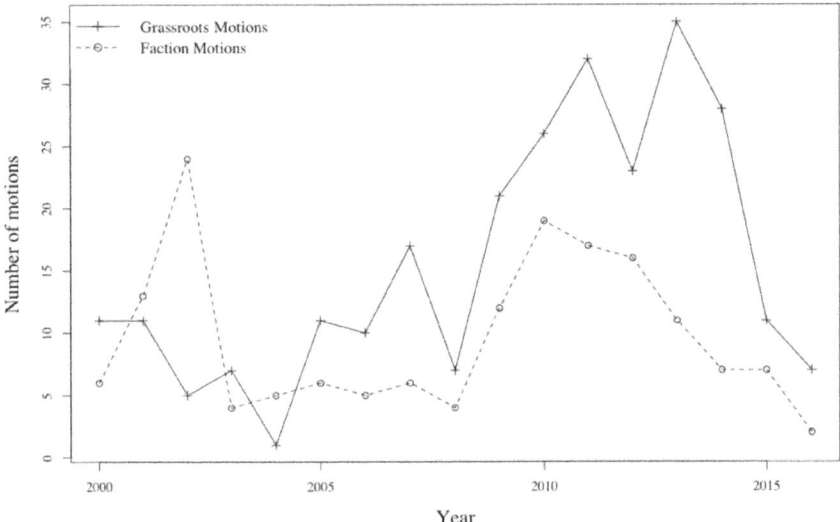

FIGURE 6.1 National Political Board motions from factions and grassroots members (2000–2016)
Source: Authors' Motions of National Political Board and National Plenary Database

suggest inviting the economic team [of the Ministry of Finance and Economy] so the team members can bring information about the issue. The delegates agreed to undertake the necessary arrangements to be able to have one representative of the economic team at a subsequent [National] Political Board meeting."[4]

Figure 6.1 presents the number of motions each year that were introduced by the faction representatives and by the grassroots members. The grassroots delegates seem to have been active and to have introduced a large number of motions. In fact, in most of the years we have surveyed, grassroots delegates seem to be more active than the faction representatives.

Minute 1-08 of the May 5, 2008 meeting of the National Plenary is a good illustration of both the relevance of the body and of the grassroots members' role in the party's decision making. The grassroots delegates from Montevideo and from abroad[5] presented the motion "Campaign to collect signatures to annul the Expiration Law: Consideration of the FA's

---

[4] Translation from Spanish by the authors.
[5] The FA has recognized Base Committees abroad, especially in Argentina.

participation and its instrumentation." This motion is significant because, as will be detailed in the following section, it shows how the grassroots members can change the party's guidelines and even change a government decision – i.e., the government and the largest factions did not support the movement toward annulling the law. The motion was supported by eighty-one votes; nine were opposed and fifty-three abstained.

In 2016, the FA discussed the need to set in motion a constitutional reform. As opposed to other countries in the region, this was not an initiative of the president or one that his government was staunchly pursuing. However, the FA discussed this issue and in the National Plenary of June 25, 2016, it convened to discuss the need for reform. It approved a motion presented by the MPP, PCU, List 711, Artiguista Current, PSU, List 738, Nuevo Espacio (New Space), Partido Obrero Revolucionario (Revolutionary Workers Party, POR), PAIS, and the grassroots delegates from Montevideo. The motion included the explicit desire of the party to implement a constitutional reform; it also recommended that this process should build upon the agreements already developed by the party commission that had been working on the constitutional reform; and that both this commission and the National Political Board should set an agenda to discuss the issue with different sectors of society and with all elements of the FA's party structure. This example illustrates the relevance of the issues that the party debates at these events, the interaction between the grassroots activists, factions, and leaders, and the potential autonomy of the party's agenda from that of the FA in government. Manuel Ferrer, a grassroots delegate from Montevideo—and a member of the Group of 41 described in Chapter 2 – said in the group interview:

At the level of political initiative we are a machine ... the Constitutional reform was dead and buried. Nobody wanted a constitutional reform. And it was a commission, the last one to take place before the printing of the booklet for the congress, and we were two grassroots delegates from Montevideo ... with a written paper and if that paper was not subjected to a vote there was going to be trouble ... the wheels began to work and there were tons of written documents, very public proposals and actions, half the congress was about that issue. And that was an initiative from below on an issue that was [allegedly] dead and buried.

(personal interview with Manuel Ferrer)

As will be detailed later in this chapter, grassroots activists frequently interact with the factions and can influence the position of the party. On some occasions, these positions are not the preferred positions of the party elites or of the largest factions. In this regard, grassroots activists prevent the concentration of power in the hands of these elites or in the largest factions. Without grassroots activists, the minority factions (usually the PCU and other leftist factions) would be constantly subjected to the will of the party elites and of the largest factions, and the conflict between the factions would be more difficult to manage, endangering the unity of the coalition. As reviewed in Chapter 3, this was true in the FA's early years and it remains true. To be clear, this does not mean that grassroots activists control the party, have extensive veto power, or that the factions' and leaders' will is completely overwhelmed by the grassroots activists. As highlighted in Chapter 5, grassroots activists' engagement is efficacious and this has consequences for public policy. They have a voice, which gives them potential influence, yet they essentially play a role in the unity of the left. The role of the grassroots delegates in promoting the unity of the party was mentioned throughout the in-depth interviews we conducted with faction leaders and grassroots activists.

## THE IDEOLOGICAL TRANSFORMATION OF THE FA

The programmatic project of the FA was modified through internal deliberative processes and thus it occurred gradually. In fact, the ideological congress is essentially an instance of bottom-up organization. In the platform the party presented for the 2004 national election, which it won, the most radical positions of the party were abandoned (Garcé and Yaffé 2005, Yaffé 2005). The organizational attributes already reviewed have also affected the way the FA processed programmatic adaptation over the years. As opposed to what happens in parties that are mere personalistic vehicles, change for the FA has been gradual and the result of intense debate.

After the authoritarian period, the FA gradually moderated ideologically and programmatically. The late 1980s and early 1990s were years of realignment within the party and the formation of new factions, some of which continue to exist today (e.g., AU). Garcé and Yaffé (2005) and Yaffé (2005) indicate that the FA gradually moderated starting in 1995. Their studies show how the party gradually adopted more centrist perspectives compared to the clearly leftist manifesto of 1971. Changes were undertaken through lively debates in party congresses and documents. This gradual and mostly deliberative process indicates a process of party adaptation. Yaffé summarizes this process, which he analyzes in detail based on party documents, as follows: "... and that change should not be interpreted as a sheer operation of electoral catch-up, or a last-minute opportunist turn, because it has been the result of a long and complex process of programmatic and ideological renovation" (2005, 97).[6] However, it is crucial to emphasize that this process did not involve abandoning the opposition to the neoliberal turn nor a distancing from the party grassroots members or the social movements.

In moderating its program, the FA did not imitate the traditional parties' centrist positions or convert the party to a professional–electoral machine (Moraes and Luján 2015). The party kept its stances regarding the main economic cleavages in Uruguayan politics. First, it retained its staunch opposition to the privatization of public-utility companies. Second, it promoted redistributive policies through tax, health, and education reforms. Third, Uruguay was one of the two countries in Latin America's left turn to implement collective bargaining as part of the labor market rules. Fourth, as extensively reviewed in the previous chapter, the most striking facet of the FA is the reproduction of the extended institutional influence of grassroots volunteer activists. The party changed as a result of a changing environment in which there was no longer a USSR, modern global capitalism had changed the structure of property, and the development process and democratization in Latin America dramatically shifted the political picture in the region, compared to the FA's early days.

The party did not obstruct the translation of the party's ideological platform into electoral platforms defined by the candidates. On the contrary, it acted as the basic organizational support for the electoral mobilization. It has interacted with campaign structures and teams as well as with other, self-mobilized networks of activists (Frenteamplistas Networks), of conjunctural life, that exist "virtually" with little or no in-person participation or face-to-face engagement. Thus, the organization proved able to react to structural, institutional, and conjunctural challenges. This contrasts with other processes of transformation reviewed in the comparative politics literature of political parties in Latin America. In general, these transformations were championed and developed by leaders and required a transformation of the role of the party's traditional social bases of support. Such transformations were seen in Argentina's PJ under Menem's leadership (Burgess and Levitsky 2003, Levitsky 2003) and in Brazil's PT beginning in the late 1990s (Hunter 2010, Ribeiro 2014).

Even though the major programmatic transformation took place during the 1990s, the ideological debate never ended and there remain

---

[6] Translation by the author. See also Lanzaro (2004).

ongoing programmatic debates. For example, on February 22, 2014 the National Plenary unanimously approved the installation of the Ideological Update Commission, comprising six representatives from the factions, four from the Montevideo grassroots activists, one from Canelones, and two from the rest of the countryside, i.e., the grassroots members had one more member on the commission than did the factions (Minute N°01-14, 2014).

Finally, during the process of programmatic and electoral realignment of the Uruguayan party system, the FA not only captured more votes, but also changed its electoral base of support (Lanzaro 2004, López Cariboni and Queirolo 2015, Luna 2007, Moreira 2000, Moreira and Delbono 2016). As in other Latin American countries in which the left accessed government, a class-based vote gradually consolidated (Handlin 2013, Madrid 2012). Since 2009, the FA has been attracting an increasing number of voters from poor sectors,[7] individuals oriented toward voting for the FA not only as a result of the economic performance of the leftist government, but also because of the individuals' position in the social structure.

EXAMPLES OF LIMITS TO STRATEGIC ADAPTATION

The literature claims that under presidential regimes, presidents have the power to appoint the cabinet and other institutional positions. This power reduces the influence of party organization. As the argument goes, there are institutional incentives to privilege the leadership of the president. Tabaré Vázquez and José Mujica (and again Tabaré Vázquez for his second term) had the power to nominate their ministers, undersecretaries, heads of state-owned public-utility companies, etc. Nonetheless, the FA shows that there is no necessary or sufficient relationship between this type of government and type of party organization. Tabaré Vázquez has been the most successful leader of the FA. He won the mayoralty of Montevideo in 1990, the first time a leftist party ever accessed office. Fourteen years later, in 2004, he was elected president, the first time a leftist president had taken office in Uruguay. Despite this impressive record of political success, the first and second times Vázquez had run for president, he had to comply with party decisions, sometimes

---

[7] Using survey data from 1989 to 2014, López, Cariboni, and Queirolo (2015) show that class voting models better explain the vote in the last national election than do traditional economic voting models (the latter fare better in explaining election results prior to 2009).

vetoing his or his government's own policy projects or choices. Two major policies where there was a staunch disagreement between Vázquez and the party were the free trade agreement (FTA) with the USA and abortion rights.

José Mujica was a "rock star" president. He was elected in the 2009 national elections after beating the PN candidate Luis Alberto Lacalle Herrera in the runoff in November. He was interviewed by all major news organizations and gave famous speeches that went viral around the world, with millions of views on YouTube.[8] Yet, even this president, who made Uruguay more visible than ever before, had to negotiate or defer to party organizational decisions. Nonetheless, activists emphasized that during Mujica's tenure the National Group of Government did not meet. Despite the fact that this informal institution did not operate, the FA formal structure nonetheless influenced the administration's policy direction, as exhibited in the previous section.

During the 2014 primary election campaign, grassroots representatives to the National Plenary of the FA from Montevideo (the Group of 41) asked to have meetings with the two candidates competing for the party's nomination to be the candidate for the national election, Tabaré Vázquez and Constanza Moreira. During the meeting with Vázquez, the grassroots representatives raised a series of issues and asked his opinion on the constitutional reform (promoted by the grassroots activists). Vázquez answered that he would do what the party platform said. (La República, November 14, 2013).[9]

## An FTA with the USA

During the first FA government (2005–2010), a controversial issue engendered differences between the FA organization and the administration in terms of the country's international relations. During the first months in office, President Tabaré Vázquez and the Economy and Finance Minister, Danilo Astori, pushed for an FTA between Uruguay and the USA. With this initiative, the government was seeking to diversify the country's international commerce, at a time when Uruguay's neighbors and main commercial partners, Argentina and Brazil, were not benefitting the

---

[8] The most frequently viewed video was his speech at the UN General Assembly in 2013.
[9] "Vázquez recibió a las bases del FA de Montevideo" (Vázquez received the FA grassroots from Montevideo), available at www.republica.com.uy/vazquez-recibio-a-las-bases-del-fa-de-montevideo/, last accessed March 22, 2019.

country. However, entering into an FTA with the USA was explicitly against the FA's government platform, with which it won the national elections in 2004.[10]

Opportunities to sign the FTA increased with the visit of US President George W. Bush in early 2006. In August of that year, President Vázquez said, in a meeting with businessmen, that: "those who in the name of principles believe that commerce is a matter of ideology are mistaken" and that "... the train ... only stops once."[11] Vázquez said this in reference to the possibility of moving forward on an FTA with the USA (El Espectador, August 9, 2006).[12] Vázquez had the support of the majority of his cabinet, especially from the Economy and Finance Minister, one of the main promoters of the FTA. Only two ministers were opposed (Reinaldo Gargano, Foreign Affairs Minister, from the PSU and Marina Arismendi, Social Development Minister and member of the PCU). Yet, the initiative generated great tensions within the FA.

The possibility that an FTA with the USA could eventually materialize activated the whole FA structure, from the Base Committees to the factions whose positions were more visible through some FA Representatives and Ministers, like Gargano (El País, September 17, 2006).[13] In July 2006, the National Plenary of the FA, based on discussion of an internal document called "Informe de análisis politico en el marco del Uruguay integrado al mundo" (Political analysis report concerning a framework for integrating Uruguay into the world), decided:

To reiterate the resolution of the Fourth Extraordinary Congress "Héctor Rodríguez," in the sense that we reject the current FTA project and the eventual bilateral agreements with the US ... which includes the contents of the FTAs already signed between the US and Latin American countries. To accept that commercial agreements can take place with different countries in the world whenever they favor our

---

[10] "... we reject the current Free Trade Area of the Americas and the eventual bilateral commercial treaties with the US conceived in this framework, since they are not favorable to our goals of consolidating a productive country." (Grandes Lineamientos Programáticos para el Gobierno 2005-2010; IV Congreso Extraordinario del Frente Amplio – Major Programmatic Guidelines for the Government 2005-2010; Fourth Extraordinary FA Congress –December 20–21, 2003). Translation from Spanish by the authors.
[11] Translation from Spanish by the authors.
[12] "Vázquez: el tren algunas veces pasa una sola vez" (Vázquez: the train sometimes stops just once), available at www.espectador.com/politica/75467/vazquez-el-tren-algunas-veces-pasa-una-sola-vez, last accessed August 24, 2017.
[13] "Vázquez sin votos en oficialismo para TLC. La mayoría del Frente mantiene rechazo." (Vázquez without votes in the government's party for the FTA. The majority of the FA retains its rejection).

participation in international commerce, do not harm our sovereignty and economy, and also do not contradict our commitments with other countries in the region, especially with the MERCOSUR treaty.

(Resolution, National Plenary, July 15, 2006)[14]

The following month, in response to a proposal of the grassroots activists from Montevideo, the National Political Board reiterated the Plenary's resolution (Political Board Resolution N° 27, August 14, 2006). In September, several leaders of the leftist factions of the FA participated in public rallies and organized events against the FTA. FA leaders were integrated into activities organized by the National Commission for the Defense of Sovereignty promoted by social organizations (the union movement, the cooperatives movement, the student movement, and the retiree organizations) as a strategy to advocate against signing an FTA (El Observador, September 17, 2006[15] and El País, September 17, 2006).[16] The Vázquez government had to abandon the idea of pursuing a FTA with the USA in light of the opposition from the party, led by the leftist factions and the grassroots activists.

### The Plebiscite on the Law Concerning the Expiration of the Punitive Claims of the State against Crimes during the Dictatorship

During the FA's first government (2005–2010), a group of social organizations (including the PIT-CNT, the student movement, groups of families of people who were detained and had disappeared during the dictatorship, some minor groups from the left and intellectuals) started a campaign to hold a plebiscite to repeal the "Ley de Caducidad" (15,848 Ley de Caducidad de la Pretensión Punitiva del Estado, Law of the Expiration of the Punitive Pretension of the State). The law was enacted in 1986, during the first democratic government after the authoritarian regime. It resulted from an agreement between the PC and PN and established amnesty for crimes committed during the authoritarian regime (1973–1984) by the military and the police. Those who supported the bill argued that it was a way to pacify the country. For those opposed

---

[14] Translation from Spanish by the authors. The resolution was approved by 115 votes, 2 opposed it and there were 5 abstentions.
[15] "Tres legisladores hablaron en contra de un acuerdo con la mayor potencia del mundo." (Three Congressmen spoke against an agreement with the major world power).
[16] "Vázquez sin votos en oficialismo para TLC. La mayoría del Frente mantiene rechazo." (Vázquez without votes in the official party for an FTA. The majority of the FA maintains its rejection).

(the political left and some minor groups within the traditional parties), the bill gave impunity to those who committed crimes and violated human rights during the dictatorship. In 1989, civil-society organizations convened a call for a referendum to repeal the law and the referendum failed to receive the necessary votes.

In 2007, in a different political context, civil-society organizations argued the need for a plebiscite to repeal the law, because repealing it through Congress (the FA had the necessary majority to do so) would not yield the desired retroactive effects and would not allow the government to put the responsible military personnel on trial. By contrast, annulling the law through a plebiscite that would establish a constitutional amendment included the retroactive effects, among which was the "negation of res judicata." It was politically difficult to argue for the annulment of the law for two main reasons: first, because the Congress of the FA prior to the 2004 national elections decided not to proceed with this since it was a delicate issue at a juncture where the FA had a good chance of winning, for the first time,[17] the national elections; second, because president Tabaré Vázquez (2005–2010) argued against it, asserting that he would respect his campaign promises.[18]

The position of the party on the human-rights policy stance of the FA's government toward the Law of the Expiration of the Punitive Pretension of the State changed when the party took office. At the 5th Ordinary Congress of 2007, a motion was approved that called on the citizenry to participate in the campaign, initiated by social organizations, to gather the required number of signatures to annul the Law of the Expiration of the Punitive Pretension of the State. This resolution was approved almost unanimously by the 1,400 grassroots delegates attending the Congress, and resulted from the synthesis of around ten different motions, all of which supported the campaign already set in motion by social organizations.[19] The position of the party was consolidated at the

---

[17] In the FA Congress, the position that prevailed was that the Executive branch should promote investigations against human rights violations during the dictatorship authorized by Art. 4 of the Expiration Law, legal authority that had not been activated by the governments of the Colorado and National party (La República, December 17, 2007, "El FA adhirió a la anulación de la Ley de Caducidad" – the FA adhered to annulation of the Law of the Expiration).

[18] "Ya no se escucha su canto. Tabaré Vázquez y la Ley de Caducidad" (His voice is no longer heard. Tabaré Vázquez and the Expiration Law), September 20, 2007, (available at www.montevideo.com.uy/auc.aspx?49753, last accessed in July 20, 2016).

[19] La República, December 17, 2007, "El FA adhirió a la anulación de la Ley de Caducidad" (The FA adhered to annulation of the Law of the Expiration).

National Plenary on April 5, 2008 when a majority of eighty-one in favor (fifty-three abstentions and nine against) decided to support the campaign to gather the required number of signatures. The motion was introduced by the grassroots activists' delegates from Montevideo and the delegates from Base Committees from abroad.

> To support and convene ... means to put all the FA structure, one more time, in the streets, in this case to collect signatures to annul the Expiration Law, as it has always done on sensitive issues that afflict our people. There is only one possible reading of the resolution of the V Ordinary Congress "Compañero Gral. Líber Seregni." It only remains to gather all our strength and finish at once with the impunity for the Uruguayan people's genocidal criminals. The National Organizational Commission recommends that the FA, as a political party, be integrated in the Coordination Commission for the Annulment of the Expiration Law.
> (Resolutions' minute No. 1-08, 5/04/2008)[20]

In this vote, the representatives of the grassroots members were decisive in changing the position of the party, putting it in opposition to the president's preferences. In the vote, the only factions that were in favor of supporting the signature-collection campaign to repeal the law were the minor more leftist factions (the POR, the Movimiento 20 de Mayo – the 20th of May Movement, the Corriente de Izquierda – Leftist Current – and the Partido Socialista de los Trabajadores – Socialist Workers Party), as well as the PCU and the New Space. The campaign had little support among faction representatives in the National Plenary of the FA. The major factions (Mujica's MPP, the FLS of Astori, and the PSU)[21] were aligned with Tabaré Vázquez's position and voted against the FA taking part in the signatures campaign. If the decision had been in the factions' hands – in the hands of their delegates to the National Plenary – the party would have remained aligned with the president's position. The grassroots activists' decision, however, made the difference. Even those grassroots delegates who were also part of the MPP or the PSU factions voted against the positions of their respective factions and therefore voted for the FA to participate in the campaign for the Annulment of the Expiration Law.[22] Thus, without the grassroots activists, the decision of the party would have been different.

---

[20] Translation from Spanish by the authors.
[21] Mujica and Astori were the candidates who competed in the party's primary election to determine the presidential candidate for the 2009 national elections.
[22] See El Espectador "La Ley de Caducidad: comienza campaña masiva para anularla" (The Expiration Law: A massive campaign to annul it begins), April 7, 2008 (available at www.espectador.com/sociedad/118946/ley-de-caducidad-comienza-campana-masiva-para-anu

## The TISA Negotiations

During the first year of Vázquez's second term in office (2015–2020), one of the conflicts that the executive confronted was its attempt to integrate the country into the Trade Service Agreement (TISA) negotiations, a free-market reform. Negotiations began during José Mujica's (2010–2015) government, but they were not made public. By the beginning of Vázquez's second term in office, these negotiations had become public and the FA reacted, trying to influence the direction of government action.

The position of Vázquez and the Ministry of Economy and Finances was to engage Uruguay in the negotiations, and then decide whether to sign the agreement. However, given the differences that the TISA generated among the FA factions, Vázquez asked the FA to discuss the issue and to take a position concerning the country's participation in the TISA negotiations. As a result, the FA directorate set a timetable that included meetings with involved ministers, and it was discussed throughout the FA structure (as recalled in the Resolutions minute N° 3-15, September 5, 2015, which also registered a decision on this issue).

The FA's National Secretary met with seven of the thirteen ministers of Vázquez's administration. Several ministers raised concerns about entering the TISA because it would undermine national sovereignty in key areas (labor, environment, state-owned companies, and telecommunications, among others). Other ministers, however, claimed that it was critical to participate in the negotiations to acquire experience in these matters, and they also emphasized the benefits of joining the TISA in areas such as professional services and software. This was the position of the Foreign Minister, Rodolfo Nin Novoa and Economy and Finance Minister, Danilo Astori. They both belong to FA's moderate factions and thought that Uruguay had to participate in the negotiations because the benefits far exceeded the costs (La Diaria, September 7, 2015).[23] The internal discussion lasted from May to September 2015.

On September 5, 2015 the issue was discussed at the National Plenary of the FA. Two motions were presented for consideration. Motion 1 was signed by the moderate factions and called for remaining in the

---

larla, last accessed July 20, 2016), and Página 12 "Desafía el Frente Amplio a Tabaré por la amnistía" (The FA challenges Tabaré over amnesty), April 7, 2008, (available at www.pagina12.com.ar/diario/elmundo/4-102011-2008-04-07.html, last accessed March 22, 2019).

[23] La Diaria "Estar o No Estar" (To be or not to be), September 7, 2015 (available at http://ladiaria.com.uy/articulo/2015/9/estar-o-no-estar/, last accessed September 28, 2018).

negotiations. Motion 2 was signed by more leftist factions and the PSU, among others, and suggested that Uruguay had to withdraw from the negotiations. It was decided that it was inconvenient "to keep participating in the TISA negotiations" in light of the "process of analysis and discussion" that the party undertook regarding the issue, and because the negotiations are "inattentive to the ... vision [of the FA] concerning the nation's development, ... the programmatic definitions, Constitutive Declaration and the party statutes."[24] One-hundred-and-seventeen members of the National Plenary voted in favor of this motion, twenty-two voted to stay in the negotiations (Resolutions minute N° 3-15, September 5, 2015). The winning motion was supported by almost all the grassroots members (with the exception of one Coordinating Group from Montevideo) and the leftist factions of the FA (MPP, PCU, PSU, and List 711). The motion to remain in the negotiations was supported by the most moderate factions aligned with the Economy and Finance Minister and Vázquez (La Diaria, September 7, 2015).[25] With the party and other organizations opposing the TISA – the union movement had called a general strike to oppose the negotiations – the president decided to abandon the TISA negotiations. The strong influence of the party on the agenda of the executive branch of government is highlighted by Víctor Rossi, then Minister of Transportation and Public Works and one of the politicians from Vázquez's inner circle. The following excerpt is from an interview with Rossi, before President Vázquez's decision to pull out from the TISA: "... at the government level there have been no discussions, and no decision has been made yet [though] the position of the National Plenary of the FA is very important [and] it is something that will likely have influence." (La Diaria, September 7, 2015).[26]

The vote of the grassroots activists was not crucial in determining the party's decision to oppose the preferences of the executive because the factions that opposed negotiations had, by themselves, more votes than those that favored the TISA negotiations.[27] Nonetheless, the votes from

---

[24] Translation from Spanish by the authors.
[25] La Diaria "Estar o No Estar" (To be or not to be), September 7, 2015 (available at http://ladiaria.com.uy/articulo/2015/9/estar-o-no-estar/, last accessed September 28, 2018).
[26] Ibid. Translation from Spanish by the authors.
[27] See El País "El Plenario del Frente otra vez bajo la mira" (The FA's Plenary is once again under scrutiny), September 13, 2015 (available at www.elpais.com.uy/informacion/plenario-frente-vez-mira.html, last accessed September 28, 2018) for data about the composition of the FA plenary and voting.

## Examples of Limits to Strategic Adaptation 141

the grassroots activists helped produce an overwhelming anti-TISA outcome. Gabriel Márquez, a grassroots delegate from Montevideo, said in the group interview:

> ... in the case of the TISA the government ended up checking with the political party [organization] ... the grassroots members played [a role] from two places. One is the natural place, as in the National Plenary [where the grassroots members have representatives]. In this case, the position and the participation perhaps are not noticeable because we do not have speakers in the press, in contrast to the factions ... they are in the media and give their explanations ... But in Montevideo we are 41 delegates, we would be the largest faction, by far [in terms of delegates to the National Plenary] ... For the people that do not participate in a Base Committee [the TISA resolution] was a product of some factions against others and not [the result of] the role the grassroots members played, we had many agreements with the grassroots members from Canelones and the rest of the countryside in this sense. Since it was an issue that had a lot of impact in the Coordinating Groups and in the Committees, many of the Congressmen that usually do not go, went, and there they left with many bruises [in a metaphorical sense]. And they saw Frenteamplista people all over, in the Cerro, Colón, as in Malvín [different neighborhoods in Montevideo, in popular and wealthy areas]. That is the case of the TISA. It was a very important influence. There were factions that were very important and had their influence and role, I have no doubts about it. There was the opinion of very influential frenteamplistas, but the role of the grassroots members in this case, I believe, was fundamental.
> (personal interview with Gabriel Márquez)

With the party and the union movement opposing his stance, President Vázquez decided to leave the negotiations. Parties in the opposition criticized Vázquez's decision, and claimed that the president was isolated and opposed by his own party. However, the socialist representative, Roberto Chiazzaro said: "... What Tabaré [Vázquez] really achieved ... was the participation and mobilization of the FA, because this [issue] was discussed throughout the country, and it was remarkable how people participated, informed and discussed politically ... Tabaré is not isolated from the FA and the FA is not isolated from Tabaré, Tabaré asked the party for its opinion." (La Diaria, September 7, 2015).[28] Other leaders also emphasized that the decision illustrated the democratic nature of the FA. Enrique Rubio, FA leader and former minister in Vázquez's first term, said in the personal interview:

---

[28] La Diaria "Estar o No Estar" (To be or not to be), September 7, 2015 (available at http://ladiaria.com.uy/articulo/2015/9/estar-o-no-estar/, last accessed September 28, 2018). Translation from Spanish by the authors.

*Are there constraints on the government, or some limits, due to this party structure? Not only that the coalition makes it necessary to build agreements to take advantage of the majority in the Legislative, but also this [structure]?*

It imposes some limits, yes. At least it is more laborious, sometimes, to propel, to materialize some proposals. In some cases, it ends up with the opposite decision, in some specific [cases]. The TISA was in one direction initially and it ended in the opposite one. In some previous international affairs, if it took the train or not [in reference to Vázquez's speech about the opportunity to sign an FTA], it ended in the opposite direction. In some cases, inside the Executive some of the factions with important influence, such as the FLS propel a position to which the president commits himself and then he realizes that in the political party there is another equilibrium. This brings the situation to an intermediate point.

*Do these limits only work as vetoes or do they also work preemptively in terms of who is in government?*

I see where the political party stops me or I have in my head, when I am deciding, that I will not be able to get there because the political party will veto it.

(personal interview with Enrique Rubio)

## CONCLUSIONS

This chapter has analyzed the role that the organizational structure exerts over one of the key dimensions of party organization: the party-in-government. In terms of the literature, we seek to advance understanding of how party organization influences the party's in-government public-policy orientation, a largely unexplored topic. We have presented evidence concerning the autonomous political action of grassroots activists in the decision-making bodies of the party. The analysis of the motions discussed in the National Plenary and among the National Political Board shows that grassroots activists are not mere observers, they are actors in the decision-making process. We have also analyzed the role grassroots activists play in the ideological transformation of the party. Finally, we have presented in-depth case and descriptive evidence to delineate the impact of the FA's peculiar structure in some very crucial areas in the context of Uruguayan politics – areas which are significant in any democratic context, including, among others, foreign policy, human rights, and the political system. The FA is a case where democratic party organization heavily influences the party's positions while in opposition and while in government. However, this does not imply that the grassroots activists work against government policy or against the leadership of the party.

# Conclusions 143

This idea was expressed by the executive secretary of Vázquez's second term in office in an in-depth interview with the authors:

If government governs, the party organization does politics. The government's responsibility is to apply the party's platform. It is not about the government saying "we are going to do this and that." The government has the platform and the political organization can check the degree of compliance, not about the everyday decisions outside the purview of the grassroots members. That is an FA characteristic, that it has a platform that has been heavily discussed previously, that it has a congress where there is a lot of discussion. Beyond its effects ... other parties do not have it ... The platform is the spine, where everyone comes from or to which one returns ... And I have heard directly from the president [Vázquez] "this thing is in the platform," and "that thing is not in the platform" ... "if it is in the party's platform framework, avanti."

(personal interview with Juan Andrés Roballo)

We have presented three in-depth case studies concerning three different issues: two related to foreign policy, an issue typically reserved for the president in presidential regimes, and one concerning human rights, one of the most sensitive political issues in Uruguayan politics since the restoration of democracy in 1985. To process-trace the role of the organization in the policy outcome, we have used different sources of evidence. We have shown instances where there is in fact an observable role of the grassroots activists, i.e., there is, as is usual in qualitative studies, a case "selection bias." The scope of the evidence simply allows us to show that the organization does indeed influence the party-in-government. The crucial variable that differentiates the FA from other comparable parties is its peculiar organizational structure, as has been emphasized throughout this book.

The same influential politician from the inner circle of Vázquez's second term said that he once received a phone call from a grassroots delegate to the National Plenary. She – the caller – was also a faction activist. He recalled that she said that there could be a difficulty with Montevideo's grassroots activists because of government decisions with a particular issue, that the grassroots activists were already mobilized. She did not claim to represent any faction, and at that point she was defending the position of the grassroots members, she was "... throwing her weight around, really, positively ... There you have a person from a faction that was 'wearing the hat' of the grassroots, she was pushing forward." (personal interview with Juan Andrés Roballo).

The decision-making process of the FA does not guarantee the best policy outcomes or that decisions will be made in a timely manner.

Party leaders and opposition politicians usually complain about the obstructive role played by the grassroots structure of the party. At the same time, the process usually brings policies further to the left, which distances the policies from the median voter preferences. This process also precludes leaders from taking strategic decisions in electoral terms. Both results can hinder democratic representation by limiting the party's ability to represent the median voter. This is the flipside of ideological coherence and the diminished probability of policy switches. The party's organizational structure can pose a challenge for strategic adaptation but it provides insurance against the risk of brand dilution (Lupu 2016).

# 7

# The FA in Comparative Perspective

## INTRODUCTION

This chapter analyzes the FA in comparative perspective. As argued in the introduction to this volume, the party-politics literature so far has not adequately addressed the critical role organizational structure plays in explaining the trajectory of party vitality. Even though there are classical texts (Duverger 1954, Panebianco 1988) and a line of the literature that explores how the internal dynamics of party organization influences organizations' fate (Anria 2018, Bermeo and Yashar 2016, Burgess and Levitsky 2003, Calvo and Murillo 2019, Cyr 2017, Levitsky 2003, Madrid 2012, Scarrow 2015), few have studied the role organizational structure per se plays in reproducing grassroots activism.

The deviant nature of the FA calls attention to how organizational structure can explain individual engagement and cooperation with the party. As a result of this endogenous property, our argument challenges the idea that the direction and nature of party organization change are inevitable. Also, it challenges the idea that organizational structure type is inevitably tied to a historical stage. In this vein, Scarrow (2015) suggests that not only is there no clear relationship between historical period and form of party organization, but also that, historically, parties with active members (especially the mass-organic party type) have been rare and that – paradoxically and contrary to conventional wisdom – this type of party has been more common in contemporary democracies.

There have been other mass-organic parties in Latin America. What happened to these party organizations? This has been a subject of extensive research in the comparative politics literature of Latin America.

Hunter (2010), Levitsky (2003), Levitsky and Roberts (2011), Roberts (1998), Roberts (2014), and Samuels (2004), and have analyzed the process of demobilization of formerly mass-organic Latin American parties. This literature has emphasized the role of exogenous factors, or the ability of party leaders to strategically "adapt," to explain the transformation of formerly mass-organic parties.

The case of the FA, which confronted similar exogenous challenges, calls attention to the relevance of organizational structure in determining party activists' levels of engagement. Organizational design is crucial for fostering and reproducing activism. Beyond exploring the individual traits that predispose activists to participate in a party organization, we have provided a theoretical argument concerning the organizational attributes that explain the reproduction of such activism – and its decline.

There are two main ways to structure a party organization's activism: one where members rely on and work for their leaders, and one where activists are stakeholders (Scarrow 2015). The FA shows how granting activists a significant *voice* in the organization can affect individual engagement. An organizational structure that ensures responsiveness; i.e., an institutionalized structure that ensures that one's voice is relevant – and not merely eventually considered for a specific decision or action – is more likely to maintain and reproduce activists' engagement. We now consider the pervasiveness of this dynamic beyond the context of Uruguayan politics. The civil-society literature, the organizational-justice literature in social psychology, and, more generally, the literature on participatory-democratic theory (c.f Rhodes-Purdy 2018), have provided convincing evidence concerning the role of perceived efficacy in the reproduction of participation and legitimacy, more generally. In our case, the organizational structure sets incentives that ensure efficacy for an activist's participation. This facilitates the reproduction of cooperation with the organization.

This chapter first examines the process of organizational change that characterized the Brazilian PT, a former mass-organic leftist party that turned into a professional–electoral party. We analyze the case of the PT because it is the case that most closely resembles the FA in its emphasis on grassroots activism; as in the case of the FA, a "basista" ideology (i.e., the critical role assigned to the grassroots activists) was part of the party's early identity. Our goal is to highlight the similarities and differences between the PT and the FA. The comparison with the PT, as a negative case, increases the theory's analytical leverage. Second, we discuss the case of the FA as a strange electoral alliance or coalition. We compare the case of the FA with other leftist coalitions in Latin America, with a special focus on the successive experiences of leftist coalitions in Chile and Argentina, showing that the FA developed a common organizational structure that is not observable in other, similar electoral alliances.

## THE BRAZILIAN PT: A NEGATIVE CASE IN LATIN AMERICA

Handlin and Berins Collier (2011) studied types of attachment between civil-society and party organizations in Brazil, Chile, Uruguay, and Venezuela. They assumed that the FA and the PT have a similar type of party organization: institutionalized leftist party organizations. They found that the linkages between the FA and civil society are significantly greater than in the case of the PT and they concluded that party organization does not explain the ties parties develop with civil society. These authors' conclusion, however, fails to take into account the difference between the "mass-organic" nature of the FA and the professional-electoral nature of the PT. We dispute the claim that both party organizations are similar and thus we emphasize the difference between the PT and the FA. The same result could be read as a proof of the difference between the two organizations. Even though Levitsky and Roberts (2011) classify both parties in the same *family* (i.e., institutionalized leftist parties), they acknowledge that the two parties do not have the same kind of organizational structure. This, we argue, explains the difference in the two parties' capacity to reproduce the engagement of their activists and their linkages with civil society.

Brazil has been described as an inchoate party system (Mainwaring 1999, 2018, Mainwaring and Scully 1995). The literature, however, has recounted a gradual process of increasing stability, especially thanks to the development of the PT (Mainwaring 2018, Piñeiro and Rosenblatt 2018, Zucco Jr 2008). The PT was founded in 1980 and, after more than thirty years, it has consolidated itself as a stable party organization (Zucco Jr 2010). Keck (1992) states that the PT was born with a mass collective identity and it was the only mass-based party born in Latin America in the 1980s. The PT in Brazil is an iconic case of a mass-based party that turned into an institutionalized professional–electoral party (Levitsky and Roberts 2011, Ribeiro 2014). In contrast with the FA, the PT is a negative case, i.e., a case of the failure to reproduce an organizational setting that promotes and ensures the engagement of grassroots activists.

In the case of the PT, the prospect of winning national elections, and the socioeconomic context in Brazil, fostered programmatic moderation and favored the strategic decisions made by its main leader, Luiz Inácio "Lula" Da Silva. Hunter (2010) rightly introduces a more nuanced perspective, where the origins of the party's organizational structure are crucial to explain the pace of such transformation. In this process, internal transformations (i.e., concentration of power in party elites) interact with exogenous factors, which range from the socioeconomic environment to institutional rules. The endpoint is the demobilization of the organization, the professionalization of its structures, and the creation of parallel structures of highly professionalized electoral campaigns. In this section, we emphasize how the PT gradually and persistently deprived activists of an efficacious voice, which facilitated power concentration in a small cadre and the transformation of the party from a mass party to a professional–electoral party.

The PT was conceived as a party having strong linkages with unions; Lula was the leader of the strong metallurgic union in São Paulo. Yet, it is not a classic union-based party in the Duverger sense. As in the case of the FA in Uruguay, the PT was not a classic leftist Leninist party; both parties placed more emphasis on their respective grassroots-activist bases, in an effort to avoid the model of democratic centralism. As with the FA, the PT comprised different factions; at one time it had sixteen of them. Hunter (2010) summarizes the groups that originally coalesced around this leftist party in Brazil: Christian base communities, intellectuals, and, most of all, labor organizers (22). The PT has always been very open and broad in its incorporation of new interest groups. This enriched the debate within the party, but also engendered problems of leadership (Keck 1992). The party emerged in the context of a repressive authoritarian regime that ruled from 1964 until 1985. Major leaders and grassroots members from the foundational groups suffered political persecution. According to Keck (1992), this context was one of the main factors that fostered the unification of the different organizations in one party. The PT fought to redemocratize the country, both in terms of the political regime and in terms of the "social question." The PT politicized the idea that the Brazilian state was built to favor the economic elite and set itself the goal of democratizing the society. Achieving this goal was difficult, both because of the authoritarian context and because the PT had to operate under regulations that severely restricted party building. PT bylaws had to follow a rigid template established by the authoritarian regime (Keck 1992, Ribeiro 2013, Samuels and Zucco Jr 2016).

In order to distance itself from other Brazilian parties, the PT created from its inception a non-elitist structure that ensured open channels for activists' participation throughout the territory. In its early years, the PT built strong ties with social movements, developing connections with NGOs, labor unions, and Catholic activists. These connections were consolidated in the base nuclei organized by the party at the municipal level. The party's stronghold in the early years was in São Paulo and Porto Alegre and, later, in Rio de Janeiro. Samuels (2006) and Ribeiro (2014) emphasize that the PT was the only party with a dense organization that worked permanently and mobilized its activists. More importantly, it was "the only party with relatively widespread member involvement in its governance" (Samuels 2006, 22). Also, the PT created sectoral secretaries, open to party activists interested in issues such as environment, women, youth, and the Afro-Brazilian movement (Samuels and Zucco Jr 2016).

Even though both the PT and the FA have had active grassroots activists and a strong ideological commitment to participatory democracy since their very inception, there is a crucial difference in the relationship between these grassroots activists and the party leaders. In the case of the FA, its grassroots activity emerged spontaneously and reproduced very fast, like "a fungus," during the party's birth (personal interview with Óscar Bottinelli, Pedro Cribari, and Martín Ponce de León). These grassroots activists were convened and constituted independently from FA factions and leaders. Although some of these grassroots activists were, individually, members of one of the coalesced factions, and others were union members, these previously existing organizations did not structure or capture the Base Committee movement. The Base Committees were not part of the CNT structure or of any of the preexisting political groups of the FA. The FA cannot be considered as merely the sum of the organizations of its constituent factions. The FA gathered many people who participated in unions, political parties, and the student movement, but it also gathered people who had no prior formal political activity. More critically, these new Base Committees and their members had no organic relationship with the direction of the party or any of its constituent groups (see Chapter 4).

In the case of the PT, the initial structure of the base nuclei was the organization already presided over by PT leaders in the union movement. Even though the base nuclei helped complete the process of gathering the required number of adherents to present to the electoral authority, activism in the PT emerged and developed from an already established organization in unions and in other groups. Those who joined the PT as party members after its foundation and after the 1982 election also did not change the previous structure. Quoting a February, 1982 official PT memo (written before the 1982 elections), Brandão (2003, 68) highlights a discrepancy between the number of base nuclei and the number of members. The same is mentioned in the January, 1983 memo, which notes that in 1981, the PT jumped from 28,000 to 300,000 members, but the number of base nuclei only increased from 623 to around 1,000 (Brandão 2003, 69). In the case of the PT, the increase in the number of members did not translate to an increase in the number of base nuclei nor to an increase in the number of people attending those base nuclei. Hence, the party leadership was not overwhelmed by a massive grassroots movement that needed an organizational structure to channel it.

In the first national conference of the PT in São Paulo on August 8–9, 1981, the party discussed whether the base nuclei would have decision-making power or an advisory role. Although the 5682 Law of July 21, 1971 (Lei Orgânica dos Partidos Políticos, Organic Law of Political Parties) strongly regulated how parties could organize, the PT figured out a way to circumvent this constraint and established a structure that allowed grassroots activists to participate. Yet, the party also decided to grant only an advisory role to the base nuclei. Ferreira (2008) recalls that the justification for this decision was that base nuclei with decision-making power could be manipulated by organized factions within the party. As in other parties with members, the PT's grassroots activists had a role in the political life of their party organizations; i.e., they participated in debates, chose party authorities, engaged in faction competition, and eventually became members of the party elite.

The PT base nuclei could select representatives to the municipal conferences, which, in turn, would elect delegates to the regional and national conferences. These bodies elected the directors of the party (diretorios) and the executive board (comisões diretivas) at each level. However, in contrast to the case of the Base Committees in the FA, the base nuclei in the PT did not have a set number of representatives to the different conferences nor a set number of seats among the directors or the executive board. Moreover, in the PT, there was no organizational provision that could make the base nuclei delegates continuously accountable to their fellow grassroots activists, as is the case for the FA (see Chapter 3). Thus, there was no distinction between those who participated in the directing bodies as grassroots delegates and those who did not have base nuclei as their referent; they all worked as trustees and not, as in the case of grassroots representatives in the FA, as delegates.

Ribeiro (2008) claims that the base nuclei developed somewhat during the PT's first three years, though that quickly halted. In his account, the fact that only 5 percent of the PT members in 1982 belonged to base nuclei indicated the difficulty of developing a participatory structure organized in base nuclei. In August 1985, the PT had 668 nuclei, a number only slightly greater than that in 1980.[1]

In 1983, the trade union group in São Paulo began to exert control over the PT's structure. This was accomplished through its faction, called Articulaçao (Articulation). In 1995, Articulation served as the base of the Campo Mayoritario (Majoritarian Camp), the faction that has controlled the party since that year. This process unfolded parallel to the growing control that the executive commissions were exerting at different levels of the party organizational structure. These commissions, especially the national commission (initially conceived as administrative and executive bodies) took over the political role previously reserved for the directors and the conferences (Ribeiro 2008). As a result, the majoritarian faction that controlled the National Executive Commission began to control the PT's organization.

The base nuclei were relevant during the initial stages of the party because they helped gather the required number of affiliates to formalize the PT as a political party. However, after this initial stage, they quickly lost relevance. They began to operate for the sole purpose of electing delegates to the conferences at the different levels. By the end of the 1980s, the base nuclei's loss of significance was evident. In 1990, a resolution of the 7th national encounter of the PT in São Paulo stated that: "The majority of the nuclei ceased to exist, or when they exist ... they have an episodic action, before the Conferences or Conventions."[2] According to Ribeiro (2008), the weakening of the base nuclei in the PT is explained by a combination of factors: the scarcity of material resources, the conflict between factions, and their instrumentalization as electoral committees for candidates.

The number of base nuclei in the PT did not significantly increase after the early years of the party, and they were not autonomous from the competition between factions. Because the internal debates in the PT have always been led by the factions, the base nuclei never had an autonomous life, and those who were elected as representatives of base nuclei

---

[1] Boletim Nacional, N° 12, São Paulo, August 1985, 4 (cited in Ribeiro 2008, 249).
[2] Construção partidária. Resoluções do 7° Encontro Nacional, São Paulo, 1990, 443. Cited in Ribeiro 2008, 250. Translation from Portuguese by the authors.

responded to their factions. They were not seen as a unified movement; rather, they were just another arena of competition between factions. By contrast, in the case of the FA, the grassroots structure was seen, from its very inception, as a source of unity for the left. The majoritarian faction, Articulation (then Majoritarian Camp), feared that radical leftist factions could gain leverage by capturing the base nuclei and, in turn, the organization. This fear led Articulation/Majoritarian Camp to oppose any attempt to grant the base nuclei a decision-making role in the party during the 1980s and early 1990s. This discussion of the possibility of Base Committees being captured by leftist factions also occurred in the FA. Moderate FA factions complained that the grassroots movement was captured by the PCU or the MPP. As a result, moderate factions viewed the positions reserved for the grassroots activists throughout the FA structure as a chance to increase the power of more leftist factions (see Chapter 3). However, this critique did not prevent grassroots activists from being granted a significant role in the decision-making bodies (see Chapter 4).

In 1995, the Majoritarian Camp achieved almost complete control over the main positions of the PT directorate (Ribeiro 2014). That year, the Organic Law of Political Parties was repealed and Brazilian parties were able to change their statutes. This intensified the discussion in the PT about statute reform. In this context, the majoritarian faction pushed forward its idea of increasing the number of affiliates, loosening the requirements to become a member, and thus reducing the political role of grassroots activists. This position triumphed and crystalized in the 2001 statute reform. The Majoritarian Camp took power away from the grassroots activists by establishing the direct election of the directors and the executive commissions. Thus, the conferences where grassroots representatives participated lost the prerogative of selecting representatives and reduced the directors' level of accountability to activists. According to Hunter (2010) and Ribeiro (2014), these rules gave more autonomy to party elites. Once the party gained the national government, the Majoritarian Camp had more access to patronage, which reinforced its leverage in the party. Neither the minority factions nor the grassroots activists were able to contest this process of power concentration and increased autonomy.

During the 1990s, the FA also underwent a process of ideological moderation (see Chapter 6), introduced the direct election of party authorities and grassroots and faction representatives to the FA structure, and reduced the size of the quorum for taking some decisions. However,

## The Brazilian PT: A Negative Case in Latin America 153

as opposed to what happened in the case of the PT, these changes, which were codified in the statute reform of 1993, were accompanied by an increase in the representation of grassroots activists on the Political Board, in the National Plenary, and in the Departmental Plenaries; grassroots delegates thereafter accounted for a third, and then half, of the total members of these bodies (see Chapters 3 and 4). The changes in the FA accord with those implemented in the PT and in other cases where mass-based parties transformed themselves into professional–electoral parties. Nonetheless, in the FA, changes were made possible only with grassroots activists' consent, in exchange for increasing their representation to maintain their relative power in the reformed organizational setting.

Even though the PT still differs from other Brazilian parties because it retains a relatively dense organizational structure, the PT reduced its relationship with Brazil's social movements and weakened the channels in the territory for direct participation (Ribeiro 2014, Samuels and Zucco Jr 2016). As Anria (2018) states, the PT organization fostered concentration of power in the elite and the party leadership became increasingly insulated. The author adds that:

> The PT is also an example of a movement-based party that has gradually suppressed social mobilization from below, a classic case of a movement-based party that confirms the tendency toward top-down control associated with party bureaucratization and concentrated executive authority.
>
> (243)

The PT exhibited a process similar to that of many European parties, described by Scarrow (2015); while parties reduce the role and power of grassroots activists in the organization, they increase the number of adherents or members that have a loose linkage with the party organization and have a consultative role at best in the decision-making structure. At the same time, this process leads to greater power for the party elites, who can easily control an atomized mass of members.

The PT lacked one critical piece that prevented the FA from changing its nature: there was no lock-in mechanism that could ensure the reproduction of the activist structure. As reviewed in previous chapters, this lock-in mechanism implies that grassroots activists have *voice* and an autonomous representation structure that gives them a veto in decisions affecting the fate of the organization. In contrast to the FA, the PT underwent the natural process described by Michels (1999 [1911]), a process he dubbed the "Iron Law of Oligarchy." In the PT, as in other mass-based parties, the activist structures became ossified and the party turned into a professional–electoral organization. In these cases, party elites had sufficient leverage to gradually change the nature of the organization; i.e., in contrast to the FA, the PT had no lock-in mechanism to prevent the natural process of oligarchization.

### THE FA AS A STRANGE ELECTORAL ALLIANCE

The FA differs not only from other institutionalized leftist parties in the region but also from similar electoral coalitions. The main difference is that the FA developed a permanent structure separate from each of the groups that formed the coalition. Lanzaro (2000, 45) describes the evolution of the FA as follows: "... what began as a coalition of parties—following the leftist front model put in practice since 1962—then became a coalition party, unified, where the whole is more relevant than its components ..." The existence of an autonomous organizational structure characterized not only the highest levels of the coalition, but also the grassroots, the Base Committees. Activists could participate regardless of their membership in any of the constitutive groups. More specifically, there are FA party locales – the Base Committees – that do not belong to any of the parties or factions that constitute the coalition (see Chapter 3). This type of organization is rare for electoral coalitions, where the amount of common structure is usually only the minimum necessary and each organizational member retains organizational autonomy.

The FA structure is even more peculiar if we consider the incentives set by the DSV (see Chapters 2 and 4) that enables factions to nominate their own candidates in separate ballots (Luján and Moraes 2017). Moreover, until the constitutional reform of 1997, parties were allowed to nominate more than one presidential candidate. However, even though the coalition members were not forced to coordinate by jointly nominating a single presidential candidate, the FA coalition has always, in fact, nominated one presidential candidate and has also developed a shared organizational structure, parallel to those of each faction. The FA shared organization is also more developed and complex than the two foundational Uruguayan parties, the PC and PN. In these latter parties, the activism is located in the constituent factions, and the shared structures are minimal (Buquet, Chasquetti, and Moraes 1998).

Chile, over the course of its history, has experienced successful leftist electoral coalitions. In the 1930s, the Frente Popular (Popular Front) was formed as a coalition between the PSCh, the Radical Party, the Partido Comunista de Chile (Chilean Communist Party, PCCh), and some unions and social movements. The Popular Front was an early example of a successful center-left electoral coalition in Latin America in the context of the popular fronts that were confronting Fascism. It won the 1938 presidential election and the Radical Party president Pedro Aguirre Cerda was the first president of a victorious center-left coalition under democracy in Latin America. Yet, the coalition lasted only a few years, because the PSCh and the PCCh abandoned the coalition in 1941 (Faúndez 1988, Gil 1966, Moulian 1993).³ In 1956, with the formation of the Frente de Acción Popular (Popular Action Front, FRAP), leftist parties – the most important being PCCh and PSCh's two factions – constituted a single unified coalition that lasted until 1969 (Gil 1966, Moulian 1993). Later, the most important instance of a politico-electoral coalition in Chile was the Unidad Popular (Popular Unity, UP).

From 1958 onward, Socialist Salvador Allende's leadership further consolidated the ideological cleavage of Chilean politics, a rare example of class cleavage under democracy in the developing world in the early twentieth century (Scully 1992, Zemelman 1971). During the 1960s and early 1970s, as in many other countries in the region, ideological polarization increased (Valenzuela 1978). In 1970 Salvador Allende was elected president under the UP alliance. The PSCh and PCCh, among other political groups and parties, formed the UP. This coalition of parties and movements supported Salvador Allende's presidential candidacy, and later presented joint lists for the congressional elections in March 1973. The violent coup that overthrew Allende in September 1973, and the seventeen-year authoritarian regime that ensued, left a profound imprint on Chile. Pinochet's authoritarian regime was characterized by its brutality and the restructuring of Chilean political institutions. Thus, Pinochet's government not only profoundly changed the socialist-era policies implemented during Allende's democratic presidency, but also exerted a violent repression that almost led to the complete disappearance of leftist parties (Roberts 1998). The shock of the authoritarian regime impacted three aspects of the party system: the political alliances, the party organizations, and the programmatic stances.

In the Third Wave of Democracy, the clearest example of a durable center-left coalition in Latin America is the Concertación (Concertation)

---

³ In the PSCh, there were internal conflicts over the its participation in the coalition. This eventually led to defections and the formation of a new party – the Socialist Workers Party, formed in 1942 (Faúndez 1988, Gil 1966, 284, Moulian 1993, 38). In 1957, the PSCh reunited.

in Chile. This coalition came into being for the 1988 Referendum to oppose Pinochet. It comprised the Partido Demócrata Cristiano (Christian Democratic Party, DC) and the PSCh as the leading partners, together with the Partido por la Democracia (Party for Democracy, PPD), the Partido Radical Social Demócrata (Radical Social Democratic Party, PRSD), and other minor parties. The transition to democracy was the main galvanizer of the coalition (see, e.g., Garretón 1995, Loveman 1995). In the 1990s, the coalition's primary goal was to avoid an authoritarian regression. It governed Chile for twenty years, from 1990 to 2010, during which time it oversaw a successful, stable democratic transition (Drake and Jaskic 1999, Ffrench-Davis 2008, Mainwaring and Scully 2010, Weyland, Madrid, and Hunter 2010).

None of these electoral alliances built a common organizational structure. In the case of the UP, the alliance that brought Allende to power did not develop a common grassroots structure. Rather, each party or organization had its own activist structure. When the FA was in its early stages (1971), the UP was the model for the FA (personal interview with Carlos Baraibar). In the discussions on how to organize the FA, some factions (the most important ones) preferred the UP model, which had no common grassroots territorial structure, like Base Committees. As Ponce de León and Rubio (2018) state, this position was defeated in the commission that discussed the organizational structure, because Base Committees were a significant reality before and during this debate (see Chapter 4).

Even those electoral alliances that are able to access government (and thus gain access to material resources) do not develop a common structure like the FA. The Concertation, Chile's most electorally successful and durable instance, convened only a single weekly meeting (every Monday) of party leaders in La Moneda (Chile's presidential palace). There were no party locales of the Concertation or any other permanent structure. The coalition never had a unified decision-making structure or a cadre of grassroots activists. In 2010, when the center-right coalition, Coalición por el Cambio (Coalition for Change), led by Sebastián Piñera, won the national elections, the Concertation entered a process of disintegration. In the opposition, the formerly allied parties found it difficult to coordinate their efforts. For the 2013 national election a new coalition was formed – the New Majority, which included the PCCh. It replicated the decision and organizational structure of the Concertation, where there was no shared structure beyond that of each of the parties participating in the coalition.

In the 1990s, Argentina had a succession of center-left coalitions that opposed the Partido Justicialista (Justicialist Party, PJ). The first of these coalitions was the Frente Grande (Grand Front), formed in 1993. It was formed by two preexisting leftist coalitions – Frente por la Democracia y Justicia Social (Social Justice and Democracy Front, FREDEJUSO) and Frente del Sur (Front of the South). These two leftist coalitions comprised former PJ members, several minor center-left parties (e.g., the Partido Intransigente – the Intransigent Party – and the Christian Democratic Party), human-rights activists, and leftist parties (e.g., Communist Party). The main leader was Carlos "Chacho" Álvarez. The Grand Front was born in opposition to the structural adjustments and market reforms undertaken by Menem beginning in 1990. It had relatively early electoral success – accomplished without constructing a dense organizational structure – and relied heavily on the popularity of its leaders. For example, Abal Medina (2009) notes that:

The FG [Grand Front] leaders always fought to have freedom of action, hoping not to be tied down by institutional procedures when making decisions. This was for two reasons. In the first place, party growth was achieved largely as a result of its leaders' popularity and media exposure, not as a result of territorial development. Second, the party's nucleus often considered Álvarez's speed of response an important requirement. His capacity to generate political initiatives enabled the FG to succeed at junctures where a weak structure would usually fail.

(Abal Medina 2009, 360)

The main organizational characteristics of the Grand Front coalition were replicated in a new Argentinean center-left coalition called Frente País Solidario (Front for a Country in Solidarity, FREPASO). The FREPASO was a coalition formed by Grand Front and the Unidad Socialista (Socialist Unity); the Partido Comunista de Argentina (Argentinean Communist Party) and the Partido Demócrata Cristiano (Christian Democratic Party) confirmed their adherence to a center-left coalition. This alliance, formed in 1995, was a product of the Grand Front's electoral success in the 1994 election of the Constitutional Assembly (Escudero 2002). The FREPASO was organized as a confederation of parties and was an alternative to the traditional two-party system which comprised the Unión Cívica Radical (Civic Radical Union, UCR), and PJ. In the 1995 presidential election, it successfully took the second place from the UCR. As in the case of the Grand Front, this alliance did not develop a shared structure like that of the FA. The FREPASO was organizationally weak and did not have a nation-wide presence; it was mainly present in the city and province of Buenos Aires and in other provinces, e.g., Santa

Fe, where center-left parties had their stronghold (Novaro 2010). The national board of the FREPASO comprised representatives of each party that participated in the confederation, and this board was the only shared structure (Escudero 2002). Throughout its short life, it relied heavily on the personalistic leadership of Chacho Álvarez.

In 1997 the FREPASO and the UCR formed the Alianza por el Trabajo, la Justicia y la Educación (Alliance for Work, Justice, and Education, henceforth Alliance). It was born in August 1997 as an anti-Menemist coalition that aimed to eliminate corruption and to improve social and labor conditions, which had been adversely affected by the neoliberal reforms applied during Menem's administrations.[4] The Alliance was an attempt to coordinate the main opposition forces to Menemismo, who saw this coalition as the only possible way to defeat Menem and the PJ.

In 1997, the Alliance won the midterm legislative elections and on December 10, 1999 it won the presidential elections with the ticket Fernando de la Rúa (UCR) and Carlos "Chacho" Álvarez (FREPASO), with 48.4 percent of the votes. Despite its electoral success, the Alliance was a coalition even less structured than the FREPASO, and it had many coordination problems. It was only an electoral coalition and was unable even to present a unified list in every Argentinean Province. As argued above, it was essentially a coalition to defeat Menem and it was vaguely unified in programmatic terms. When it governed, it could not articulate a coherent economic policy, which was critical in the context of the severe economic crisis that Argentina faced in 2000 and 2001. As the crisis worsened and social unrest increased, the Alliance proved increasingly unable to coordinate and govern. The clearest manifestation of this incapacity was the resignation of Carlos "Chacho" Álvarez as vice-President. The economic situation worsened and the inability of De la Rúa's government to weather it ended with his resignation and the collapse of the Argentinean economy and its political system in 2001 (Leiras 2007, Lupu 2016, Novaro 2010, Rosenblatt 2006). In contrast to the FA, the Alliance did not develop a common shared structure. Neither the Grand Front, the FREPASO, nor the Alliance had a shared body of grassroots members nor did any of these coalitions have a dense common organizational structure (i.e., rules, programmatic documents, and party locales) beyond those of each party participating in the coalition.

---

[4] Carlos Saúl Menem was President of Argentina from 1989 to 1995 and from 1995 to 1999. For an analysis of his presidencies, see Palermo and Novaro (1996) and Novaro and Palermo (2004).

## CONCLUSIONS

This chapter closes the empirical assessment section of this volume. We have presented evidence in support of our argument by examining cases from several other Latin American countries. We analyzed Brazil's PT as a comparable, contrasting case, and we discussed other cases of electoral coalitions that did not develop the kind of common grassroots structure that characterizes the FA, such as the Concertation in Chile and the different center-left coalitions that existed in Argentina during the 1990s and early 2000s.

The PT is usually compared with the FA because they are institutionalized leftist parties. The PT also used to be a party with activists. However, the PT's linkage with activists weakened over time. It turned into an electoral–professional party (Levitsky and Roberts 2011). The PT, as has happened to other mass-based party organizations in the region or worldwide, lost activists. Some former activists left the organization, essentially turning into simple rank-and-file voters of the party, or remained as members without any activity in the party. The FA also has lost activists, but the grassroots structure remains alive and politically relevant. Yet, beyond the number of activists, the distinctive feature of the FA's organizational structure is the existence of mechanisms and positions that ensure activists' efficacy up to and including the party's highest and most significant decision-making institutions. In the PT, the structure became elitist, oligarchized, and increasingly disconnected from the party's grassroots. Activists have no influence in the direction of the party.

As shown in this chapter, the FA also differs from other Latin American coalitions or electoral alliances. Other electoral alliances, even those electorally successful alliances that accessed government, such as Concertation in Chile and the Alliance in Argentina, did not develop common organizational structures, nor did they engender a common cadre of grassroots activists. As extensively discussed throughout this volume, the FA developed a complex organizational structure that includes regular gatherings of the coalition members that go far beyond electoral coordination. This has characterized the FA since its very inception. The FA also very early on developed a cadre of FA activists who do not belong to any of the factions or parties that formed the FA.

# 8

# Theoretical Conclusions and Political Implications

INTRODUCTION

The FA has maintained high levels of activism and organizational vitality for more than forty-eight years. This has occurred in the context of a generalized decline of party organizations qua valued channels of democratic representation and, more specifically, in the context of a party organization that has been in government for three terms. This volume has sought to identify what facilitates the reproduction of a party organization that grants an important role to grassroots activists. Also, the volume surveys about the effect of party's organizational traits on political engagement and its reproduction. To answer these questions, we have employed a mixed method research strategy, combining thick description, process tracing, and experimental survey research.

Our study has focused on the historical and constant causes that explain the production and reproduction of this type of party organization and its impact at the individual level. We claim that the FA's distinctive organizational attributes are explained by historical causes. The FA was born as a coalition of left-of-center political organizations in a context of high polarization and political violence. From its inception, it attracted many citizens, who joined the party as activists, forming Base Committees. This forced the nascent coalition's leaders to develop a common structure to include the grassroots movement in the organizational structure. It privileged consensus and balance among factions, which resulted in institutionalized channels for decision making. More importantly, this was complemented by a distinctive grassroots autonomous organization that gradually gained an institutionalized political role in the decision-making structure of the party. This institutional setting, which grants *voice* to grassroots activists throughout an autonomous channel of representation, was consolidated and reproduced through feedback mechanisms. We claim that the early consolidation of a dense and complex organizational structure that ensured activists a significant voice in the organization is the key to understanding the ability of a mass-organic party to reproduce such a high level of commitment and avoid oligarchization.

In this chapter, we summarize the evidence presented in this volume that supports our descriptive and causal hypotheses of the production and reproduction of activism in the FA. Although the FA has managed for more than four decades to reproduce itself as a party with activists, it faces considerable challenges ahead. We review some of the challenges for the future of the FA, which also apply to other parties that seek to reproduce high levels of activism. Finally, we discuss some general theoretical and policy implications of our study.

## REVIEW OF EMPIRICAL FINDINGS

The FA is a deviant case. It is a successful case of party reproduction, both in electoral terms and as a vibrant organization (Rosenblatt 2018). Compared to other parties in Latin America, and more specifically with other (formerly) mass-organic leftist parties – especially the PT, the most studied case – the FA still convenes a considerable number of volunteer activists who continue to work and meet regularly, even between electoral cycles.

As is the case with other parties in the region and worldwide, the FA has been influenced by exogenous challenges. The end of the Cold War and the technological revolution, among other societal changes, affected the levels of activism observed in the FA. The loss of activists is also explained by domestic factors: the reduction of the intensity of political polarization that was so pervasive during the FA's early years; the consolidation of democracy; and the stabilization of the economy. This global and local context has undoubtedly influenced the decrease in the absolute number of activists. However, activists still play a central role in the party's life, and especially in the decision-making structure. This continued vitality is observable in the everyday activities of the party and its Base Committees. Thus, this case study has provided an opportunity to test several hypotheses about the reproduction of activists' engagement beyond the impact of exogenous processes. The FA is a deviant case that enables us to focus on endogenous factors involved in explaining both the reproduction of the organizational structure that gives voice to grassroots activists and the reproduction of activism at the individual level.

The PT, the iconic leftist mass-organic party in Latin America that shared with the FA the ideological commitment to participatory democracy, became a professional–electoral party. This supports the claim that the FA is not simply a deviant case, but that it is also exceptional. As emphasized in the recent comparative historical analysis literature, context is crucial to understanding the causal effect of a given mechanism (Falleti and Lynch 2009). This is illustrated by the case of the FA, which reinforces the idea that promoting strong party organizations is not simple.

Our study yielded three main empirical findings. First, the FA's organizational structure was built in a specific historical context and it produced a lock-in effect that made it very difficult to reduce the role grassroots activists play in the party's structure. Second, the FA has channels of participation that still convene activists throughout the territory who work as volunteers during the year. Even though the party has professionalized its structure and introduced new technologies, much of the everyday and campaign activities rely heavily on these volunteers. These activists are not simply members of the organization – they act like organizers. These organizers are more willing to dedicate time and resources to the organization than are mere adherents. Third, the channels for effective voice are critical to explain the willingness of volunteer activists to reproduce their cooperation with the organization.

This volume has described the activism in the FA. Approximately 7,000 activists meet on a weekly basis in the Base Committees and in other organizational structures of the FA. The deliberation that occurs in the Base Committees is vertically transmitted to the FA's decision-making bodies. Also, the decisions that are made at the top are channeled throughout the structure. This bi-directional process is executed by activists who are engaged in those bodies.

This volume has also shown that ambitious politicians satisfy their career goals through the factions. It is not efficacious to pursue a political career through the grassroots structure. Factions are the sole channel for recruiting candidates and for appointing people to government positions (Buquet and Chasquetti 2008, Moraes 2008). The grassroots Base Committees do not participate in either the recruitment and selection of electoral candidates or in the appointment of government officials. Therefore, the power that faction leaders have to control their factions by controlling candidate selection and government appointments is not replicated in the grassroots structure; faction leaders do not have the ability to control the grassroots structure, either by delivering resources for pursuing a political career or by influencing the selection of grassroots delegates to the FA structure.

Delegates from the grassroots activists integrate all bodies within the FA structure and they coexist with delegates from the FA factions and party leaders. Delegates' fate cannot be controlled by the elites. This confers autonomy on the grassroots delegates. At the same time, for grassroots activists, the only way to reproduce their political clout in the FA is by keeping their grassroots organization alive. This vertical structure that connects different bodies of the FA and in which grassroots activists play a crucial role has low barriers to entry. There are known and open channels through which to engage with the party; this, in turn, facilitates efficacious participation.

Both the comparative historical analysis literature in general and the literature on the origin of political parties in particular show that the origin of an organization or institution, and its early steps, determine its long-term trajectory (Mahoney and Rueschemeyer 2003, Panebianco 1988, Pierson 2004). This includes the combination of context, structural conditions, and, more critically at this stage, agency. As argued elsewhere, the origin of the FA was strongly influenced by a context of intense polarization and political violence. At the organization's very inception, FA leaders were overwhelmed by an autonomous, bottom-up grassroots movement whose members demanded a role in a permanently democratic organization. This gradually led to the incorporation of grassroots activists throughout the decision-making structure. Given the institutionalization of the activists' role, a strong lock-in effect was set in place. This is critical for understanding the reproduction of the mass-organic nature of the party, even after levels of activism waned.

The book has highlighted the interaction between organizational setting (qua rules) and individual behavior. In the FA, rules engender selective incentives (associated with individual's perceived efficacy). The existence of organizational structures that grant voice to activists generates the necessary incentives to remain engaged. This perspective on the nature of selective incentives differs from its conventional use in the literature. For example, Panebianco (1988) conceptualizes selective incentives as individual material rewards, related to patronage or private goods distribution. In the case of the FA, rules generate a selective incentive (perceived efficacy) that favors the development of the organization and is not associated with the distribution of scarce resources within the party or the creation of a captive clientele in the hands of party leaders.

Using a survey instrument, we collected evidence to support the claim that activists systematically differ from adherents in their willingness to engage in volunteer activism and in the elasticity of their engagement. Also, through survey experiments, our study showed how perceived efficacy explains the reproduction of activism, i.e., the decision to cooperate with the party organization. The results support the claim that perceived efficacy – especially a reduction in perceived efficacy – significantly affects engagement: depriving activists of a significant role in party decision making reduces their willingness to cooperate with the organization in the future. The effect of diminishing the political role of rank-and-file members is stronger among those who are activists than among those who are merely adherents.

This case study challenges three assumptions in the party-politics literature. First, it challenges the assumption that party organizations follow an inevitable trajectory; i.e., all parties will eventually become cartel or professional–electoral organizations (Katz and Mair 1994). Second, it challenges the assumption that internal party democracy is primarily about candidate selection. Thus, in the literature, internal party democracy is often reduced to the process of nominating and selecting candidates among the elite (e.g., Kitschelt 1994). However, this obscures the decision-making process that takes place within the party organization, aside from the power of elected representatives. Third, contrary to the conclusion of Freidenberg and Levitsky (2007) or of Levitsky (2003) about the unimportance of formal party rules, the case of the FA shows how parties' formal rules can be crucial for explaining individual behavior, party survival over time, and party adaptation. Another lesson of the case of the FA is that, apart from organizational structure, there are many paths by which parties may adapt to exogenous challenges. Yet, some of those potential paths, as in the case of the Peronism described by Levitsky (2003), conflict with democratic representation. In contrast, in the case of the FA, the critical factor that enabled the party to adapt over time without risking democratic governance is the party rules, which ensure the constant incorporation of activists' demands and consideration of their views.

The main theoretical lesson of the case of the FA is that reproducing a political organization, one of the main challenges facing political organizations in contemporary democracies, is possible when the organization affords grassroots activists a potentially significant role, through rules and actors that ensure the enforcement of such rules. Nevertheless, the second main theoretical contribution is that this level of engagement can only be reproduced in a structure that is autonomous of the power of the party elite. This autonomy, in the case of the FA, derives from the creation of an organizational structure that is parallel to that of the factions. Individuals do not participate in this common structure to obtain clientelistic goods or to pursue a political career.

The case of the FA challenges the idea that parties based on volunteer activism are dead and that attempts to build a democratic party organization inevitably end up producing an oligarchic organization. Moreover, if organizational structure can foster activism, there is a chance for policy interventions to reverse the declining role of party activists in contemporary democracies. By focusing on the role of organizational structures, this volume sheds light on the potential effects of policy reforms aimed at improving the link between parties and society. This is an important lesson, because it provides a focus for efforts aimed at improving an allegedly crucial channel for reproducing democratic representation.

### THE CHALLENGES AHEAD

The analyses presented in this volume, as with all case-study research, can only offer provisional evidence – i.e., it tells us the story "so far." The analysis did not aim to predict whether this organizational structure will continue to reproduce itself or the levels of engagement grassroots activists will display in the future. A critical juncture may greatly alter current observed levels of engagement. In addition to the possibility of currently unforeseen future shocks, the FA faces numerous evident challenges that also characterize other active political organizations.

The FA's organizational and governance structure is a permanent subject of debate. Some indicate that this structure is inconvenient for confronting the challenges of today's society, especially for channeling new means of participation (Bimber, Flanagin, and Stohl 2012). However, the organizers' tasks require their presence and thus cannot be supplanted by online participation, which usually produces a simple adhesion to an organization without commitment of time or an activist role (Han 2014). Organizers can, of course, use Internet tools to do their work or to try to increase the number of party adherents. The problem arises when traditional activists (who organize), as opposed to those who participate or mobilize through cyber-activism, are unable to perform their function within the organization. While cyber-activism can usefully complement the mobilization tasks developed by factional leaders, grassroots activists carry out a great number of tasks for the organization and guarantee their presence and articulation of political activism in the territory. Privileging adherents and cyber-activism over spaces for in-person activism would change the FA from a mass-organic party to a professional–electoral party.

The FA, like other social and political organizations throughout the world, is subject to the temptation of transforming its (costly) internal structure into a broad network of adherents (with low levels of participation). This change would reduce the incentives to develop the organization. This transformation, while it might promote a (perhaps superficially) more democratic organization by adding more adherents, would make the FA more elitist, i.e., controlled by leaders with the capacity to mobilize high numbers of supporters. At the same time, the FA would lose its capacity to benefit from the participation structures that allow the emergence of new leaders, especially at the local and community level (McKenna and Han 2014). As Han (2014) claims, mobilization can work if an organization does not need to constantly engage a great number of people, does not need intense activist commitment on the part of its members, or if it has other sources of power besides the power of the people.

For Uruguay's younger generation, the FA has always been the party in government. At the time of writing this book, the FA has been in government for over fourteen years. The members of the younger generation have not experienced the political development of the party during its resistance to the authoritarian regime in the 1970s and 1980s or during the pro-market reforms in the 1990s. This creates a challenge for the FA to create a narrative that preserves its transformative vision of the future, its ability to reproduce Trauma and Purpose to fuel party life (Rosenblatt 2018). This is also related to the fact that, even though becoming the country's ruling party is the manifestation of the FA's success, this success has siphoned off the organization's best leadership cadres. This was a problem also in the case of Chile, where leaders from the Concertation[1] increasingly became detached from their party organizations. The crucial difference is that the FA is much more than a coalition or a professional–electoral party. It has a grassroots activist structure comprising volunteers

---

[1] The center-left coalition that governed Chile from 1990 to 2010.

who still have a relevant place and influence and who maintain the party's vitality outside of government functioning.

The FA has led three consecutive governments thus far. As a result, it has new political economy challenges. The FA's experience in government throughout the current economic cycle reflects the political constraints of leftist parties that attain office in Latin America (Murillo, Oliveros, and Vaishnav 2011, Campello 2015). The challenge of the permanent incorporation of changes and demands is also related to the evolution of at least four major issues that confront leftist political parties in Latin America, or that confront any successful political organization in a developing country: (1) the tension between growth and redistribution (Campello 2015), (2) the incorporation and political organization of the poor and the informal sectors, (3) security issues, and (4) corruption – all hot topics in Latin American politics.

The political economy literature has extensively documented the challenges posed by the potential conflict between growth and wealth redistribution (Campello 2015, Korpi and Palme 1998, Murillo, Oliveros, and Vaishnav 2011, Przeworski and Sprague 1986). For the left, the paradox of redistribution and growth is especially significant, because leftist parties must redistribute. Presidents elected from the left are different from those with an economically liberal agenda. Presidents from leftist parties are forced to redistribute, as that typically is the promise under which they are elected. To do so, without conflict, they need growth. In a time of economic expansion, redistribution is easier than in a context of economic recession; social spending can increase and poverty can be reduced as a result of economic growth. In contrast, when recession strikes, the redistribution agenda is constrained. Campello (2015) writes that in the context of an economic crisis, leftist governments are subjected to the dilemma of whether to advance interventionist and redistributive policies, which are what its voters expect, or to satisfy investors' interest in promoting pro-market reforms. The greater the government's dependence on foreign capital, the greater is its incentive to develop an agenda that fulfills the investors' needs.

In an economy that since 2015 has been growing more slowly, the demands of the unions can only be fulfilled by increasing fiscal deficits or increasing the levels of taxation on capital. The first option is not viable for a left that seeks to preserve macroeconomic stability, and it would increase inflation. The second option could engender a contraction of production and capital flight – as a result of less favorable conditions for investors – aggravating the problem of growth. If the left restricts its redistributive agenda, it closes the perceived gap between the political left and the right. Without redistribution, the agenda of the left dilutes.

Another political economy challenge to the left is the incorporation of the informal sectors, those who were not incorporated by the first expansion of the welfare system. Additionally, the informal sectors in Latin America in general, including in Uruguay, have never been politically organized – with the exception of the classic populist experiences in the region (Collier and Handlin 2009). This is a structural problem throughout Latin America, as well as in other peripheral economies. The informal sector has been one of the main beneficiaries of the FA's expansive social policies during the FA's first three governments (Pribble 2013, Rossel 2016). This sector of society did not traditionally support the left and only gradually came to support the FA (Luna 2004, 2014). The main challenge for the FA is to engender deep roots politicizing these sectors. This was one of the main deficits of the Concertation parties in Chile. To accomplish this, the FA would need its organizers to work in the territory and to change adherents into activists, building trust without relying on a clientelist exchange. Handlin (2013) analyzes the politicization of these sectors and how leftist parties can attract those who are the main beneficiaries of its policies in Venezuela, Brazil, and Chile. Chavismo was the main organizer of the informal sectors. However, the mechanism for ensuring the loyalty of the grassroots activists in these sectors is clientelism. In contrast, the PSCh and the PT have a technocratic approach to the incorporation of these sectors. These parties' main difference with Chavismo is that there is no direct relationship between the welfare policies they pursue and the party organization. The challenge for leftist parties is to arouse the loyalty of these sectors. In the case of the FA, the real challenge, as regards obtaining electoral support among the informal sectors, is not just to gather more people but to penetrate beyond the urban periphery.

Leftist governments in Latin America face another challenge. Traditionally, leftist parties access office promising to avoid repressive policies and to tackle security issues with an inclusive perspective. As a consequence, one of the reform mechanisms that they have implemented is the creation of community police, whose responsibilities include intensive patrolling, conflict resolution with alternative procedures – to avoid repression – and the incorporation of civil-society organizations from the territory, as a way to reaching out to citizens. Nevertheless, these types of interventions may clash with the pressing need to solve security issues in red zones; i.e., areas with high levels of criminality and the presence of organized crime (e.g., narcocriminals). These kinds of problems are usually ranked among the most important in public-opinion polls, especially for middle sectors. This usually puts leftist governments in the uncomfortable position of having to implement repressive measures as a short-term response in order to avoid the loss of voters.

Finally, the history of Latin America exhibits the pervasive presence of rampant corruption among political elites. The oligarchic republics of the nineteenth century often saw a complete conflation of private and public interest; the authoritarian regimes that ruled the region throughout the twentieth century were plagued with corruption; the market-oriented governments of the 1990s privatized public utilities using very dubious procedures. Leftist governments have not escaped this nefarious trend that is often found among the rulers of unequal societies that are undergoing the conflictive process of development (Huntington 1968). Since leftist parties were very critical of the rampant corruption of the predecessors of the "neoliberal" wave, corruption scandals that occur during their own terms greatly endanger the legitimacy of the leftist parties and of the party system as a whole.

## A DECADENT ORGANIZATION OF THE PAST OR DEMOCRACY IN THE TWENTY-FIRST CENTURY?

Having parties with activists, as opposed to having only professional–electoral parties, is more critical for contemporary democracies than conventional wisdom assumes. Even though activists are less necessary than they once were for mobilizing voters, the existence of democratic organizations is critical, especially for democracies with more demanding citizens , (Inglehart and Welzel 2005, Norris 1999). If Norris's (1999) and Inglehart and Welzel's (2005) hypotheses are correct, and modern democracies must face the challenge of more demanding citizens, the FA's organizational structure is well-suited to adapt to it. An organizational structure that promotes activists' *voice* is critical for modern democracies, because this structure limits leaders' discretion and enables a demanding citizenry to have a say, thus making the citizenry more willing to engage with a party organization. This structure of dense territorial penetration makes the organization more accessible for those groups and citizens who, without necessarily joining the party, want to interact with it, in order, for example, to channel a local demand.

More generally, most authors of the comparative-politics literature of Latin America in the 1990s and early 2000s valued positively the capacity of governments to implement market reforms. This bias was translated into an argument that successful party adaptation was a function of the structure's flexibility to enact a policy switch. This flexibility was associated with a structure in which leaders have the necessary autonomy to impose their policy preferences, betraying their mandates (Stokes 1999). In this vein, parties in which leaders are accountable to a complex structure and, more critically, to volunteer grassroots activists, are constrained in their ability to enact strategic adaptation and the policies supposedly necessary to stabilize the economy (Burgess and Levitsky 2003, Levitsky 2003).

This literature overlooked the inherent tension between programmatic moderation and policy switches vis-à-vis the logic of responsible party government (Adams 2001). The programmatic changes that many parties enacted weakened democratic representation and left citizens only with the option to evaluate policies ex-post. As Downs (1957) states, when parties moderate to the point that they become indistinguishable to citizens, alienation and indifference toward politics ensue. According to Lupu (2016) these processes led to the dilution of the value of the brands in Latin American party systems. When a party leapfrogs the position of its rivals, it loses its reputation. This kind of change affects parties' role in reducing the costs of information for citizens. From this perspective, if leaders are restricted by the organization and by grassroots activists, policy switches that change the nature of a party are less likely and party systems remain relatively polarized, allowing responsible party government and substantive democratic representation.

The flipside of these positive effects of the FA's organizational structure is the inability to act decisively when there is no consensus and difficulty choosing the most strategic course of action. As the literature on the role of veto players has demonstrated, the existence of multiple actors reduces the decisiveness of the institution and the leadership (Tsebelis 1995). Also, as the literature on party politics highlights, granting a role to activists in the decision-making structure of the organization both reduces the possibility of taking strategic decisions and increases polarization – activists are more radical than leaders, adherents, and voters (Hazan and Rahat 2010). Decision-making processes to design public policy might, in some cases, be too slow or suboptimal in technical terms. Pribble (2013) describes the case of educational reform in Uruguay as a case of tension between the party organizational structure and public policy making. Pribble analyzes the degree of progress in terms of universalism in middle schools (reforms that effectively incorporate more students) during the

PSCh government in Chile (together with the rest of the Concertation coalition) and the FA in Uruguay. The author concludes that while Chile made significant progress in terms of ensuring universal, though unequal, coverage, in Uruguay: "...the FA's reform to education policy had a neutral effect for universalism" (Pribble 2013, 114). The author argues that the FA's organizational structure, which she labels "a constituency-coordinating party of the left," explains this outcome. Specifically, the party has strong ties with unions, as opposed to the case of the PSCh, a professional–electoral party.

The educational reform was a top priority in the FA's first government (2005–2010). In substantive terms, it implied a change in organizational and curricular policy that the teachers' union opposed. Pribble (2013) shows how, in the context of a "bottom-up" model of designing public policy that contrasts with the Chilean "top-down" model, the staunch opposition of the teachers' union was crucial. The teachers' union was part of the FA's social base. Before the FA gained the government for the first time in 2005, these unions helped to locate the FA as a party that opposed the neoliberal model. Moreover, after the FA assumed government, these unions gained power as a consequence of a significant increase in the education budget and the role the FA granted unions in state agencies that oversee education policy. Since the FA had to listen to the opinion and interests of its social bases, this reform was extremely slow. Nevertheless, in other complex major-policy issues, reforms were successful and there have been significant advances.

The case of the FA illustrates the virtues of a party organization having a dense democratic structure that promotes activists' engagement. At the same time, it also shows the difficulties such an organization encounters when it tries to promote structural reforms that affect its social bases. Nevertheless, this trade-off is inherent to democracy. Democratic representation is not – or not only – about policy success or efficiency. It is, rather, concerned with the ongoing cycle of channeling demands and translating citizens' preferences into policies.

# Appendix – Interviewees

| Name | Position | Date |
|---|---|---|
| Miguel Aguirre Bayley | Historian specialized in FA's history | August 18, 2016 |
| Alberto Couriel | Former senator and FA founder | September 28, 2016 |
| Alberto Roselli | Former Montevideo's City Hall Secretary | October 4, 2016 |
| Alfredo Curbelo | Former FA's Organization Secretary | September 23, 2016 |
| Álvaro García | Former Minister of Economy and Finances | September 16, 2016 |
| Juan Andrés Roballo | Former Representative and President Vázquez Secretary | October 1, 2016 |
| Carlos Baráibar | Senator and FA founder | August 23, 2016 |
| Carmen Fernández | Grassroot activist- Montevideo | June 5, 2017 |
| Daniela Stanisich | Grassroot activist- Montevideo | August 11, 2016 |
| Eduardo Alonso | Grassroot activist- Montevideo | June 14, 2017 |
| Eduardo Bonomi | Minister of the Interior | September 26, 2017 |
| Eduardo Lorier | Senator | September 22, 2016 |
| Enrique Rubio | Senator | September 22, 2016 |
| Gabriel Márquez | Grassroot activist- Montevideo | June 8, 2017 |
| Gabriel Otero | Mayor | September 23, 2016 |
| Gerardo Rey | President of Electricity National Administration | September 19, 2016 |
| Gonzalo Zuvela | Grassroot activist- Montevideo | May 8, 2017 |
| José Bayardi | Former Minister of Defense and Representative | September 20, 2016 |
| José López | Grassroot activist- Montevideo | August 29, 2016 |
| Juan Castillo | Former Union Leader and Secretary General of the PCU | September 16, 2016 |

(*continued*)

*(continued)*

| Name | Position | Date |
|---|---|---|
| Lucía Topolansky | Vice president of the Republic | February 9, 2017 |
| Luis Casal Beck | Journalist specialized in the FA | August 9, 2016 |
| Manuel Mugico | Grassroot activist- Montevideo | June 5, 2017 |
| Marcos Carámbula | Former Mayor of Canelones and Senator | March 28, 2017 |
| Mariano Arana | Former Mayor of Montevideo | February 15, 2017 |
| Mariano Bianchino | Grassroot activist- Canelones | September 20, 2016 |
| Mario Bergara | Former Minister of Economy and Finances and President of the Central Bank | September 21, 2016 |
| Martín Ponce de León | FA founder | September 21, 2016 |
| Miguel Fernández Galeano | Health Viceminister | March 24, 2017 |
| Miriam Rodríguez | Mayor | September 19, 2016 |
| Mónica Xavier | Senator and former FA president | September 20, 2016 |
| Oscar Botinelli | Líber Seregni's advisor | September 20, 2016 |
| Pedro Cribari | Grassroot activist (1971–1984) | July 26, 2016 |
| Raúl Calixto | Grassroot activist- Montevideo | June 7, 2017 |
| Rodrigo Arcamone | Mayor | September 20, 2016 |
| Sergio Prato | Grassroot activist- Montevideo | June 12, 2017 |
| Jorge Pasculli | Editor Weekly "Las Bases" | March 11, 2019 |
| Wilfredo Penco | Founding father and minister of Electoral Justice | February 23, 2017 |
| Ana Fleitas | Grassroot activist- Montevideo | June 6, 2017 |
| Liliam Kechichián | Grassroot activist and Minister of Tourism | November 10, 2016 |
| Sandra Nedov | Mayor | September 19, 2016 |
| Sergio Prato (group interview) | Grassroot activist- Montevideo | September 23, 2016 |
| Gabriel Márquez (group interview) | Grassroot activist- Montevideo | September 23, 2016 |
| Manuel Ferrer (group interview) | Grassroot activist- Montevideo | September 23, 2016 |
| Verónica Piñeiro (group interview) | Grassroot activist- Montevideo | September 23, 2016 |
| Ana Cabral (group interview) | Grassroot activist- Montevideo | September 23, 2016 |
| José López (group interview) | Grassroot activist- Montevideo | September 23, 2016 |
| Andrés Domínguez (group interview) | Grassroot activist- Montevideo | September 23, 2016 |
| Selva Silvera (group interview) | Grassroot activist- Montevideo | September 23, 2016 |
| Matías Robalez | Grassroot activist- Montevideo | January 17, 2018 |

# References

Abal Medina, Juan Manuel. 2009. "The Rise and Fall of the Argentine Centre-Left: The Crisis of Frente Grande." *Party Politics* 15 (3):357–375.
Adams, James. 2001. *Party Competition and Responsible Party Government*. Ann Arbor: University of Michigan Press.
Aguiar, César A. 2000. "La Historia y la Historia: Opinión Pública y Opinión Pública en el Uruguay." *Prisma* (15):7–45.
Aguirre Bayley, Miguel. 2001. *1971–1975 de Febrero-2001. 30 Años de Compromiso con la Gente*. Montevideo: La República.
2005. *Frente Amplio. La Admirable Alarma de 1971*. Montevideo: Ediciones de Cauce.
Aldrich, John H. 1995. *Why Parties?: the Origin and Transformation of Political Parties in America*. Chicago: University of Chicago Press.
Altman, David. 2010. *Direct Democracy Worldwide*. New York: Cambridge University Press.
Anria, Santiago. 2016. "Democratizing Democracy? Civil Society and Party Organization in Bolivia." *Comparative Politics* 48 (4):459–478.
2018. *When Movements Become Parties: The Bolivian MAS in Comparative Perspective*. New York: Cambridge University Press.
Astori, Danilo. 2001. "Estancamiento, Desequilibrios y Ruptura, 1955-1972." In *El Uruguay del Siglo XX: La Economía*, edited by Benjamín Nahum, 65–94. Montevideo: Instituto de Economía-Ediciones de la Banda Oriental.
Axelrod, Robert. 1984. *The Evolution of Cooperation*. New York: Basic Books.
Baggetta, Matthew, Hahrie Han, and Kenneth T Andrews. 2013. "Leading Associations: How Individual Characteristics and Team Dynamics Generate Committed Leaders." *American Sociological Review* 78 (4):544–573.
Barrán, José Pedro and Benjamín Nahum. 1985. *Batlle, los Estancieros y el Imperio Británico, Tomo VI: Las Primeras Reformas 1911-1913*. Montevideo: Ediciones de la Banda Oriental.
Bennett, Andrew and Jeffrey T. Checkel, eds. 2015. *Process Tracing: From Metaphor to Analytic Tool*. New York: Cambridge University Press.

Bergara, Mario. 2015. *Las Nuevas Reglas de Juego en Uruguay: Incentivos e Instituciones en una Década de Reformas*. Montevideo: DECON, Facultad de Ciencias Sociales, Universidad de la República - Fin de Siglo.

Bermeo, Nancy and Deborah Yashar. 2016. *Parties, Movements, and Democracy in the Developing World*. New York: Cambridge University Press.

Bértola, Luis. 1991. *La Industria Manufacturera Uruguaya, 1913-1961: Un Enfoque Sectorial de su Crecimiento, Fluctuaciones y Crisis*. Montevideo: CIEDUR.

Bidegain, Germán and Víctor Tricot. 2017. "Political Opportunity Structure, Social Movements, and Malaise in Representation in Uruguay, 1985–2014." In *Malaise in Representation in Latin American Countries: Chile, Argentina, and Uruguay*, edited by Alfredo Joignant, Mauricio Morales and Claudio Fuentes, 139–160. New York: Palgrave Macmillan.

Bidegain Ponte, Germán. 2013. "Uruguay: ¿El Año Bisagra?" *Revista de Ciencia Politica* 33 (1):351–374.

Bogliaccini, Juan A. 2019. "The Reconstruction of Business Interests after the ISI Collapse: Unpacking the Effect of Institutional Change in Chile and Uruguay." *Third World Quarterly*:1–20.

Bimber, Bruce, Andrew Flanagin, and Cynthia Stohl. 2012. *Collective Action in Organizations*. New York: Cambridge University Press.

Brandão, Marco Antonio. 2003. *O Socialismo Democrático do Partido dos Trabalhadores: A História de uma Utopia (1979-1994)*. Sao Paulo: Annablume.

Bueno de Mesquita, Bruce, Alastair Smith, Randolph M. Siverson, and James D. Morrow. 2003. *The Logic of Political Survival*. Cambridge, MA: The MIT Press.

Bulmer-Thomas, Victor. 2013. *The Economic History of Latin America Since Independence*. Third ed. New York: Cambridge University Press.

Buquet, Daniel and Daniel Chasquetti. 2008. "Presidential Candidate Selection in Uruguay, 1942-2004." In *Pathway to Power in Latin America*, edited by Peter Siavelis and Scott Morgenstern, 316–342. University Park: Penn State University Press.

Buquet, Daniel, Daniel Chasquetti, and Juan Andrés Moraes. 1998. *Fragmentación Política y Gobierno en Uruguay: ¿Un Enfermo Imaginario?* Montevideo: Facultad de Ciencias Sociales.

Buquet, Daniel and Gustavo De Armas. 2005. "La Evolución Electoral de la Izquierda: Crecimiento Demográfico y Moderación Ideológica." In *La Izquierda Uruguaya: Entra la Oposición y el Gobierno*, edited by Jorge Lanzaro, 109–138. Montevideo: Editorial Fin de Siglo-Instituto de Ciencia Política.

Buquet, Daniel and Rafael Piñeiro. 2014. "La Consolidación de un Nuevo Sistema de Partidos en Uruguay." *Revista Debates* 8 (1):127–148.

Burgess, Katrina and Steven Levitsky. 2003. "Explaining Populist Party Adaptation in Latin America: Environmental and Organizational Determinants of Party Change in Argentina, Mexico, Peru, and Venezuela." *Comparative Political Studies* 36 (8):881–911.

Caetano, Gerardo. 2005. *La Fundación del Frente Amplio y las Elecciones de 1971*. Vol. Tomo I, *Colección Liber Seregni*. Montevideo: Taurus.

Caetano, Gerardo and Gustavo De Armas. 2011. "Diez Años del Informe de Coyuntura. Del Uruguay de la Crisis a las Posibilidades y Exigencias de Desarrollo." In *Política en Tiempos de Mujica. En Busca del Rumbo. Informe de Coyuntura N° 10*, edited by Gerardo Caetano, María Ester Mancebo, and Juan Andrés Moraes, 11–41. Montevideo: Estuario Editora.
Caetano, Gerardo and José Rilla. 1998. *Breve Historia de la Dictadura*. Montevideo: Ediciones de la Banda Oriental.
Caetano, Gerardo, José Rilla, and Roméo Pérez. 1987. "La Partidocracia Uruguaya. Historia y Teoría de la Centralidad de los Partidos Políticos." *Cuadernos del CLAEH* 44 (4):37–62.
Calvo, Ernesto and Maria Victoria Murillo. 2019. *Non-policy Politics: Richer Voters, Poorer Voters, and the Diversification of Electoral Strategies*. New York: Cambridge University Press.
Campello, Daniela. 2015. *The Politics of Market Discipline in Latin America: Globalization and Democracy*. New York: Cambridge University Press.
Cancela, Walter and Alicia Melgar. 1985. El Desarrollo Frustrado. 30 Años de Economía Uruguaya 1955-1985, Serie Argumentos. Montevideo: CLAEH-Ediciones de la Banda Oriental.
Carneiro, Fabricio and Federico Traversa. 2018. "Uruguay 2017: Reactivación Económica y Nuevos Conflictos Políticos." *Revista de Ciencia Política* 38 (2):379–407.
Castiglioni, Rossana. 2005. *The Politics of Social Policy Change in Chile and Uruguay: Retrenchment versus Maintenance 1973-1998*. New York: Routledge.
Cavatorta, Francesco and Fabio Merone. 2013. "Moderation through Exclusion? The Journey of the Tunisian Ennahda from Fundamentalist to Conservative Party." *Democratization* 20 (5):857–875.
CEPAL. 2016. *Panorama Social de América Latina 2015*: United Nations Economic Commission for Latin America and the Caribbean.
Chasquetti, Daniel. 2014. "Parlamento y Carreras Legislativas en Uruguay: Un Estudio Sobre Reglas, Partidos y Legisladores en las Cámaras. Montevideo: Instituto de Ciencia Política - Facultad de Ciencias Sociales - Universidad de la República.
Colafranceschi, Marco, Elisa Failache, and Andrea Vigorito. 2013. Desigualdad Multidimensional y Dinámica de la Pobreza en Uruguay en los Años Recientes. In *El Futuro en Foco. Cuadernos Sobre Desarrollo Humano* Montevideo: PNUD Uruguay.
Collier, David. 1999. "Data, Field Work, and Extracting New Ideas at Close Range." *Newsletter of the Organized Section in Comparative Politics of the American Political Science Association* 10 (1):1-2, 4–6.
  2011. "Understanding Process Tracing." *PS: Political Science & Politics* 44 (4):823–830.
Collier, David, Henry Brady, and Jason Seawright. 2010. "Sources of Leverage in Causal Inference: Toward an Alternative View of Methodology." In *Rethinking Social Inquiry. Diverse Tools, Shared Standards*, edited by David Collier and Henry Brady, 161–200. Lanham, MD: Rowman & Littlefield.

Collier, David and Ruth Collier. 1991. *Shaping the Political Arena. Critical Junctures, the Labor Movement, and Regime Dynamics in Latin America.* Princeton, NJ: Princeton University Press.

Collier, Ruth Berins and Samuel Handlin. 2009. *Reorganizing Popular Politics: Participation and the New Interest Regime in Latin America.* University Park, PA: The Penn State University Press.

Coppedge, Michael. 1998a. "The Dynamic Diversity of Latin American Party Systems." *Party Politics* 4 (4):547–568.

1998b. "The Evolution of Latin American Party Systems." In *Politics, Society, and Democracy: Latin America*, edited by Scott Mainwaring and Arturo Valenzuela, 171–206. Boulder, CO: Westview Press.

Cyr, Jennifer. 2017. *The Fates of Political Parties: Crisis, Continuity, and Change in Latin America.* New York: Cambridge University Press.

D'Elía, Germán. 1982. *El Uruguay Neobatllista 1946-1958.* Montevideo: Ediciones de la Banda Oriental.

Dal Bó, Pedro. 2005. "Cooperation Under the Shadow of the Future: Experimental Evidence from Infinitely Repeated Games." *American Economic Review*, 95 (5):1591–1604.

Dalton, Russell and Martin Wattenberg, eds. 2000. *Parties Without Partisans: Political Change in Advanced Industrial Democracies.* Oxford: University Press Oxford.

Dargent, Eduardo and Paula Muñoz. 2011. "Democracy Against Parties? Party System Deinstitutionalization in Colombia." *Journal of Politics in Latin America* 3 (2):43–71.

Downs, Anthony. 1957. *An Economic Theory of Democracy.* New York: Harper and Row.

Drake, Paul and Iván Jaskic, eds. 1999. *El Modelo Chileno. Democracia y Desarrollo en los Noventa.* First ed, *Colección Sin Norte*. Santiago de Chile: LOM Ediciones.

Dunning, Thad. 2012. *Natural Experiments in the Social Sciences: A Design-based Approach.* New York: Cambridge University Press.

2016. "Transparency, Replication, and Cumulative Learning: What Experiments Alone Cannot Achieve." *Annual Review of Political Science* 19: 541–563.

Duverger, Maurice. 1954. *Political Parties.* London: Methuen.

Escudero, Laura. 2002. "Argentina." In *Partidos Políticos de América Latina. Cono Sur*, edited by Manuel Alcántara Saez and Flavia Freidenberg, 33–116. Salamanca: Ediciones Universidad de Salamanca.

Etchemendy, Sebastián. 2019. "The Rise of Segmented Neo-Corporatism in South America: Wage Coordination in Argentina and Uruguay (2005-2015)." *Comparative Political Studies* 52 (10): 1427–1465.

Falleti, Tulia and Julia Lynch. 2009. "Context and Causal Mechanisms in Political Analysis." *Comparative Political Studies* 42 (9):1143–1166.

Faúndez, Julio. 1988. *Marxism and Democracy in Chile: From 1932 to the Fall of Allende.* New Haven, CT: Yale University Press.

Ferreira, Jaqueline. 2008. "O Partido dos Trabalhadores e os Núcleos de Base." Dissertação de Mestrado apresentada ao Programa de Pós-Graduação em Ciências Sociais da Faculdade de Filosofia e Ciências, Universidade Estadual Paulista.

Ffrench-Davis, Ricardo. 2008. *Entre el Neoliberalismo y el Crecimiento con Equidad. Tres Décadas de Políticas Económicas en Chile*. Santiago: Dolmen Ediciones.
Filgueira, Carlos H. and Fernando Filgueira. 1994. *El Largo Adiós al País Modelo: Políticas Sociales y Pobreza en el Uruguay*. Montevideo: Arca.
Finch, Henry. 1980. *Historia Económica del Uruguay Contemporáneo*. Montevideo: Ediciones de la Banda Oriental.
Fiorina, Morris P. 1980. "The Decline of Collective Responsibility in American Politics." *Daedalus* 109 (3):25–45.
Freidenberg, Flavia, and Steven Levitsky. 2007. "Organización Informal de los Partidos en América Latina." *Desarrollo Económico* 46 (184):539–568.
Garcé, Adolfo and Jaime Yaffé. 2005. *La Era Progresista*. Montevideo: Editorial Fin de Siglo.
Garretón, Manuel Antonio. 1995. *Hacia una Nueva Era Política: Estudio Sobre las Democratizaciones*: Fondo de Cultura Económica.
Gil, Federico Guillermo. 1966. *The Political System of Chile*. Boston: Houghton Mifflin.
Goertz, Gary and James Mahoney. 2012. *A Tale of Two Cultures: Qualitative and Quantitative Research in the Social Sciences*. Princeton, NJ: Princeton University Press.
González, Luis E. 1991. *Political Structures and Democracy in Uruguay*. Notre Dame, IN: University of Notre Dame Press.
  1995. "Continuity and Change in the Uruguayan Party System." In *Building Democratic Institutions: Party Systems in Latin America*, edited by Scott Mainwaring and Timothy Scully, 138–163. Stanford, CA: Stanford University Press.
González, Luis E. and Rosario Queirolo. 2000. "Elecciones Nacionales del 2004: Posibles Escenarios." In *Elecciones 1999/2000*, edited by Oscar Botinellli, Daniel Buquet, Gerardo Caetano, Agustín Canzani, Antonio Cardarello, Daniel Chasquetti, Gustavo De Armas, Adolfo Garcé, Luis Eduardo González, Aldo Guerrini, Jorge Lanzaro, Altair Magri, Constanza Moreira, Romeo Pérez Antón, Rosario Queirolo and Jaime Yaffe, 299–321. Montevideo: Ediciones de la Banda Oriental-Instituto de Ciencia Política.
Gunther, Richard and Larry Diamond. 2003. "Species of Political Parties: A New Typology." *Party Politics* 9 (2):167–199.
Haggard, Stephan and Mathew D. McCubbins, eds. 2001. *Presidents, Parliaments, and Policy*. New York: Cambridge University Press.
Hagopian, Frances and Scott Mainwaring. 2005. "Introduction: The Third Wave of Democratization in Latin America." In *The Third Wave of Democratization in Latin America: Advances and Setbacks*, edited by Frances Hagopian and Scott Mainwaring, 1–13. New York: Cambridge University Press.
Han, Hahrie. 2014. *How Organizations Develop Activists: Civic Associations and Leadership in the 21st Century*. New York: Oxford University Press.
  2016. "The Organizational Roots of Political Activism: Field Experiments on Creating a Relational Context." *American Political Science Review* 110 (2):296–307.

Handlin, Samuel. 2013. "Social Protection and the Politicization of Class Cleavages during Latin America's Left Turn." *Comparative Political Studies* 46 (12):1582–1609.

Handlin, Samuel and Ruth Berins Collier. 2011. "The Diversity of Left Party Linkages and Competitive Advantages." In *The Resurgence of the Latin American Left*, edited by Steve Levitsky and Kenneth Roberts, 139–161. Baltimore, MD: The Johns Hopkins University Press.

Hazan, Reuven and Gideon Rahaţ. 2010. *Democracy within Parties: Candidate Selection Methods and Their Political Consequences*. Oxford: Oxford University Press.

Heidar, Knut. 1994. "The Polymorphic Nature of Party Membership." *European Journal of Political Research* 25 (1):61–86.

Hersh, Eitan D. 2015. *Hacking the Electorate: How Campaigns Perceive Voters*. New York: Cambridge University Press.

Hirschman, Albert. 1970. *Exit, Voice, and Loyalty. Responses to Decline in Firms, Organizations, and States*. New York: Harvard University Press.

   1982. *Shifting Involvements: Private Interest and Public Action*. Princeton, NJ: Princeton University Press.

Huber, Evelyne and John D. Stephens, eds. 2012. *Democracy and the Left: Social Policy and Inequality in Latin America*. Chicago, IL: University of Chicago Press.

Hunter, Wendy. 2010. *The Transformation of the Workers' Party in Brazil, 1989-2009*. New York: Cambridge University Press.

Huntington, Samuel. 1968. *Political Order in Changing Societies*. New Haven, CT: Yale University Press.

Inglehart, Ronald and Christian Welzel. 2005. *Modernization, Cultural Change, and Democracy: The Human Development Sequence*. New York: Cambridge University Press.

Issenberg, Sasha. 2012. *The Victory Lab: The Secret Science of Winning Campaigns*. New York: Broadway Books.

Jäger, Kai. 2017. "The Potential of Online Sampling for Studying Political Activists around the World and Across Time." *Political Analysis*:1–15.

Jones, Mark. 2005. "The Role of Parties and Party Systems in the Policymaking Process." State Reform, Public Policies, and Policymaking Processes, IADB-Washington DC, February 28–March 2.

Katz, Richard S. and Peter Mair, eds. 1994. *How Parties Organize: Change and Adaptation in Party Organizations in Western Democracies*. Thousand Oaks, CA: Sage.

Katz, Richard S. and Peter Mair. 1995. "Changing Models of Party Organization and Party Democracy: The Emergence of the Cartel Party." *Party Politics* 1 (1):5–28.

Keck, Margaret E. 1992. *The Worker's Party and Democratization in Brazil*. New Haven, CT: Yale University Press.

Kirchheimer, Otto. 1966. "The Transformation of the Western European Party System." In *Political Parties and Political Development*, edited by Joseph LaPalombara and Myron Weiner, 177–200. Princeton, NJ: Princeton University Press.

Kitschelt, Herbert. 1994. *The Transformation of European Social Democracy*. New York: Cambridge University Press.
Kitschelt, Herbert and Steven Wilkinson, eds. 2007. *Patrons, Clients and Policies. Patterns of Democratic Accountability and Political Competition*. New York: Cambridge University Press.
Korpi, Walter and Joakim Palme. 1998. "The Paradox of Redistribution and Strategies of Equality: Welfare State Institutions, Inequality, and Poverty in the Western Countries." *American Sociological Review* 63(5):661–687.
Lanzaro, Jorge. 1986. *Sindicatos y Sistema Político: Relaciones Corporativas en el Uruguay, 1940-1985*. Montevideo: Fundación de Cultura Universitaria.
  2000. "El Frente Amplio: Un Partido de Coalición entre la Lógica de Oposición y la Lógica de Gobierno." *Revista Uruguaya de Ciencia Política* 12: 35–67.
  2004. "La Izquierda se Acerca a los Uruguayos y los Uruguayos se Acercan a la Izquierda. Claves de Desarrollo del Frente Amplio." In *La Izquierda Uruguaya Entre la Oposición y el Gobierno*, edited by Jorge Lanzaro, 13–107. Montevideo: Fin de Siglo-FESUR.
  2007. "The Uruguayan Party System: Transition within Transition." In *When Parties Prosper: The Uses of Electoral Success*, edited by Kay Lawson and Peter H. Merkl, 117–140. Boulder, CO: Lynne Rienner.
  2011. "Uruguay: A Social Democratic Government in Latin America." In *The Resurgence of the Latin American Left*, edited by Steven Levitsky and Kenneth Roberts, 348–374. Baltimore, MD: Johns Hopkins University Press.
  2012. "Continuidad y Cambios en una Vieja Democracia de Partidos." *Cuadernos del CLAEH* 100: 37–77.
Leiras, Marcelo. 2007. *Todos los Caballos del Rey: La Integración de los Partidos Políticos y el Gobierno Democrático de la Argentina, 1995-2003*. Buenos Aires: Prometeo.
Levitsky, Steven. 2003. *Transforming Labor-Based Parties in Latin America: Argentine Peronism in Comparative Perspective*. New York: Cambridge University Press.
Levitsky, Steven, James Loxton, Brandon Van Dyck, and Jorge Domínguez. 2016. *Challenges of Party-Building in Latin America*. New York: Cambridge University Press.
Levitsky, Steven and Kenneth Roberts, eds. 2011. *The Resurgence of the Latin American Left*. Baltimore, MD: Johns Hopkins University Press.
Linz, Juan. 1990. "The Perils of Presidentialism." *Journal of Democracy* 1: 51–69.
  1994. "Democracy, Presidential or Parliamentary: Does It Make a Difference?" In *The Failure of Presidential Democracy: The Case of Latin America.*, edited by Juan Linz and Arturo Valenzuela, 3–87. Baltimore, MD: John Hopkins University Press.
López Cariboni, Santiago and Rosario Queirolo. 2015. "Class Voting versus Economic Voting: Explaining Electoral Behavior before and after the 'Left Turn' in Latin America." 8ª Congreso Latinoamericano de Ciencia Política, ALACIP, Lima, Perú, July 22–24, 2015.
Loveman, Brian. 1995. "The Transition to Civilian Government in Chile, 1990–1994." In *The struggle for democracy in Chile*, edited by Paul W. Drake and Ivan Jaksic, 305–337. Lincoln, NE: University of Nebraska Press.

Luján, Diego and Juan A. Moraes. 2017. "Why Fusions? The Role of Electoral Coordination in the Frente Amplio's Formation." *Departamento de Ciencia Política, Universidad de la República, Uruguay.*
Lumley, Thomas. 2011. *Complex Surveys: A Guide to Analysis Using R.* Hovoken, NJ: Wiley.
Luna, Juan Pablo. 2004. "¿Entre la Espada y la Pared? La Transformación Reciente de las Bases Sociales del Frente Amplio y sus Implicancias para un Eventual Gobierno Progresista." In *La Izquierda Uruguaya Entre la Oposición y el Gobierno*, edited by Jorge Lanzaro, 195–250. Montevideo: FESUR-Fin de Siglo.
  2007. "Frente Amplio and the Crafting of a Social Democratic Alternative in Uruguay." *Latin American Politics and Society* 49 (4):1–30.
  2014. *Segmented Representation: Political Party Strategies in Unequal Democracies.* Oxford: Oxford University Press.
Luna, Juan Pablo and David Altman. 2011. "Uprooted but Stable: Chilean Parties and the Concept of Party System Institutionalization." *Latin American Politics & Society* 53 (2):1–28.
Lupu, Noam. 2014. "Brand Dilution and the Breakdown of Political Parties in Latin America." *World Politics* 66 (4):561–602.
  2016. *Party Brands in Crisis: Partisanship, Brand Dilution, and the Breakdown of Political Parties in Latin America.* New York: Cambridge University Press.
Madrid, Raúl L. 2012. *The Rise of Ethnic Politics in Latin America.* New York: Cambridge University Press.
Mahoney, James and Dietrich Rueschemeyer, eds. 2003. *Comparative Historical Analysis in the Social Sciences.* New York: Cambridge University Press.
Mahoney, James and Kathleen Thelen. 2015. *Advances in Comparative-Historical Analysis.* New York: Cambridge University Press.
Mainwaring, Scott. 1999. *Rethinking Party Systems in the Third Wave of Democratization: The Case of Brazil.* Stanford, CA: Stanford University Press.
Mainwaring, Scott, ed. 2018. *Party Systems in Latin America: Institutionalization, Decay, and Collapse.* New York: Cambridge University Press.
Mainwaring, Scott and Edurne Zoco. 2007. "Political Sequences and the Stabilization of Interparty Competition." *Party Politics* 13 (2):155–178.
Mainwaring, Scott and Matthew Shugart. 1997. "Presidentialism and Democracy in Latin America: Rethinking the Terms of the Debate." In *Presidentialism and Democracy in Latin America*, edited by Scott Mainwaring and Matthew Shugart, 12–54. New York: Cambridge University Press.
Mainwaring, Scott and Timothy Scully, eds. 1995. *Building Democratic Institutions: Party Systems in Latin America.* Stanford, CA: Stanford University Press.
  2010. *Democratic Governance in Latin America.* Stanford, CA: Stanford University Press.
Marchesi, Aldo. 2017. *Latin America's Radical Left: Rebellion and Cold War in the Global 1960s.* New York: Cambridge University Press.
McKenna, Elizabeth and Hahrie Han. 2014. *Groundbreakers: How Obama's 2.2 Million Volunteers Transformed Campaigning in America.* New York: Oxford University Press.

Michels, Robert. 1999 (1911). *Political Parties: A Sociological Study of the Oligarchical Tendencies of Modern Democracy*. New Brunswick, NJ: Transaction Publishers.

Monestier, Felipe. 2011. *Movimientos Sociales, Partidos Políticos y Democracia Directa desde Abajo en Uruguay: 1985-2004*. Buenos Aires: Consejo Latinoamericano de Ciencias Sociales.

Moraes, Juan Andrés. 2008. "Why Factions? Candidate Selection and Legislative Politics in Uruguay." In *Pathways to Power: Political Recruitment and Candidate Selection in Latin America*, edited by Peter M. Siavelis and Scott Morgenstern, 164–185. University Park, PA: Pennsylvania State University Press.

Moraes, Juan Andrés and Diego Luján. 2015. "The Heft of the Uruguayan Left: A Case of Party Adaptation without Moderation." *Paper Prepared for the Project Reforming Communism: Cuba in Comparative Perspective.*

Moreira, Constanza. 2000. "Las Paradojales Elecciones del Fin de Siglo Uruguayo: Comportamiento Electoral y Cultura Política." In *Elecciones 1999/ 2000*. Montevideo: Ediciones de la Banda Oriental.

2004. *Final de juego: Del bipartidismo tradicional al triunfo de la izquierda en Uruguay*. Montevideo: Ediciones Trilce.

Moreira, Constanza and Andrea Delbono. 2016. "Diferenciación Social, Generacional y Geográfica del Voto del Frente Amplio en las elecciones nacionales de 2014. Revisando la Hipótesis del Policlasismo de los Partidos Políticos Uruguayos." In *Permanencias, Trancisiones y Rupturas. Elecciones en Uruguay 2014/15*, edited by Adolfo Garcé and Niki Johnson, 119–139. Montevideo: Editorial Fin de Siglo.

Morgan, Jana. 2011. *Bankrupt Representation and Party System Collapse*. University Park, PA: Penn State Press.

Morley, Samuel A., Roberto Machado, and Stefano Pettinato. 1999. "Indexes of Structural Reform in Latin America." *Serie Reformas Económicas-ECLAC Economic Development Division* (12).

Moulian, Tomas. 1993. *La Forja de Ilusiones: El Sistema de Partidos 1932-1973*. Santiago de Chile: Universidad de Artes y Ciencias Sociales (ARCIS) y Facultad Latinoamericana de Ciencias Sociales (FLACSO).

Murillo, Maria Victoria. 2001. *Labor Unions, Partisan Coalitions, and Market Reforms in Latin America*: New York: Cambridge University Press.

2009. *Political Competition, Partisanship, and Policy Making in Latin American Public Utilities*. New York: Cambridge University Press.

Murillo, María Victoria, Virginia Oliveros, and Milan Vaishnav. 2011. "Economic Constraints and Presidential Agency." *The Resurgence of the Latin American Left*: 52–70.

Nahum, Benjamin, Ana Frega, Móncia Marona, and Ivette Trochón. 1993. *Historia Uruguaya. El Fin del Uruguay Liberal. Tomo 8 1959-1973*. Montevideo: Ediciones de la Banda Oriental.

Nichter, Simeon. 2008. "Vote Buying or Turnout Buying? Machine Politics and the Secret Ballot." *American Political Science Review* 102 (1):19–31.

Norris, Pipa. 1999. *Critical Citizens: Global Support for Democratic Governance*. Oxford: Oxford University Press.

Novaro, Marcos. 2010. *Historia de la Argentina, 1955-2010*. Buenos Aires: Siglo Veintiuno.
Novaro, Marcos and Vicente A Palermo. 2004. *La Historia Reciente: Argentina en Democracia*. Buenos Aires: Edhasa.
Padrón, Álvaro and Achim Wachendorfer. 2017. *Trade Unions in Transformation Uruguay: Building Trade Union Power*. Berlin: Friedrich-Ebert Stiftung.
Palermo, Vicente and Marcos Novaro. 1996. *Política y Poder en el Gobierno de Menem*. Buenos Aires: Norma.
Panebianco, Angelo. 1988. *Political Parties: Organization and Power*. New York: Cambridge University Press.
Panizza, Francisco. 1990. *Uruguay, Batllismo y Después: Pacheco, Militares y Tupamaros en la Crisis del Uruguay Batllista*. Montevideo: Ediciones de la Banda Oriental.
Paolillo, Claudio. 2004. *Con los Días Contados*. Montevideo: Editorial Fin de Siglo.
Pérez, Verónica and Rafael Piñeiro. 2016. "Uruguay 2015: Los Desafíos de Gobernar por Izquierda cuando la Economía se Contrae." *Revista de Ciencia Política* 36 (1):339–363.
Pierson, Paul. 2004. *Politics in Time: History, Institutions, and Social Analysis*. Princeton, NJ: Princeton University Press.
Piñeiro, Rafael. 2014. "Cartelización Clientelar y Estabilidad de la Democracia en América Latina pre-1974." Doctor en Ciencia Política, Instituto de Ciencia Política, Pontificia Universidad Católica de Chile.
Piñeiro, Rafael and Fernando Rosenblatt. 2016. "Pre-analysis Plans for Qualitative Research." *Revista de Ciencia Política* 36 (3):785–796.
 2018. "Stability and Incorporation: Towards a New Concept of Party System Institutionalization." *Party Politics*:1–12. doi: 10.1177/1354068818777895.
Piñeiro, Rafael and Jaime Yaffé. 2004. "El Frente Amplio por dentro. Las fracciones frenteamplistas 1971-1999." In *La izquierda uruguaya entre la oposición y el gobierno*, edited by Jorge Lanzaro, 297–319. Montevideo: Fin de Siglo/FESUR.
Piñeiro, Rafael, Verónica Pérez, and Fernando Rosenblatt. 2016. "Pre-analysis Plan: The Broad Front: A Mass-Based Leftist Party in Latin America: History, Organization and Resilience." Available at: http://egap.org/registration/1989.
Pizzorno, Alessandro. 1970. "An Introduction to the Theory of Political Participation." *Social Science Information* 9 (5):29–61.
Ponce de León, Martín and Enrique Rubio. 2018. *Los GAU. Una Historia del Pasado Reciente (1967-1985). Vivencias y Recuerdos*. Montevideo: Ediciones de la Banda Oriental.
Pribble, Jennifer. 2013. *Welfare and Party Politics in Latin America*. New York: Cambridge University Press.
Przeworski, Adam. 2010. *Democracy and the Limits of Self-Government*. New York: Cambridge University Press.
Przeworski, Adam and John Sprague. 1986. *Paper Stones. A History of Electoral Socialism*. Chicago, IL: Chicago University Press.

Przeworski, Adam, Michael Alvarez, José Antonio Cheibub, and Fernando Limongi. 2000. *Democracy and Development: Political Institutions and Well-Being in the World, 1950-1990*. New York: Cambridge University Press.
Queirolo, Rosario. 2001. "La Organización Interna del Frente Amplio a Treinta Años de su Fundación: 1971-2001." Tesis de Maestría en Ciencia Política en Iberoamérica, Universidad Internacional de Andalucía-Sede Iberoamericana Santa María de la Rábida.
  2013. *The Success of the Left in Latin America: Untainted Parties, Market Reforms, and Voting Behavior*. Notre Dame, IA: University of Notre Dame Press.
Rama, Germán. 1971. *El Club Político*. Montevideo: Arca.
  1987. *La Democracia en Uruguay: Una Perspectiva de Interpretación*. Buenos Aires: Grupo Editor Latinoamericano.
Real de Azúa, Carlos. 1964. *El Impulso y su Freno: Tres Décadas de Batllismo y las Raíces de la Crisis Uruguaya*. Montevideo: Ediciones de la Banda Oriental.
Remmer, Karen. 1991. "The Political Impact of Economic Crisis in Latin America in the 1980's." *American Political Science Review* 81 (3):777–800.
Rhodes-Purdy, Matthew. 2017. *Regime Support Beyond the Balance Sheet: Participation and Policy Performance in Latin America*. New York: Cambridge University Press.
  2018. "Procedures Matter: An Organizational Justice Model of Regime Support." 76th Annual Conference of the Midwest Political Science Association, Chicago, IL, April 5–8.
Ribeiro, Pedro Floriano. 2008. "Dos Sindicatos ao Governo: A Organização Nacional do PT de 1980 a 2005 " Programa de Pós-Graduação Em Ciência Política Centro de Educação e Ciências Humanas Universidade Federal de São Carlos.
  2013. "Organização e Poder nos Partidos Brasileiros: Uma Análise dos Estatutos." *Revista Brasileira de Ciência Política* 10: 225.
  2014. "An Amphibian Party? Organisational Change and Adaptation in the Brazilian Workers' Party, 1980–2012." *Journal of Latin American Studies* 46 (1):87–119.
Riedl, Rachel. 2008. "Institutions in New Democracies: Variations in African Political Party Systems." PhD, Political Science, Princeton University.
  2014. *Authoritarian Origins of Democratic Party Systems in Africa*. New York: Cambridge University Press.
Roberts, Kenneth. 1998. *Deepening Democracy? The Modern Left and Social Movements in Chile and Peru*. Stanford, CA: Stanford University Press.
  2002. "Social Inequalities Without Class Cleavages in Latin America's Neoliberal Era." *SCID* 1 (36):3–33.
  2014. *Changing Course in Latin America: Party Systems in the Neoliberal Era*. New York: Cambridge University Press.
Roberts, Kenneth and Erik Wibbels. 1999. "Party Systems and Electoral Volatility in Latin America: A Test of Economic, Institutional, and Structural Explanations." *American Political Science Review* 93 (3):575–590.

Rosenblatt, Fernando. 2006. "El Dispar Desenlace de la Crisis Económica en Argentina y Uruguay (2001-2002): Una Explicación Desde la Teoría de las Prospectivas." *Revista de Ciencia Política* 26 (2):97–119.

2018. *Party Vibrancy and Democracy in Latin America*. New York: Oxford University Press.

Rossel, Cecilia. 2016. "De la Heterogeneidad Productiva a la Estratificación de la Protección Social." In *Hacia un Desarrollo Inclusivo. El caso del Uruguay*, edited by Verónica Amarante and Ricardo Infante. Santiago: Comisión Económica para América Latina y el Caribe (CEPAL).

Rovira Mas, Jorge. 2001. "¿Se debilita el Bipartidismo?" In *La Democracia de Costa Rica Ante el Siglo XXI*, edited by Jorge Rovira Mas, 195–232. San José: Editorial de la Universidad de Costa Rica.

Samuels, David. 2004. "From Socialism to Social Democracy: Party Organization and the Transformation of the Workers' Party in Brazil." *Comparative Political Studies* 37 (9):999–1024.

2006. "Sources of Mass Partisanship in Brazil." *Latin American Politics & Society* 48 (2):1–27.

Samuels, David and Cesar Zucco Jr. 2016. "Party-Building in Brazil. The Rise of the PT in Perspective "In *Challenges of Party-Building in Latin America*, edited by Steven Levitsky, James Loxton, Brandon Van Dyck and Jorge Domínguez, 331–355. New York: Cambridge University Press.

Samuels, David and Matthew Shugart. 2010. *Presidents, Parties, and Prime Ministers: How the Separation of Powers Affects Party Organization and Behavior*. New York: Cambridge University Press.

Sartori, Giovanni. 1976. *Parties and Party Systems: A Framework for Analysis*. New York: Cambridge University Press.

Scarrow, Susan. 2015. *Beyond Party Members: Changing Approaches to Partisan Mobilization*. Oxford: Oxford University Press.

Scarrow, Susan, Paul Webb, and Thomas Poguntke. 2017. *Organizing Political Parties: Representation, Participation, and Power*. Oxford: Oxford University Press.

Scarrow, Susan and Burcu Gezgor. 2010. "Declining Memberships, Changing Members? European Political Party Members in a New Era." *Party Politics* 16 (6):823–843.

Schattschneider, Elmer. 1942. *Party Government*. New York: Holt, Rinehart, and Winston.

Schlesinger, Joseph A. 1994. *Political Parties and the Winning of Office*. Ann Arbor, MI: University of Michigan Press.

Scully, Timothy. 1992. *Rethinking the Center: Party Politics in Nineteenth and Twentieth-Century Chile*. Standford, CA: Standford University Press.

Seawright, Jason. 2012. *Party-System Collapse: The Roots of Crisis in Peru and Venezuela*. Stanford, CA: Stanford University Press.

Selle, Per and Lars Svasand. 1991. "Membership in Party Organizations and the Problem of Decline of Parties." *Comparative Political Studies* 23 (4):459.

Senatore, Luis, Natalia Doglio, and Jaime Yaffé. 2004. "Izquierda Política y Sindicatos en Uruguay (1971-2003) " In *La Izquierda Uruguaya entre la Oposición y el Gobierno*, edited by Jorge Lanzaro. Montevideo: Fin de Siglo.

Senatore, Luis and Gustavo Méndez. 2011. "La Política Salarial en el Bienio 2010-2011." In *Política en Tiempos de Mujica. En Busca del Rumbo. Informe de Coyuntura N° 10*, edited by Gerardo Caetano, María Ester Mancebo and Juan Andrés Moraes, 113-123. Montevideo: Estuario Editora.

Shefter, Martin. 1994. *Political Parties and the State: The American Historical Experience*. Princeton, NJ: Princeton University Press.

Solari, Aldo. 1991. *Uruguay, Partidos Políticos y Sistema Electoral*. Montevideo: Fundacion de Cultura Universitaria.

Solari, Aldo and Rolando Franco. 1983. *Las Empresas Públicas en el Uruguay: Ideología y Política*. Montevideo: Fundación de Cultura Universitaria.

Stinchcombe, Arthur. 1968. *Constructing Social Theories*. New York: Harcourt Brace & World.

Stokes, Susan. 1999. "What Do Policy Switches Tell Us about Democracy?" In *Democracy, Accountability and Representation*, edited by Adam Przeworski, Susan Stokes and Bernard Manin, 98-130. New York: Cambridge University Press.

Stokes, Susan C, Thad Dunning, Marcelo Nazareno, and Valeria Brusco. 2013. *Brokers, Voters, and Clientelism: The Puzzle of Distributive Politics*. New York: Cambridge University Press.

Strom, Kaare. 1990. "A Behavioral Theory of Competitive Political Parties." *American Journal of Political Science* 34 (2):565.

2000. "Parties at the Core of Government." In *Parties Without Partisans: Political Change in Advanced Industrial Democracies*, edited by Russell Dalton and Martin Wattenberg, 180-207. New York: Oxford University Press.

Tavits, Margit. 2008. "Party Systems in the Making: The Emergence and Success of New Parties in New Democracies." *British Journal of Political Science* 38 (1):113-133.

2013. *Post-Communist Democracies and Party Organization*. New York: Cambridge University Press.

Thelen, Kathleen. 1999. "Historical Institutionalism in Comparative Politics." *Annual Review of Political Science* 2 (1):369-404.

Thorp, Rosemary. 1998. *Progreso, Pobreza y Exclusión: Una Historia Económica de América Latina en el Siglo XX*. New York: Banco Interamericano de Desarrollo / Unión Europea.

Tsebelis, George. 1995. "Decision Making in Political Systems: Veto Players in Presidentialism, Parliamentarism, Multicameralism and Multipartyism." *British Journal of Political Science* 25 (3):289-325.

Uruguay, Central Bank of. 2015. Informe de Política Monetaria. Cuarto Trimestre. Montevideo: Central Bank of Uruguay.

Valenzuela, Arturo. 1978. *The Breakdown of Democratic Regimes: Chile*. Baltimore, MD: Johns Hopkins University Press.

Van Haute, Emilie and Anika Gauja. 2015. "Introduction. Party Members and Activists " In *Party Members and Activists*, edited by Emilie Van Haute and Anika Gauja, 1-17. New York: Routledge.

Vanger, Milton. 1963. *José Batlle y Ordoñez of Uruguay: The Creator of His Times, 1902-1907*. Cambridge, MA: Harvard University Press.

Verba, Sidney, Kay Schlozman, and Henry Brady. 1995. *Voice and Equality: Civic Voluntarism in American Politics*. Cambridge, MA: Harvard University Press.
Webb, Paul and Stephen White, eds. 2007a. *Party Politics in New Democracies*. Oxford: Oxford University Press.
Webb, Paul and Stephen White. 2007b. "Political Parties in New Democracies: Trajectories of Development and Implications for Democracy." In *Party politics in new democracies*, edited by Paul Webb and Stephen White, 345–369. Oxford: Oxford University Press.
Wettstein, Germán. 1980. *La Autoridad del Pueblo. General Seregni*. México: Mex-Sur.
Weyland, Kurt. 2002. *The Politics of Market Reform in Fragile Democracies: Argentina, Brazil, Peru, and Venezuela*. Princeton, NJ: Princeton University Press.
Weyland, Kurt, Raúl Madrid, and Wendy Hunter, eds. 2010. *Leftist Governments in Latin America: Successes and Shortcomings*. New York: Cambridge University Press.
Wills Otero, Laura. 2015. *Latin American Traditional Parties, 1978-2006*. Bogotá: Universidad de los Andes, Facultad de Ciencias Sociales, Departamento de Ciencia Política, Ediciones Uniandes.
Yaffé, Jaime. 2005. *Al Centro y Adentro: La Renovación de la Izquierda y el Triunfo del Frente Amplio en Uruguay*. Montevideo: Linardi y Risso.
  2016. "Izquierda y Democracia en Uruguay, 1959-1973: Un Estudio sobre Lealtad Democrática en Tiempos de la Guerra Fría Latinoamericana." Doctorado en Ciencia Política, Facultad de Ciencias Sociales- Departamento de Ciencia Política, Universidad de la República.
Zemelman, Hugo. 1971. "Génesis Histórica del Proceso Político Chileno." In, edited by Enzo Faletto, Eduardo Ruiz and Hugo Zemelman, 33–118. Santiago, Chile: Quimantú.
Zucco Jr, Cesar. 2008. "Stability without Roots: Party System Institutionalization in Brazil." Institucionalización de los Sistemas de Partidos en América Latina, CIDOB-Barcelona, November 20–21.
  2010. Stability without Roots: Party System Institutionalization in Brazil. In *Working Paper Series*, edited by SSRN. Available at SSRN: http://ssrn.com/abstract=2002359

# Index

activism
  cyber-, 165
  decay of, 5
  determinants, 15
  in-person, 166
  network, 132
  reproduction, 11, 15, 17, 19, 99, 122–123, 145–146, 162
  spontaneous, 149
activists. *See also* Base Committees
  vs. adherents, 7, 15, 110, 162
  autonomy, 8, 79, 149, 161
  as buffer, 78–79
  characteristics, 56
  as delegates, 2, 12
  grassroots structure, 14
  independence, 77–78
  influence, 6, 79, 127, 130, 142
  integration, 108, 163
  involvement in decision-making, 82
  as organizers, 162
  perceived efficacy, 7, 16
  representation, 100
  role of, 6–7, 12, 88, 150
  source of power, 14
  veto power, 6–8, 12, 14, 16, 71, 100, 116, 131, 153
  as volunteers, 13–14, 49, 56, 100, 162
adaptation, 146
adherents, 15, 108, 153, *See also* activists
Administración Nacional de Combustibles, Alcohol y Portland, 44
Africa, 20

Aguirre Bayley, Miguel, 33
Aguirre Cerda, Pedro, 155
*Ahora*, 95, 97
Alianza por el Trabajo, la Justicia y la Educación, 158–159
Allende, Salvador, 155
Alonso, Eduardo, 50, 70
Álvarez, Carlos, 157–158
amnesty, 136
Annulment of Amnesty for Human Rights Crimes Law, 38, 138
Annulment of Privatization of State Companies Law, 38
Arce, Liber, 35
Argentina, 22, 31, 38–39, 132, 134, 157–159
Arismendi, Marina, 135
Articulaçao, 151
Artiguista Current, 130
Asamblea Uruguay, 71, 131
Asia, 20
Astori, Danilo, 73, 134, 139
authoritarian regime, 86, 148, 155, 166, 169
authoritarianism, 30, 35
axolotl, 21

Baliñas, Arturo, 85
Baraibar, Carlos, 156
Base Committees
  access to officials, 55
  activity, 3, 47, 50, 54, 104
  attendees, 51

Base Committees (cont.)
  criticism of, 3
  delegate accountability, 69–70, 150
  demographic characteristics, 51
  distribution, 50, 57
  finances, 60
  independence, 154
  location, 50
  names, 60
  number, 2, 50, 57
  open access, 62–64, 80, 99, 121, 163
  physical description, 1, 47, 60
  representation, 50
  requirements for forming, 59
  role of, 3, 86, 94–97
  types, 49, 86
  visibility, 121
  voter mobilization, 56, 89, 91, 94
  yearly assembly, 66
Batalla, Hugo, 103
Batllismo, 31
Bella Unión, 59
Bergara, Mario, 49, 75
Bianchino, Mariano, 52, 61, 107
Bolivia, 11, 22, 39
Bottinelli, Óscar, 33, 35, 88, 94, 96, 149
Brazil, 31, 38–39, 83, 132, 134, 147
Bruschera, Óscar, 93
Buenos Aires, 157
bureaucratization, 100
Bush, George W., 135

Call of October 7, 1970. *See* Declaración del 7 de Octubre
Campo Mayoritario, 151–152
Camusso, Rodríguez, 84
candidate selection, 8, 13, 47, 49, 164
Canelones, 52
cannabis, 41
Casa Grande, 73
case selection, 19
causal process observation, 24, 83, 91, 97, 104
causation, 6, 11, 14, 99, 160
Chavismo, 168
Chiazzaro, Roberto, 141
Chile, 22, 36, 38, 77, 147, 154–157, 159, 166, 168, 171
China, 44, 52
Christian Democracy Party. *See* Partido Demócrata Cristiano

civil society, 15, 47, 56, 111, 137, 146–147, 168
clientelism, 168
CNT. *See* Convención Nacional de Trabajadores
Coalición por el Cambio, 156
Cold War, 46
collective bargaining, 41–42, 46, 132
Colombia, 38
Colonia, 84
Comando Caza Tupamaros, 32
Comité Ejecutivo Provisorio, 85
Comités de Apoyo al Frente Amplio, 84, 88
commodity boom, 43
Compromiso Frenteamplista, 73
Concertación, 42, 155–157, 159, 166, 168
conditional cash transfers, 41
Congreso del Pueblo, 30, 33
Constitutive Declaration of the Frente Amplio, 85
Convención Nacional de Trabajadores, 30, 33, 38, 85, 91, 136
Corriente de Izquierda, 138
corruption, 169
Costa Rica, 22, 38
Council of Ministers, 74
Couriel, Alberto, 88–89
Cribari, Pedro, 89, 94, 149

D'Elía, José, 85, 91
Da Silva, Luiz Inácio, 148
de la Rúa, Fernando, 158
dealignment crisis, 39
debt crisis, 36
decisiveness, 7, 12, 170
Declaración del 7 de Octubre, 83, 85
demobilization, 146, 148
democracy
  internal, 8, 28, 164
  representation, 16
  restoration, 36
  role of parties, 4–5, 8, 16, 160, 170
democratic transition, 20, 38, 96, 156
demographic shift, 40
Día del Comité de Base, 60
digital divide, 41
Domínguez, Andrés, 121
double simultaneous vote, 30, 71, 81, 154
Doubly Decisive test, 100
dual transition, 10, 23, 35–40

# Index

Eastern Europe, 20
Economic Commission for Latin America and the Caribbean, 42
economic crisis, 10, 33, 35, 40, 44, 158
economic stagnation, 30
Ecuador, 39
*El Espectador*, 135
*El País*, 135
*El Popular*, 84
elites, 79, 126, 152–153, 163
Encuentro Progresista, 103
engagement
  civic, 15
  determinants, 17, 146
  types, 12, 48
Erro, Enrique, 33
experiment, 4, 25
Expiration Law, 129, 136–138

Facebook, 25–26
feedback mechanism, 6, 11, 14, 28, 83, 99, 161
Fernández, Carmen, 70
Ferrer, Manuel, 50, 122, 130
fiscal deficit, 167
foreign direct investment, 42
free trade agreement, 52, 77
Frente Amplio
  activists, 2, 12
  administrative data, 3, 50, 57, 61, 90
  as case study, 20, 23, 28
  as deviant case, 7, 19, 145, 161
  as movement, 13, 48
  Bases Programáticas de la Unidad, 86
  challenges facing, 161, 165
  channels of participation, 162
  characteristics, 23
  Compromiso Político, 86–87, 94, 96
  Congress, 68, 100
  consensus decision-making, 91
  coordinating groups, 54, 66–67, 87
  direct democracy campaigns, 36–37, 46
  distinctiveness, 4, 7, 14–15, 24, 47, 81, 91, 132, 159
  dual structure, 6, 13, 49
  dues, 60–61
  educational reform, 171
  electoral performance, 3, 19, 46, 89
  factions, 65, 71–79
  fiscal challenges, 42, 44, 46
  governmental performance, 42
  Grupo de los 41, 67, 71, 130, 134
  ideological moderation, 40, 127, 131, 152
  Ideological Update Commission, 133
  internal elections, 49
  member characteristics, 1–2
  membership, 61
  Mesa Ejecutiva Provisoria, 86
  Mesas Ejecutivas Departamentales, 66, 87
  National Assembly of Base Committees, 94
  national commissions, 70
  National Organizational Commission, 59, 66, 69, 93
  National Plenary, 2, 27, 50, 67–68, 77, 87, 99–100, 127, 134
  National Political Board, 2, 27, 50, 67–68, 87, 100, 127
  organizational structure, 6, 8, 11, 48, 65, 86–87, 125
  origin, 6–7, 13, 30, 46, 48, 160, 163
  platform, 132
  political economy, 40–46, 167
  programmatic moderation, 39
  regional influence, 22
  Regionales, 67
  Reglamento de Organización, 86
  role of activists, 12, 17
  role of elites, 13
  role of factions, 8, 12, 162
  size, 3
  social spending, 41
  tax reform, 41
  vitality, 3, 160–161
  volunteers, 7
Frente de Acción Popular, 155
Frente de Izquierda de Liberación, 33, 83
Frente del Pueblo, 84
Frente del Sur, 157
Frente Grande, 157
Frente Líber Seregni, 73, 138
Frente País Solidario, 157
Frente Popular, 154
Frente por la Democracia y Justicia Social, 157
Frenteamplistas Networks, 132

García, Álvaro, 75
Gargano, Reinaldo, 135
Gestido, Oscar, 33

Gini index, 42
Great Britain, 20
Group of 41. *See* Frente Amplio
Grupo de los Cinco, 83
Grupos de Acción Unificadora, 57, 85

health care system, 41
Hoop test, 90
Hoop Test, 87, 97
Hospital de Clínicas, 59

Import Substitution Industry, 10, 31, 36, 38, 46
incentives, 15–17, 28, 109, 116, 119, 146, 154, 163
inequality, 42
inflation, 10, 32, 34, 42, 44, 167
informal sector, 42, 168
institutional design, 16
internal dynamics
   internal dynamics, 145
iron law of oligarchy, 8–9
Iron Law of Oligarchy, 153
ISI. *See* Import Substitution Industry
issue database, 27, 127–128

Juan Lacaze, 84
Juventud Uruguaya de Pie, 32

*La Hora*, 88
La Paloma, 56
La Paz, 84
*La República*, 134
labor, 46
labor organizers, 148
labor unrest, 34
Lacalle Herrera, Luis Alberto, 38, 134
Latin America, 20, 147, 159, 167
Law of Voluntary Interruption of Pregnancy, 41
left turn, 22, 46, 132
Lei Orgânica dos Partidos Políticos, 150, 152
liberalization, 36
libertarian policies, 41
linear regression, 111
List 711, 73, 130
List 738, 130
lock-in effect, 12, 14, 28, 83, 99, 106, 153, 162–163
López, José, 50

*Marcha*, 35
market reform, 10
market reforms, 10, 37–38, 139, 166, 170
Márquez, Gabriel, 63, 141
Menem, Carlos, 132, 157–158
MERCOSUR, 73
México, 21, 38
Michelini, Zelmar, 84–85, 95, 97
mobilization, 38
Montevideo, 1–2, 50, 52, 54
Moreira, Constanza, 134
Movement to Socialism. *See* Movimiento al Socialismo
Movimiento 20 de Mayo, 138
Movimiento al Socialismo, 11
Movimiento Blanco Popular y Progresista, 83
Movimiento de Liberación Nacional-Tupamaros, 32
Movimiento de Participación Popular, 71, 130, 138, 152
Movimiento Herrerista, 85
Movimiento por el Gobierno del Pueblo, 83, 103
Movimiento Revolucionario Oriental, 33, 85
Movimiento Socialista, 85
Mujica, José, 22, 41, 73, 78, 133, 139
Mujico, Manuel, 49, 57, 61

National Commission for the Defense of Sovereignty, 136
National Group of Government, 134
National Plenary, 2
neoliberalism, 23, 38–39, 46, 132, 158
New Majority, 156
Nin Novoa, Rodolfo, 139
Nuevo Espacio, 130, 138

oligarchization, 8–9, 11, 13, 23, 79, 83, 100, 106, 109, 154, 159, 161
One Laptop Per Child program, 41
Organización Nacional de Independientes, 93
organization
   as independent variable, 23
   attachment, 7
   form, 23
   reproduction, 6–7, 11, 162, 164
   rules, 12, 14, 20
   structure, 5
   vitality, 16

# Index

organized crime, 169
organizers, 13, 49

Pacheco Areco, Jorge, 33, 35, 46, 83
parliamentarism, 11, 126
Partido dos Trabalhadores, 9, 11, 14, 22, 24, 42, 83, 106, 132, 146–154, 159, 162, 168
Partido Colorado, 6, 13, 30, 36, 83, 136, 154
Partido Comunista de Argentina, 157
Partido Comunista de Chile, 154
Partido Comunista del Uruguay, 13, 33, 71, 83, 130, 138, 152
Partido Demócrata Cristiano, 13, 35, 83, 103, 156–157
Partido Intransigente, 157
Partido Justicialista, 125, 132, 157
Partido Nacional, 6, 13, 30, 36, 83, 134, 136, 154
Partido Obrero Revolucionario, 130
Partido Obrero Trotskista, 85
Partido por la Democracia, 156
Partido por la Victoria del Pueblo, 73
Partido Radical Social Demócrata, 156
Partido Socialista de Chile, 24, 106, 154, 156, 168, 171
Partido Socialista de los Trabajadores, 138
Partido Socialista del Uruguay, 13, 33, 71, 130, 138
party system stability, 23
Pasculli, Jorge, 96
patronage, 152
pensions, 32–33
perceived efficacy, 17, 19, 28, 109, 118, 120, 123, 146, 163–164
Peronism, 164
Perú, 22, 38
Petroleum Company Monopoly, 38
Pinochet, Augusto, 155
Piñera, Sebastián, 156
PIT. *See* Plenario Intersindical de Trabajadores
Plan Ceibal. *See* One Laptop Per Child program
Plenario Intersindical de Trabajadores, 38
polarization, 155
political parties
 adaptation, 5–6, 11, 131, 144, 164, 170
 cadre, 5
 cartel, 9, 126

clientelistic, 7, 17, 33
contemporary challenges, 5, 8–9
contraints on, 10
evolution, 5, 27
importance, 20
in developing societies, 10
leftist, 133, 147, 154–155, 167
links to society, 11, 165
mass-organic, 4–5, 7, 20, 82, 106, 145
moderation, 148, 170
organization, 147
organizational change, 5, 9, 145
organizational structure, 11
professionalization, 9, 16, 109, 126, 148
realignment, 33
representation function, 10
resilience, 20
rules, 18, 164
system, 11, 147
trajectory, 8, 11, 163–164
types, 4–5
vs. civic associations, 16
political violence, 46
polyarchy, 20, 31
Ponce de León, Martín, 33, 57, 84, 149
popular initiatives, 37–38
populist regimes, 17
Porto Alegre, 149
post-stratification, 25
poverty, 42, 167
Pratto, Sergio, 62
pre-analysis plan, 4
presidentialism, 7, 10, 126, 133
Primeras Líneas Uruguayas de Navegación Aérea, 45
privatization, 38
process tracing, 4, 24, 83, 143

qualitative research, 4

Radical Party, 154
redistribution, 41, 132, 167–168
referendum, 37–38, 137
representation, 144
repression, 46, 155, 168
research methods, 4
Rio de Janeiro, 149
Robalez, Mathias, 59
Roballo, Juan Andrés, 143
Rodríguez, Héctor, 90
Rodríguez, Miriam, 96

Roselli, Alberto, 69, 96
Rossi, Víctor, 140
Rubio, Enrique, 141
rural workers, 41, 46

same-sex marriage, 41
Sanguinetti, Julio Maria, 35
São Paulo, 148
Sayago, 84
Schattschneider, Elmer, 4
selectorate, 124
Sendic, Raúl, 45, 54
Seregni, Líber, 82, 86, 88, 94–95
single-case methodology, 23
Smoking Gun test, 88, 90–91, 127
social mobilization, 36
social movements, 37
social spending, 167
Stanisich, Daniela, 63
state of emergency, 35
Straw in the Wind test, 97, 103
students, 35
survey, 25, 164
survey experiment, 117–120, 164

tax reform. *See* Frente Amplio
technology, 5, 9
Terra, Juan Pablo, 35, 95
thick description, 4, 22, 28, 48
Third Wave of Democracy, 10, 155
Trade Service Agreement, 139–142
trustees, 12

unemployment, 42, 44
Unidad Popular, 42, 93, 155
Unidad Socialista, 157

Unión Cívica Radical, 157
Unión Nacional y Popular, 33
unionization, 41
unions, 35, 42, 90, 103, 140, 148–149, 167, 171
United Paper Mill, 54
United States, 20, 134
unity of the left, 83, 95, 106, 131, 152
Universidad de la República, 59
UPM. *See* United Paper Mill
Uruguay, 6, 20, 25, 38, 147
    authoritarian regime, 35–36
    economy, 13, 31–32, 44
    electoral system, 81
    exports, 43
    polarization, 13, 32, 46, 160
    political characteristics, 31
    social emergency, 41
    violence, 35

Vázquez, Tabaré, 22, 41, 45, 61, 125, 133–134, 137–142
Venezuela, 38–39, 147
voice, 6, 9, 12, 16, 71, 99, 107–108, 122, 131, 146, 148, 153, 161–162
voluntary work, 111

wages, 32–34
workers' rights, 41

Xavier, Mónica, 49

YouTube, 134

Zuvela, Gonzalo, 116

Lightning Source UK Ltd.
Milton Keynes UK
UKHW010855050722
405332UK00007B/205